Praise From Readers
of *The Slight Edge*

As an instructor of a management course in a master's program at NYU, I made *The Slight Edge* required reading. It serves as the foundation for all other course content because I believe the philosophy is key to understanding success.
—*David G. Rosenthal, Advisory Board Member, Member Curriculum Committee; Adjunct Instructor; Chief Executive Officer, Shepard Communications Group, Inc.*

The Slight Edge is the book that makes every other personal-development book actually work. This is the REAL secret!
—*Jesse Macpherson, Los Angeles, CA*

The Slight Edge was the single most formative influence on my career, health and happiness. I have gone back and read it over and over so many times that my copy is in complete tatters.
—*Reed Herreid, Minneapolis, MN*

The Slight Edge freed me from the pressure I had put on myself for not maintaining the progress I made. For instance, all the years spent trying to lose weight and maintain. It was always a roller coaster, up and down, never any stability. But along came *The Slight Edge*. This put everything in perspective. I can go after anything and know that without a doubt I will be successful, because of *The Slight Edge*.
—*Jimmy Williams, Austin, TX*

A unique view on how small changes or actions done repeatedly can change your personal, family and business life. An amazing and simple strategy anyone can apply, if they are willing.
—*Pierre Rattini, North Myrtle Beach, SC*

I had read self-help books before and they did very little for me, so at first I didn't think this book would be much different. I was very wrong. This book has given me the power of wanting to have some failure in my life, and made me see the point behind the one penny. Before reading this book, I thought being average and unhealthy and overweight was just the life I was meant to live. I was very wrong. This book moved me in ways I never thought I could be. I wish I would have had it when I was 17.
—*Tyra Snider, Canon City, CO*

It has created a sense of calm and peace for us, knowing we are on this Slight Edge journey to greatness. *The Slight Edge* has taught us the principle to be patient with ourselves, to look toward improving 1 percent at a time. It has taught us that positive and negative results don't happen overnight, but are cultivated through simple daily disciplines.
—*Haas & Tahera Khaku, Anaheim Hills, CA, co-author, Power of Mentorship for the 21st Century*

The Slight Edge is the best personal-development book I have ever read.
  —*Michael Clouse, Seattle, WA*

This book is a treasure and I use it in every aspect of my life—business, personal, and fun!
  —*Shenna Shotwell, Creedmoor, NC*

The Slight Edge is a life philosophy that should be taught as soon as children take their first steps. I wish someone had taught me this when I was young.
  —*Jane Lehman, Lexington, MI*

I use this philosophy throughout my day. I've become a better person all around. I was able to correct my negative outlooks. I'm a better role model for my children, my health is getting better, I'm more connected spiritually, my relationships are improving, and my business is thriving. It is a must-have and a must-read.
  —*Pedro Garcia, Middletown, NY*

I, like many people, get frustrated when I do not see quick results. Through the Slight Edge mentality, I was able to lose 25 pounds in just under three months. I also convinced my father, 69, who lost 20 pounds in less than three months. My father and I are both testimony to the fact that *The Slight Edge* works!
  —*Christopher Mangano, Boynton Beach, FL*

I find the book to be one of the best "diet books" I have ever read, and I have read quite a few of them through the last few years. So it is not willpower that is helping me to lose weight, it is *The Slight Edge*. What an amazing revelation this has been!
  —*Carol Chandler, Denver, CO*

Before I read *The Slight Edge*, I never understood why my efforts seemed to be a degree off. *The Slight Edge* showed me how to get that last edge I needed!
  —*Lynda Cromar, Aurora, CO*

The Slight Edge has had a profound effect on my life. After having it recommended four different times from four different people in one month, I finally purchased it. It was the first nonfiction book that I can remember not wanting to get to the end of because I loved what I was learning!
  —*Laura Jo Richins, Mesa, AZ*

I was born and raised in Albania. I came to America 13 years ago at age 18 by myself, with nothing but a dream. I didn't speak English, and had no money or connections. I am a college dropout and a former pizza delivery driver. A friend gave me *The Slight Edge* book and by implementing its simple principles, I am today living the American Dream.
  —*Andi Duli, Oklahoma City, OK*

The Slight Edge is truly a gift to the planet.
  —*Mark Skovron, Tampa Bay, FL*

I was bankrupt, had my car repossessed, and was on Medicaid and applying for food stamps. After putting the principles of *The Slight Edge* in place, I have made over a million dollars and it has also helped me in every area of my life.
  —*Darin Kidd, Appomattox, VA*

Reading *The Slight Edge* is perhaps one of the most eye-opening things one can do. It's such a simple concept that you realize you've overlooked every day of your life. Easy to do, easy not to do. Suddenly it's shocking how many things you really haven't been doing. The examples Jeff Olson provides are easy to understand and truly show how *The Slight Edge* affects the world.
     —*Julie Jonak, Houston, TX*

I have read numerous personal-development books through the years, and by far, this is one of the best! By applying the principles of *The Slight Edge*, I've lost 35 pounds in just three months, and am still going strong. I'm also working them into my job, part-time pursuits and every area of my life. I have quit focusing as much on the goals, and am focusing more on the little things I do every day, since I can control those. As a result, my life is going SO much better than it ever has!
     —*Richard Green, Franklin, TN*

This is a very simple, easy-to-follow book that can lead anyone from where they are to whatever level of success they want to achieve.
     —*Alex Serrano, Las Vegas, NV*

Over the course of the last year, by putting the Slight Edge concepts in practice, I have stopped using tobacco, and lost 25 pounds through diet and exercise.
     —*Bob Sutton, Ft. Collins, CO*

Following the principles outlined in Jeff Olson's *The Slight Edge* has helped me become a millionaire—several times over. Thanks for refining the processes into an understandable and workable format, Jeff.
     —*Rex LeGalley, Albuquerque, NM*

The Slight Edge principles apply to everything.... My wife and I have used it to improve our health and now we have lost over 100 pounds combined!
     —*BJ Baker, West Manchester, OH*

I led a life of errors in judgment until I came across this magnificent book. A blueprint for life can be founded on the Slight Edge philosophy. I found myself discarding old bad habits and replacing them with new positive habits; the result is a successful life. I was very reckless in my daily decisions, as well as my family positioning. My son noticed a huge change in my character and life perception. I no longer spend money haphazardly and my priorities are up to par.
     —*Simon Ponce, Irvine, CA*

As a student of personal progress for the past 40 years, I consider this work to be one of the foundational keys to the application of literally every other resource in this incredibly important area of life.
     —*Stephen McBroom, Floyd, VA*

The Slight Edge gives you that extra kick to push you beyond your wish list and into achieving your highest potential. I am able to apply the tools from *The Slight Edge* to balance my full-time work, while completing my bachelor's degree.
     —*Mark Roberts, Redmond, WA*

The Slight Edge is a phenomenal book. It makes you aware of the unwritten rules that we all live by and just weren't aware of! A definite MUST READ for EVERYONE, from student to executive. Wondering why you can't pass a class? *The Slight Edge*! Tried those diets but just can't seem to lose the weight? *The Slight Edge*! Have a savings plan but your bank account just refuses to grow? *The Slight Edge*! When applied correctly, *The Slight Edge* will show you how to get things back on track in your life. You will now be aware of what you're doing and be armed with the knowledge to correct the important things in your life, from relationships to getting that executive promotion. The principles have definitely helped my life. Here's to your success!
    —*Leonard Taylor, Las Vegas, NV*

Before reading *The Slight Edge*, my mindset for my life was not where it needed to be. I was a broke college student conforming to the masses. This book has changed the direction of my life dramatically by mentoring me on a new path filled with positive and disciplined philosophy.
    —*Tim Walter, San Diego, CA*

After applying the Slight Edge, my life began to change for the better and I found myself harnessing the powers of completion and momentum every day. It was amazing to see results in my business, in my health, and in my personal life.
    —*Carl Coffin, Goose Creek, SC*

I was searching for many answers to my life, when all of a sudden, I came across this magnificent and truthful information. It expanded my vision and took the fog away from my eyes.
    —*Michael Huerta, San Jacinto, CA*

As a successful leadership coach, I recommend two books to all of my clients. *The Slight Edge* is one of them!
    —*Dennis Antoine, Coral Springs, FL*

The Slight Edge kept me going on those days when I felt like I was not making progress by reassuring me that taking even the smallest positive action would eventually pay off.
    —*Susan Mix, Santa Clara, CA*

What an incredible masterpiece! *The Slight Edge* challenges me daily in business and in life. An absolute "must read" and "must apply" in every area.
    —*Dr. Vanessa R. Booker, Glendale, AZ*

The Slight Edge principles are so powerfully uplifting and inspirational that they are a catalyst for action. The Slight Edge gives me the momentum to achieve my daily goals in life.
    —*Antoinette Mims, New York, NY*

I have read personal-development books for over 20 years, and I can say this is the one that tied them all together, because it is so easy to read and understand, and so powerful in its simplicity.
    —*Mike Bishop, Wilsonville, OR*

The Slight Edge has been a philosophical staple in my life, and in the lives of those I mentor. I have started a business, and have gotten in better physical shape. The most memorable anecdote I use is, "What you do matters. What you do today matters. What do you every day matters."
—David Mack, Sacramento, CA

I LOVE THIS BOOK! As a former professional athlete, coach for over 25 years and wellness consultant, I strongly recommend *The Slight Edge* to everyone. If you want success in your health, finances and relationships, embrace this book and create a new mindset, thereby a new future for yourself. *The Slight Edge* is empowering! The philosophies and thoughts will hit home with everyone who reads it.
—Lucy Del Sarto, Olathe, KS

The Slight Edge is serving as a timeless way for me to help share the principles in which one must live to succeed in life. I have literally shared the concepts in this book with thousands.
—Ryan Chamberlin, Belleview, FL

As a full-time police officer, I believe *The Slight Edge* mentality should be a part of the educational system across America.
—Bobby Garcia, Tucson, AZ

This book has given me the vision to look past my current circumstances and into my desired results!
—Steven Joseph, St. Louis, MO

The Slight Edge took years of personal-development study and rolled it all into one, easy to understand book. Jeff Olson did an awesome job of communicating how anyone in any profession can improve his/her productivity, personal relationships and family life. WOW!
—Brian Kennedy, Jacksonville, NC

I would recommend *The Slight Edge* to anyone who is looking to understand why they have not been able to achieve their goals. They will understand that it is not all the fancy words many of the television hosts talk about, but the small things Mr. Olson writes about in his book—things that make absolute sense and are easy to do. I enjoy this book and have plans to make it part of my daily routine. I plan to give my family and myself a slight edge lifestyle. Thanks Mr. Olson.
—Glenn Watkins, Cibolo, TX

I use the Slight Edge philosophy every day in my personal life and especially in my business. Doing the daily activities compounded over time has led me to the kind of success most people only dream about. As a single mother of three boys, it is the principles in this book that have made me over a million dollars in just a few short years, and have allowed me to achieve levels of success in business and in life. *The Slight Edge* will help anyone.
—Christa Aufdemberg, Orange County, CA

The Slight Edge has given me and my family the secrets to a successful and abundant life. Practicing the basic philosophies of mastering the mundane has given my entire world a complete paradigm shift. There's a one-degree difference between hot and boiling, and this book has given me the necessary degrees to go from Good 2 Great. *The Slight Edge* is a lifer in my arsenal of personal development.
   —*Ken Hills, Syracuse, NY*

I found *The Slight Edge* to be a remarkable book. It was refreshingly different than other self-help books, as it focused on the hundreds of little daily and weekly decisions that build up to deliver the big hairy goals that one wants in life. My problem was that I can dream big and expect a lot from myself. But saying I wanted something huge next month and failing month after month just led to reluctance overall. Instead, after reading *The Slight Edge*, it was easier for me to focus on the daily schedule and on making daily progress.
   —*Timothy Sharpe, Redmond, WA*

I have used the principles of *The Slight Edge* to improve my physical fitness. I have used it to help pay off debt, build my savings and investments, and improve my relationships with my children.
   —*Stan Snow, North Yarmouth, ME*

I came across *The Slight Edge* and it instantly captured my attention. As an actress living in New York, it is so easy to get overwhelmed by everything that comes with this competitive business. *The Slight Edge* helped me to understand that the small choices I make every moment of every day make a huge impact on my life. Living in a society with so much emphasis on success, I found that *The Slight Edge* redefined what success is for me. It helps me to take the next step forward in my everyday life and do the next right thing. This ultimately leads to a very successful and fulfilling life. I attribute much of my success to the simple principles this book has outlined.
   —*Cara Cooley, Spokane, WA*

THE
SLIGHT
EDGE

Eighth Anniversary Edition

JEFF OLSON

with John David Mann

GREENLEAF
BOOK GROUP PRESS

This publication is designed to provide general information regarding the subject matter covered. However, laws and practices often vary from state to state and are subject to change. Because each factual situation is different, specific advice should be tailored to the particular circumstances. For this reason, the reader is advised to consult with his or her own advisor regarding their specific situation.

The author and publisher have taken reasonable precautions in the preparation of this book and believe the facts presented in the book are accurate as of the date it was written. However, neither the author nor the publisher assumes any responsibility for any errors or omissions. The author and publisher specifically disclaim any liability resulting from the use or application of the information contained in this book, and the information is not intended to serve as legal, financial or other professional advice related to individual situations.

Published by Greenleaf Book Group Press
Austin, Texas
www.gbgpress.com

Copyright ©2005-2013 Jeff Olson

Distributed by Greenleaf Book Group LLC

For ordering information or special discounts for bulk purchases, please contact Greenleaf Book Group LLC at PO Box 91869, Austin, TX 78709, 512.891.6100.

Composition by Tim Kuck
Cover design by Greenleaf Book Group LLC

Publisher's Cataloging-In-Publication Data
(Prepared by The Donohue Group, Inc.)

Olson, Jeff A.
    The slight edge / Jeff Olson ; with John David Mann.—8th anniversary ed.

    p. ; cm.

    "Turning simple disciplines into massive success & happiness."—Cover.
    Includes bibliographical references.
    Issued also as an ebook.
    ISBN: 978-1-62634-046-6

    1. Success. 2. Self-actualization (Psychology) I. Title.

BF637.S8 O47 2013
158.1   2013945596

Printed in the United States of America

15 16 17 18   10 9 8 7

8th Anniversary Edition

Contents

Preface xi

Part I: HOW THE SLIGHT EDGE WORKS

1. The Beach Bum and the Millionaire 1
2. The First Ingredient 15
3. The Choice 29
4. Master the Mundane 47
5. Slow Down to Go Fast 63
6. Don't Fall for Quantum Leap 81
7. The Secret of Happiness 93
8. The Ripple Effect 111
9. But You Have to Start with a Penny 127

Part II: LIVING THE SLIGHT EDGE

10. Two Life Paths 141
11. Mastering the Slight Edge 159
12. Invest in Yourself 175
13. Learn from Mentors 191
14. Use Your Slight Edge Allies 205
15. Cultivate Slight Edge Habits 217
16. Three Steps to Your Dreams 237
17. Living the Slight Edge 253
18. Where to Go from Here 269

A Personal Invitation. 273

Life-Transforming Books 275

Acknowledgments 277

About the Author. 279

Preface

When the first edition of *The Slight Edge* came out in 2005, I had no idea how popular it would become. There was no media campaign, no bookstore placement, no press release. We just published it. Promoted by word of mouth, from person to person, soon it was spreading like a grassfire, and before we knew it hundreds of thousands of people had read it and told others about it. Clearly, there was something in these pages that had struck a chord.

Since that time we have received thousands of personal letters and emails from readers, of all ages and from all walks of life, telling us how *The Slight Edge* has touched their lives. Now it was our responsibility, as we saw it, to make sure we kept making the book as relevant and as available as possible.

In 2008 we helped produce an adaptation of the book aimed at teenagers. Titled *SUCCESS for Teens: Real Teens Talk about Using the Slight Edge*, the book presented the core slight edge material in a more teen-friendly format, accompanied by dozens of stories from real-life teens about their experiences applying the principles in their lives. Through the efforts of the SUCCESS Foundation, the book has since been given to nearly two million teenagers.

In 2011 we produced a revised and expanded edition of the original book, with some additional principles I'd developed in the course of giving slight edge talks and new material by my daughter, Amber Olson Rourke, along with the inclusion of many personal experiences by *Slight Edge* readers.

With 2015 only a few years away, we started thinking about a tenth anniversary edition, which would incorporate a few new and critical concepts based on observations and experiences that had unfolded with *The Slight Edge* in the years since it first appeared. But we soon realized we couldn't wait until 2015. Too much had happened in the meantime.

So we decided to pull the trigger and make the Tenth Anniversary Edition into the *Eighth* Anniversary Edition you now hold in your hands.

This edition offers a complete rewriting and reorganization of the original material. For example, the discussion that revolves around the "roller coaster" graph that appears in chapter 1 (The Beach Bum and the Millionaire) presents an evolving understanding of where success and failure come from, and why, which did not appear in the earlier books for the simple reason that I hadn't yet articulated it. The "seven slight edge habits" in chapter 15 build on ideas that first appeared in the 2011 edition and take those ideas to their logical conclusion. Ongoing experiences in business led to several new story-illustrations, as did formative experiences from early in my career that I haven't shared until now.

Probably the most significant change in this edition is the addition of two entirely new chapters—The Secret of Happiness and The Ripple Effect—that take the concept of the slight edge to new levels of depth and breadth. These chapters explore the effect the slight edge has on two critical areas of life, everyday happiness and long-term impact, and insights from these two chapters play out throughout the rest of the book as well.

I hope you enjoy it.

Part I

HOW THE SLIGHT EDGE WORKS

1. The Beach Bum and the Millionaire

> "The only person you are destined to become is the person you decide to be."
>
> —*Ralph Waldo Emerson (attrib.)*

I want to tell you about two friends I've known since I was a kid, guys from my old neighborhood in New Mexico. These two characters grew up together, went to school together, graduated together, and roomed in college together. They were both pretty personable guys, and I got along with both of them. They had identical childhoods, though, and by high school they had both earned reputations as mischief-makers. Still, they both had more than enough drive and ambition to make up for whatever strikes they had against them. When you add it all up, in terms of their skills and potential, I would say they were evenly matched. In fact, they were almost identical in every way.

Every way except one—which was the different paths they took, and where they led.

The first friend dropped out of college, moved from New Mexico to Daytona Beach, Florida, the spring break capital of the world, where he became a beach bum, lifted weights, chased girls, and let his blond hair grow long and curly. People started calling him Gorgeous George, after the WWE wrestler who brought pro wrestling into America's living rooms. My friend was pretty popular, in a big-fish-in-a-small-pond way. But he was a beach bum, cutting golf greens to make ends meet, sweating in the sun while he lugged around bags of golf clubs for the wealthy. Frustrated and unhappy, he eventually left Daytona Beach and went back to New Mexico, where he went into business for himself. And what happened? The business failed and Gorgeous George lost everything.

Then there was my other friend, Gorgeous George's buddy. As an adult, this guy led a charmed life. Graduating from college as an A-student, he went on to business school and graduated in the top of his class, then got recruited by a gigantic tech firm, built a stellar résumé, and went on to create a string of entrepreneurial ventures, each one more successful than the last. Today his life is rich in every way. He has a beautiful, amazing daughter, thousands of friends around the world, runs a record-breakingly successful company, and is happy beyond measure. Yet he still stays in touch with his childhood friend the beach bum.

In fact, they stay in *very* close touch.

I often think about these two guys, because I know that I could have been either one of them. Matter of fact, I *was*. Because here's the one piece of the story I left out: the reason those two guys were roommates all those years, and the reason they are still in constant contact today, is that they are one and the same person.

They're both me.

That college dropout who became a frustrated beach bum, who eventually took his shot at business but bottomed out there too? That was yours truly.

That straight-A college graduate who went on to create one business success after another, who became a millionaire with a fabulous family, friends all over the world and a richly happy, fulfilled life? Guilty as charged.

I've been blessed with a lot of success in my life. But I sure didn't start out that way. I started out as Gorgeous George the college-dropout golf-greens-cutter. And I'll tell you a secret: I'm the same person today that I was then. Not that I haven't changed a lot through my experiences; we all do that. What I mean is, deep down inside, I'm really no different than I was then. It's not as if I had any sort of lightning-strike overnight transformation. I did not go to a mountaintop, did not experience enlightenment, did not have a near-death experience that showed me the truth of universal brotherhood. (Although I did go through some pretty terrible failures that at the time sure *felt* like near-death experiences.)

I didn't change who I *was* as much as I changed what I *did*.

I didn't change who I am, because no matter what the gurus and therapists might tell you, I don't believe any of us can really do that. I mean, we are who we are. The kid who became a frustrated beach bum was never anything but average: average at schoolwork, average at sports, average in social skills. The incredibly fortunate and deeply happy man I am today is still that average kid, no more, no less, and I say that without an ounce of false modesty. The only reason I've made the transformation from there to here is that, somewhere along the way, I've had the good fortune of being exposed to the slight edge.

How I got from there to here—and how *you* can get from wherever you are to wherever you want to be—is what this book is about.

My Day of Disgust

The transition from beach bum to millionaire did not happen overnight. It was a long, slow, at times painful roller-coaster process, because frankly, I didn't know what I was doing. I didn't yet have the key you're getting in this book: I didn't know about the slight edge.

I was working it out by trial and error. Lots of error.

I was born and raised in Albuquerque. My dad died when my brother, sister, and I were just kids, and somehow my mom held everything together. She was a terrific mother, a loving and constant presence in our lives. But it was still a rough way to grow up, as a fatherless, blond-headed kid in a Hispanic neighborhood where he didn't fit in. I didn't know what to do with it all, so I channeled my energy into mischief and misbehavior. A few years before my dad died, when I was in the third grade, my teachers had informed my mom that I had a low IQ. Now I started proving the point, and pretty quickly had gained that mischief-maker reputation. While my mom worked her way through the years, I struggled my way through school.

By age eighteen, it was clear to anyone who knew me that I didn't have much of a future.

I begged my way into the University of New Mexico. At college, I built upon my previous academic career and succeeded in taking my C average down to a D average. I did learn one thing, though: I learned that when spring break came, all the students went out east to Daytona Beach for a week to party hard. I thought I could do them one better—I quit school altogether and moved there.

In Daytona Beach I pursued my first calling, as the beach bum with the long curly locks. To make ends meet, if you can call it that, I took a job at the Orlando Country Club cutting the golf course grass.

One day, as I was cutting the greens under the scorching Florida sun, I paused to watch the wealthy club members playing golf all over the porcelain-smooth grass I had just cut for them. Watching them hum to and fro in their zippy golf carts, in their dapper golf outfits, with their classy golf bags filled with expensive golf clubs, I felt a burning question simmer up inside:

Why is it that they're over there riding in carts, and I'm over here working? I don't get it!

How come they were over there putting, while I was over here cutting? Hey, I was as good as these people were. Why did they get to have it ten times, twenty times better than me? *Were* they twenty times better than me? Were they twenty times smarter, or did they work twenty times harder? I didn't think so. I felt like there was something going on here that I should get, something that ought to be crystal clear, but that for me was as clear as mud.

It all just seemed so … unfair.

For whatever reason, as happens in so many people's lives, I found myself staring squarely at a fork in the road, a point I now refer to as *my day of disgust*: that moment of impact we sometimes hit in our lives when we come smack face to face with our circumstances and, without having a clue to the what or how of it, make a decision to change.

In that instant, standing there sweltering in the brutal Florida heat, I came to just such a moment of decision. I suddenly knew that I'd had it up to here with where I was and what I was. Something clicked; the tumblers in the lock fell into place; and I knew that I could never go back to where I'd been only moments earlier. I knew that for things to be different, I had to *do* something different.

I had found one piece of the puzzle. Only a piece, and not nearly enough to find my way to genuine lasting success. But enough to get started on the path of pursuit.

The Superachiever

On the heels of that day-of-disgust epiphany, I walked away from the golf course, loaded my stereo and clothes into my 1964 Dodge Dart slant-six (all my possessions fit easily into the back seat with room left over for a passenger), and took off for Albuquerque. The car kept overheating so bad that it took me six days just to get to Texas. It was the longest trip of my life—and not just because of the crappy car, but because of the distance I traveled in my heart and soul. When I arrived in New Mexico, I had resolved that I was going to forever leave behind the land of mediocrity and start inhabiting the world of high achievement. I was going to pour it on, go on all eight cylinders (okay, for the moment that would be all *six* cylinders), and do whatever it took to move my life ahead.

As I said, all my life I had been no better than average at anything I'd done: average grades, average in athletics, average social skills. I knew that the only way I could ever become anybody was by working harder and being more persistent. If I wanted to have a prayer of a chance of getting on the team, I had to work harder in the practices. If I wanted to impress somebody in the social world, I had to work harder at it. If I was going to get good grades, I would have to study harder. So I did. That semester, for the first time in my life, I got straight A's. I went on to business school and graduated in the top of my class—and the rest, you could say, was history.

Except that it wasn't. I didn't know it yet, but just working harder doesn't do it. If it did, then everyone who works hard would have made it. All you have to do is look around you and you can see that this isn't the case. The world is chock full of people who are working their butts off—and still getting their butts kicked by circumstances.

I was about to find this out.

Fresh out of college, I went to work at the Albuquerque International Airport, where I continued to pour it on and work my tail off. In what seemed like no time at all, I had become one of the youngest international airport managers in the country. I was such hot management material that I was recruited away from the airport by the Dallas-based tech giant Texas Instruments, where I worked for the next five years and advanced to the management level as a manager in the company's intelligence systems division. But corporate America wasn't for me. There was a lot of politics, which I hated, and it didn't feel like I'd yet found the place where I belonged. And I was clearly on a superachieving roll, right? Honestly, it felt like I could accomplish anything I put my mind to. Like I'd learned the magic words, found the secret formula.

So I struck out on my own and set my foot on the entrepreneurial path.

Moving back to Albuquerque again, I started a solar energy company. I knew nothing about solar energy; I barely knew whether the sun came up in the east or in the west. (East, it turns out.) But with four hundred solar companies in the state, New Mexico was the capital of the budding new industry, so ignorance or not, the smart course of action seemed clear.

And at first it looked like I had indeed made a very smart decision. Within two years, my company was one of the top in the nation, and before long we became one of the largest solar energy companies in America.

I was thrilled. On top of the world.

What I didn't yet know was that nothing ever stays the same. Everything is in motion, always. Everything changes. And that was what happened next. Times changed. Tax laws changed. Our industry was hit hard. Before I knew what was happening, my company had collapsed and I had lost everything, gone back to zero and below—owing more money than I could ever even hope to make again.

I couldn't believe it. My superachievements had turned to dust right before my eyes. My millionaire life had evaporated, leaving me right back in beach bum land: the guy with nothing.

They even took my car.

My Night of Despair

The night my car was towed away I sat there despondent, in disbelief. Years earlier as a failed college student I'd had my day of disgust. Now the other shoe had dropped, and as a failed entrepreneur I'd just arrived at my *night of despair.*

I could not comprehend what had just happened to me. After living as a failure all my life, one day I awoke and came to my senses, went back to college, applied myself like crazy, entered at the bottom and graduated at the top, worked for a major corporation for five years and went to the very top *there*, built my own company in less than five years and went to the top *there*. I had built myself from a failure into a success. And now, after fourteen long years of upward travel, I'd somehow arrived *back at the bottom*?

I was more broke than I'd been when I was Gorgeous George strutting on the beach in his cut-offs.

Twelve years of blood and guts, and for what? I just could not wrap my head around it. I couldn't see the justice or even the logic of it, of *any* of it. I felt like that teenager again, confused and angry at a world where nothing made sense. Was life just inherently unfair, with no rhyme or reason to it? Was there no point in even trying?

That was when I began to examine more carefully what had happened in my life.

This time, it was no epiphany. This time, it wasn't like that moment on the Orlando golf course. There was no switch I could throw in my life, no sudden resolution to make things better. I'd already done that, and look at where it had gotten me.

No, this time I needed to sit down and start carefully, methodically, systematically sorting through the mixed up pieces of my shattered life. There had to be some logic here, and I had to find it.

So, let's see…

I had been a college dropout, a beach bum, and complete financial failure. And I had also been a straight-A student, top corporate manager, superachieving entrepreneur in a cutting-edge industry and complete financial success. And all of those had been the same person. So what was the difference? It made no sense.

Or did it?

The more I looked at it, the more it seemed to me that this roller coaster was not a matter of bad luck or a fluke of circumstance. It couldn't be. There was something about what *I was doing* that wasn't working. But on the other hand, there had obviously been times when what *I was doing* had totally worked.

So what was the difference?

For the first time, I began to see that over the years of my career I had gone through a sequence of experiences that held the secrets to success as well as to failure. I began to see that the seeds of both beach bum and millionaire lay in the simple actions I took every day.

Escaping the Curse of the Roller Coaster

Up to that point, I knew I was average. If I had continued accepting that as simply the way things were, then nothing much in my life would have turned out for me. The shift in my life began happening when I stopped taking it for granted that just because I was an average guy, that meant I was doomed to no more than average results.

I now started questioning whether this was true. I began doing a systematic review of my life and taking a very close look at my actions and my results.

Here is what I saw:

When people are looking down the barrel of failure in their lives, they will do whatever it takes to get themselves moving, something, anything, to start climbing upward toward the point of survival. And then, once they get to the point where they're keeping their heads above water, they start heading back down again. As they start getting close enough to the failure line that they can see it coming, they go, "Whoops, I'm headed towards failure!" and then they do whatever it takes to turn their trajectory around and start heading back up … and the cycle repeats.

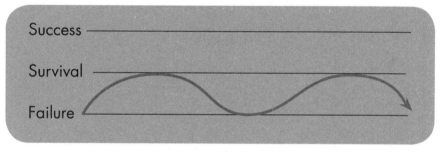

That's what I'd been doing. And that's what so many people do, living their entire lives like this, oscillating between failure and survival, striving toward success and maybe even *reaching* the level of success, but then invariably turning back and heading downward again. We do this in our finances, in our health, in our relationships, and in our lives as a whole.

Why?

Well, you could say it's because we sabotage ourselves, for all kinds of reasons. Our father was mean to us, so now we're mean to ourselves. We're conflicted, because society sends us mixed messages. We've fallen into a pattern of self-sabotage because for some reason we don't feel we deserve success. And you know, maybe some of those things are true for you. Heck, maybe they're all true. I have no idea, and truthfully, I don't really care. Because *none of that matters*. The truth is, whatever other factors may or may not be there, the only reason we keep following this roller coaster of almost-success and nearly-failure, this sine wave of mediocrity, this curse of the average, is that we're missing one simple point.

That was the point I stumbled on.

As I began examining my successes and failures, what I gradually realized was that the very same activities that had rescued me from failure, that had carried me from the failure line up to the survival line, would also rescue me from average and carry me from the survival line to the success line—*if I would just keep doing them.*

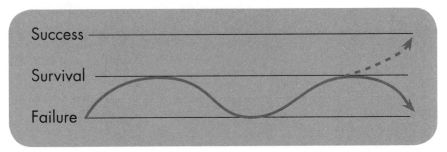

And that was exactly the point: that was exactly what I *wasn't* doing.

Once I got a little way above survival and was starting to head up into the warmer waters of success, without realizing it or thinking about it, I would stop doing the things that had gotten me there. Naturally, I would then start sinking back down again, back down toward survival and beyond, back down toward the failure line. And I did that every time.

Every time.

That's the only reason our lives follow that roller coaster. It's that simple. As soon as we get away from failure and up past the line of survival, we quit doing the things that got us there.

You know what that means? It means *you already know* how to do everything it takes to make you an outrageous success. That's how you've survived up to this point. And if you can survive, then you can succeed. You don't need to do some brilliant, impossible thing. You don't need to learn some insanely difficult skills, or have some genius-level brainstorm of an innovative idea. All you have to do is keep doing the things that got you this far.

Which is exactly what 99.9 percent of people *don't* do.

What those things are, why most people don't do them, and how you can live an outrageously happy and successful life by doing them, is what this book is all about.

I began to realize that there was a profound success secret hidden within that roller coaster: if we would just keep doing the things that got us from failure up to survival in the first place, *the things we already know how to do and were already doing*, they would eventually carry us all the way to success.

What exactly are those things? What are the actions that move us upward on that curve—and what are the actions that drive us down? I'll tell you what they are, in a single word.

Simple.

The things that take you out of failure and up toward survival and success are *simple.* So simple, in fact, that it's easy to overlook them. *Extremely* easy to overlook them. It's easy to overlook them because when you look at them, they seem insignificant. They're not big, sweeping things that take huge effort. They're not heroic or dramatic. Mostly they're just little things you do every day and that nobody else even notices. They are things that are so simple to do—yet successful people actually *do* them, while unsuccessful people only look at them and don't take action.

Things like taking a few dollars out of a paycheck, putting it into savings, and leaving it there. Or doing a few minutes of exercise every day—and not skipping it. Or reading ten pages of an inspiring, educational, life-changing book every day. Or taking a moment to tell someone how much you appreciate them, and doing that consistently, every day, for months and years. Little things that seem insignificant in the doing, yet when compounded over time yield very big results.

You could call these "little virtues" or "success habits." I call them *simple daily disciplines*. Simple productive actions, repeated consistently over time.

That, in a nutshell, is the slight edge.

Beach Bum or Millionaire?

The reason I'm telling you the story of the beach bum and the millionaire is that it's not only the story of my life.

It's the story of your life, too.

You have both a beach bum and a millionaire inside you, a potential failure and a potential success. We all do. What makes the difference in how things turn out? Actually, you do. The truth is, you have complete control over the direction that the rest of your life takes.

Since that night of despair I have built some very successful businesses and earned more money than I ever dreamed of back when I was a corporate manager or solar-energy entrepreneur. I've also experienced more joy and fulfillment in my relationships than I knew was possible. As I write these words, I am healthier, more energized, and more alive today than I was ten years ago. I am happier today, have better relationships, and a more satisfying professional life, than I did ten years ago. (And ten years ago, things were already going pretty well!) In fact, my life today is better in every way than it was ten years ago. And I expect to be saying the same thing ten years from now.

Of course, I could lose it all tomorrow. It's happened before; I'd survive. But there is something I cannot lose, and with that one thing I could start from scratch and build it all back up again, and do it in record time. That one thing is the slight edge.

One more thing: when I say "millionaire" I'm not talking purely about money or financial success. I'm using the term here as a label for *success*, but it's only a label, a metaphor, just as "beach bum" is only a metaphor. When I say *millionaire* I mean someone with a million-dollar smile, with a million friends, with a million dollars' worth—heck, a billion, a trillion dollars' worth—of joy, love, contentment, fulfillment, great relationships, curiosity and fascination, passion and enthusiasm, excitement and accomplishment … a fortune's worth of *life* in their life.

I want that life for *you*.

Personal Stories from
The Slight Edge Readers

When *The Slight Edge* first came out, I sent it around to a few friends who had asked for copies, and figured that would pretty much be that. Then I started getting calls from them, saying how much they'd gotten out of it. I discounted much of what they were saying because, after all, they were friends. But then I started hearing from people *they* had given the book to, people I didn't know.

Things started taking off from there. Before long we were hearing from hundreds of people about how the simple principles in *The Slight Edge* had touched and even changed their lives. As the hundreds turned into thousands, it occurred to us that sharing even a few of these stories, right here on these pages, might bring the material to life in a different way and help you apply it in *your* life, too.

Starting with the next chapter, and at the end of every chapter, we'll share one or two stories from *Slight Edge* readers, talking about how the slight edge has had an impact on their lives.

Essential Points from Chapter 1

The same activities that take us from failure to survival would also take us from survival to success—if we would just keep doing them.

You *already know* how to do everything it would take to make you an outrageous success. All you have to do is keep doing the things that have gotten you this far.

You have complete control over the direction that the rest of your life takes.

There is a beach bum and a millionaire inside each one of us. What makes the difference in how things turn out? *You* do.

2. The First Ingredient

> **"Do the thing, and you shall have the power."**
> —*Ralph Waldo Emerson* Essay on Compensation

L et me tell you what actually happened starting the day *after* that night of despair, after my solar energy company collapsed and they towed away my nice car. I had no resources, no savings or capital, nothing I could start over with. The only option I had was to go to work for someone else. So I did something that Gorgeous George cutting those golf greens in his cut-offs would never have dreamed he'd be doing.

I went into sales.

You have to understand, I *hated* sales. When I was starting out, that was the last thing I wanted to do. When I first went to work for Texas Instruments, my intention was to work my way up in management. They had other ideas. "If you want to be in management," they told me, "you have to start in sales."

I was horrified. I knew absolutely nothing about sales, and the idea terrified me. I had no natural gift for it. I didn't have the patience. And I am no natural-born silver-tongued smooth-talker. But, sales they wanted, so sales it was. And over time, I got used to it.

And then something ironic happened: over time, sales changed my life.

Not the process of sales itself. It was the *training* involved. In the course of going through all kinds of courses, workshops, and sales-related training material, I was exposed to a huge amount of valuable information. But it wasn't even the information itself that changed my life. Ironically, it was the thing that I eventually realized was *missing* in all that training and information, the thing that was far more valuable even than all that priceless information.

It was what I call *the first ingredient.*

After that night of despair, having no resources of my own, I went to work for a direct marketing company. In time I built up a good-sized sales force and then went on to build a couple of other successful businesses, one of which eventually appointed me CEO. Based on that experience, I then started a personal development training company called The People's Network (TPN). At TPN we produced nearly a thousand television programs on all sorts of topics, from finance to relationships, and had the opportunity to work with some of the greatest authors, thinkers, and thought leaders of our time. Because of the position I was in, I found myself at the epicenter of the personal development movement, spending time with such legendary figures as Jan Miller, the famous literary agent for personal development authors; Dick Snyder, then CEO of Simon & Schuster, the biggest personal development publisher; Jimmy Bowen, the music producer; and Oprah Winfrey.

During those years we produced and provided some of the best information on how to become successful available anywhere. And thousands of people used that information to improve their lives a little, or even a lot. But for many others—*so* many others—that golden, priceless, incredibly insightful information seemed to have hardly any effect, or no effect at all.

It was mystifying.

I had learned so much and gained so much from this stuff. These teachings were life-altering. Yet I was seeing all these people eagerly taking it all in … and not really getting much benefit from it.

In the course of that experience, I came to a sobering realization. Everything these great teachers were talking about *worked*—but it wasn't *working.* People would try to follow it, but when the quantum leap they were looking for didn't happen in the first thirty, sixty, or ninety days, they would quit.

No matter how much information there is, and no matter how good that information is, if the person consuming it doesn't have the right catalyst, the catalyst that will allow them to *apply* that information effectively, then success will still elude their grasp.

It's like eating the best food in the world without the intestinal capacity to digest or absorb it. It may be fantastic, incredibly accurate information with amazing insights and a track record of proven success, but it just goes right through you, leaving you as weak and hungry as you were before you ate it. I saw it happen hundreds, thousands of times.

It wasn't for lack of trying, and it wasn't for want of desire. If you've ever been told, "You'll get it if you just *want* it bad enough," I'm here to let you off the hook: it simply isn't true. Just wanting something doesn't necessarily get it for you, not even when you combine wanting with trying really hard and working really hard. You can want all you want, and *try* yourself blue in the face.

But it still won't happen—not without the first ingredient.

Why Diets Don't Work

Over the past few decades I've worked with thousands of people from every imaginable background and walk of life, from doctors and lawyers to bus drivers and manual laborers. They have all had the exact same opportunity. Some of these people have become millionaires, and many more have gone on to earn a good, solid living. But the majority of them, faced with exactly the same opportunities, have gone nowhere.

Why? It's not a matter of luck. It's not timing or fate. Not a matter of intelligence, skill or talent, either.

During these same years, I've gone to the very top with a range of different companies and different product lines (which I knew next to nothing about when I started) and in different countries and different languages (which I didn't speak, and still don't). And you already know it wasn't my natural gift for sales (which I don't have).

The truth is, there's been nothing brilliant about anything I've done. Quite the opposite, in fact. In every case, I've done the exact same thing every time, using ridiculously simple strategies made up of ridiculously simple lists of ridiculously simple actions. The strategies I used (none of them invented or devised by me, by the way) are so simple that if you and I sat down together in a room for twenty minutes, I could show you exactly what I did to create four different, separate multimillion-dollar organizations—and teach you how to do the exact same thing. In twenty minutes.

And chances are, it wouldn't work for you.

Why not? Because *how to do it* is not the issue. Because if we don't fundamentally change the way you think, then you'll have rearranged what I said by the time you leave the room. You'll have reinvented it by the time you go to bed that night, and in the morning you won't even recognize it as the same information.

It's the same reason diets don't work. The same reason gym memberships don't magically make you more fit. Because a diet without the slight edge, a gym membership without the slight edge, a solid and intelligently designed business plan without the slight edge, is like a plant without water.

People everywhere are clamoring for the formula, the secret, the path to improve their lives. And as I found during my years with TPN, there's more good, solid how-to information available today about all those things than there's ever been before. But that's not how it works. If you're one of the millions looking for cookie-cutter answers to the great questions in life, you can call off the search right now. *How to do it* is not the issue.

If "how to do it" were the answer, it'd be done. It's how you *do* the "hows" that's most important. If access to the right information were the answer, we'd all be rich, healthy, happy, and fulfilled. And most of us are none of those things.

Why not? Because the answer is only the answer—it isn't actually doing the thing. It isn't *applying* the answer, *living* the answer. It's only information.

It's not that how-to books are not valuable; they are. In fact, there are some wonderful ones that I'll even recommend to you at the end of this book. It's just that another how-to book is not what you need. It's not what any of us need. We already have enough of those—maybe more than enough. Because what you need to transform your life is not more information. Besides, we're all so different, and my how-to may work for me but may not be the how-to that works for you. As much as we'd all love to quantify a precise, specific, paint-by-the-numbers approach to life, love, and happiness, we are out of luck in that department, because there is no universal, one-size-fits-all method to anything.

However, there *is* a secret ingredient.

An ingredient that, once you grasp it, will cause you to find those answers, apply them, live them, and achieve those results you want. A secret ingredient that will allow you to achieve lasting success in any area of your life you choose.

The Missing Ingredient

Time to pull away the curtain and share that secret.

Ready?

Here it comes.

This is it.

(The secret ingredient is *your philosophy*.)

Now, before you react: I'm not talking about some esoteric, intellectual thing here. Not some complex, elaborate, or heady system of ideas. No long lists of bullet points you have to remember, with clever acronyms you have to memorize. And I'm definitely not talking about some kind of self-hypnosis, or about conjuring up the impossible out of thin air through some mystical power of attraction or any other kind of hocus-pocus.

And most important of all, what I'm talking about is *not hard to do*.

By "your philosophy," all I mean is changing the way you think about simple everyday things. Once you do, then you will take the steps you need to take, to lead you to the how-to's you need.

Let me put it this way. If you *don't* change how you think about these simple everyday things, then no amount of how-to's will get you anywhere or give you any true solutions. Because it's not the *hows* that do it, it's how you *do* the hows. The reason diets and self-help courses and weight-loss programs and other how-to's don't work for most people is the same reason most how-to books and courses don't work for most people. It isn't that the actions are wrong. It's that people don't keep doing them.

Focusing on the actions, the what-to-dos and the how-to-do-its, is not enough, because it's the *attitude behind the actions* that keep those actions in place.

"Aha, so all I need is an attitude adjustment?"

Unfortunately, no—it's not that simple.

Here's the problem. You can adjust your attitude by getting inspired, by listening to a great speaker, by reading an inspiring story, or by your best friend giving you a pep talk. By giving *yourself* a pep talk. Any of those things can get you moving in the right direction. So far so good. The problem is, it won't last. Remember that roller coaster diagram?

You may get inspired by that uplifting story or inspirational pep talk, but you can't freeze that feeling or glue the emotions of the moment into place. Emotions change like the wind, and you can't stop them. No one can. They keep moving; that's why they're called *emotions* and not e-*standingstills*. You can't dictate how you feel. No matter how much you may tell yourself to feel positive about this how-to step or that how-to step, what if you just don't? Today, you're excited about getting fit. You feel like doing your twenty minutes on the treadmill. Great! But what if tomorrow you just don't feel like doing it?

To find the path to success, you have to back up one more step. It's the understanding behind the attitudes that are behind the actions.

It's the philosophy. That's the missing ingredient, the secret ingredient.

The *first* ingredient.

Yes, you have to know the winning how-to actions, and you have to possess the winning attitudes—but what generates all that and keeps it all in place is your philosophy. Your philosophy is what you know, how you hold it, and how it affects what you do. How you think about simple, everyday things. That's what this book is about.

your **PHILOSOPHY** creates your **ATTITUDE** your **ACTIONS** your **RESULTS** creates your **LIFE**

A positive philosophy turns into a positive attitude, which turns into positive actions, which turns into positive results, which turns into a positive lifestyle. A positive *life*. And a negative philosophy turns into a negative attitude, which turns into negative actions, which turns into negative results, which turns into a negative lifestyle.

Life Wisdom

You don't have to go to graduate school, learn Greek, or read thick books with extremely long paragraphs by nineteenth-century German authors to change your philosophy. A life philosophy is something so simple, so basic a six-year-old child can understand it.

Here is an example of a life philosophy; it comes from Ralph Waldo Emerson in his *Essay on Compensation*:

> *Do the thing, and you shall have the power.*

Profoundly simple and just as powerful. The sort of wisdom you can actually apply in everyday life. Nike said pretty much the same thing, only with fewer words: *Just do it.* But I like the Emerson version better, and we'll be using it again later on when we talk about applying the slight edge in your life.

There are two prevalent types of attitudes: entitled and value-driven. A value-driven attitude says, "What can I do to help you?" An entitled attitude says, "What have you done for me lately?" An entitled attitude says, "Pay me more, and then maybe I'll work harder." A value-driven attitude says, "I'll work harder, and then I expect you'll pay me more."

Which of these attitudes is driven by Emerson's philosophy, "Do the thing and you'll have the power"?

Your philosophy is *what you know, how you hold what you know, and how it affects what you do.* You can look at anyone's actions and trace back, through the attitudes behind those actions, to their source: the philosophy behind the attitudes. Show me what a man does, and I'll show you his philosophy.

Here's another example of a life philosophy, this one from Thomas J. Watson, the founder of IBM:

> *The formula for success is quite simple:*
> *Double your rate of failure.*

These days we aren't often taught that the key to success is to double our rate of failure. On the contrary, we're taught to avoid failure like the plague. You've probably heard the expression, "Failure is not an option." Oh, really? Well, here's a reality check: failure had *better* be an option, because whether or not you consider it an option, it's going to happen! If you go through life with the philosophy that "failure is not an option," then you'll never have any good opportunities to learn.

If Babe Ruth had lived by the philosophy that *failure is not an option*, then you and I would have never heard of him. Why? Because Babe Ruth not only set a world record for home runs, he also led the league in strikeouts.

Michael Jordan, considered by many as one of the greatest basketball players of all time (winning six NBA titles with the Chicago Bulls), didn't make his high school team as a sophomore because they thought he was too small. The next two years he grew four inches, honed his game, and went on to do pretty well.

Over the course of his career, Abraham Lincoln had a staggering record of lost elections and public-office failures. For the ungainly lawyer from Illinois, failure was not only an option, it was practically his specialty. If it hadn't been, he would never have made it to the White House, and who knows what the United States would look like today. Or if there would even be such a thing as the United States.

And it's hard to imagine just what our lives would be like today if Thomas Edison had subscribed to the *failure is not an option* philosophy. In his efforts to find a stable filament to make his electric light bulb invention work, he tried out thousands of different versions and every single one failed. His famous comment: "I have not failed. I've simply discovered ten thousand ways that don't work."

Successful people *fail* their way to the top.

Why Lottery Winners Lose

Your philosophy is your view of life, something beyond feelings and attitudes. Your philosophy drives your attitudes and feelings, which drive your actions.

By and large, people are looking in the wrong places. They are looking for a big break, that lucky breakthrough, the amazing "quantum leap" everyone keeps talking about. I call it the philosophy of the craps table and roulette wheel, and I don't believe they'll ever find it. I've seen an awful lot of remarkable successes and colossal failures up close, and in my experience, neither one happens in quantum leaps or "breaks," whether the lucky or unlucky kind.

They happen through the slight edge.

You've probably heard the stories about lottery winners losing it all. They're not urban legends; they really happen. The depths people fall to after big lottery winnings are heartbreaking and mindboggling. And it isn't only lottery winners. You've also heard the stories about famous movie stars, recording stars, or star athletes who make incredible fortunes, literally hundreds of millions of dollars, and somehow manage to wind up broke and in debt. And when you heard those stories, you probably thought the same thing I did: "Man, I don't know how they pulled *that* off, but if *I* made that kind of money I sure wouldn't squander it all like that!"

But let me ask you a tough question: are you sure about that? Speaking as one who's made it to the top and then seen it all evaporate, all I can say is, you might be surprised.

There's a reason those lottery winners lose it all again, a reason those shining stars plummet to those dark places: they may have had the big breaks, but they didn't grasp the slight edge. Their winnings changed their bank account balance—but it didn't change their philosophy.

The purpose of this book is to show you the slight edge philosophy, show you how it works, give you plenty of examples, and show you exactly how to make it a core part of how *you* see the world and how you live your life every day.

Throughout this book, if you look carefully you'll find dozens of statements that embody this philosophy, statements like "Do the thing, and you shall have the power." Here are a few more examples that you'll come across in the following pages:

Success is the progressive realization of a worthy ideal.

Successful people do what unsuccessful people are not willing to do.

There is a natural progression to everything in life: plant, cultivate, harvest.

Here's a suggestion that can maximize how much you get out of this book, that will help you not only read it but also absorb it and apply it in your life: every time you come to a fundamental statement of philosophy, highlight it. Then go back regularly and read through just those highlighted sections: your own personal guide to the slight edge philosophy.

Diets Actually *Do* Work

I've heard people describe the slight edge as sort of a magic bullet, but that's not quite accurate. The slight edge is not a magic bullet, because you don't need a magic bullet. There is no magic bullet, no quick-fix path to success. All you need is good information, which is already available everywhere, and the right catalyst that will allow you to absorb and apply that information. The slight edge is that catalyst.

Marketing tactics try to seduce you with the promise that you will lose thirty pounds in three weeks, or make money while you sleep. But you won't. You might have some success at first, but the results won't last long. And when that happens time after time, it's tempting to just give up on great information like that—which is a genuine tragedy, because with the right catalyst that information *could* give you fantastic results.

Diets *do* work. Gym memberships *do* pay off. Solid business plans *can* make you a wealthy person. And there's a great deal of personal development material out there that *will* make you a happier, more productive, more successful, more fulfilled person.

Just not without the slight edge.

The Slight Edge is not just more good information. It's not another self-help success book packed with some revolutionary "new best way" of doing things. You don't need that. Nobody needs that. All the "new and better" information is already available. It has been for years. This book isn't more information—it is the catalyst that will help you put that good information to use. It is the missing ingredient you need for all the personal-development books, how-to's, and life guides to work.

The Slight Edge will help you apply all the information you learn from the health book, the sales book, the investment book, the positive attitude book. *The Slight Edge* is the book you need to read, highlight, and reread along with your fitness class, your career planning, your continuing education, and pursuit of new skills.

The Slight Edge will prepare you to be able to absorb all that other information, guidance, and education from all those other books, classes, situations, and experiences.

You don't need more how-to's.

You need something to make the how-to's *work* for you.

This book will help you take whatever information you want, whatever how-to's or strategies or goals or aspirations, and turn them into the life you want to be living. This book is what I wish I'd had in my hands back on that golf course when I realized I wasn't living the life I wanted, what I wish I'd had in my hands the night they towed my car away.

Whatever your deepest desires are in life, I want you to have them, and I know you can. That is my passionate belief—and I've seen it happen too many times to doubt it. But you need a place to start. *The Slight Edge* is that starting point. It's the first ingredient.

Personal Stories from
The Slight Edge Readers

After reading *The Slight Edge* I decided to apply the philosophies into every area of my life. As a father, I bought a copy for my kids and started imparting the wisdom of things that are easy to do/easy not to do. As a doctor, I started giving copies of the book to my patients who were dealing with hopelessness. (I tell them it's Prozac in paperback form.) As an author, I implemented the slight edge principles into my books as well. For every role in your life there are slight edge applications that will make a huge difference.

—*Baker Fore, D.O., Edmond, Oklahoma*

I have used the principles of *The Slight Edge* to improve my physical fitness, starting with one push-up and one sit-up a day, adding another each day and building to over 100 per day. I have used it to help pay off debt, build my savings and investments, and improve my relationships with my children.

—*Stan Snow, North Yarmouth, Maine*

Essential Points from Chapter 2

No matter how good the information is, it won't do you any good unless you have the right catalyst that will let you apply it effectively.

Your philosophy creates your attitudes, which create your actions, which create your results, which create your life.

Successful people fail their way to the top. *Do the thing, and you shall have the power.*

The slight edge is the first ingredient, the catalyst you need that makes all the how-to's work.

3. The Choice

> "I guess it comes down to a simple choice, really. You get busy living, or get busy dying."
>
> —*Andy Dufresne in* The Shawshank Redemption

A wealthy man nearing the end of his days summoned his twin sons to his bedside and told them that before he died, he wanted to pass on to them the opportunity to experience the richness of life that he had enjoyed for his many years on earth.

"If I could do so, I would give you both the world," he told his boys, "but of course, I can't. Instead, I am leaving you both with a gift."

The boys both wept to hear their father speak of his approaching death, but he bade them hush with a wave of his hand.

"I am giving you each a purse to finance your adventures. What goes into each purse is your choice."

The man lifted a pair of beautiful lacquer boxes from the bedside table onto his lap, then reached inside one and held out his hands to his sons. One hand grasped a sheaf of one thousand crisp, new $1,000 bills—one million dollars, cash. In the palm of his other hand sat a shiny new copper penny.

"I offer the same choice to you both. This million dollars; or this single penny. Whichever you choose, you must leave it in your purse under my butler's care for one full month to give you time to think about how you will use it. Whatever you do not take will be returned to my estate, which I'll leave to charity.

"One more thing," he added. "If you choose the million, you may, if you wish, draw against it as credit with my bank in town. If you choose the penny, you can also draw against it, but every day you choose to leave the penny's line of credit untouched, my butler has instructions to double the contents of your purse, for as long as it is under his care.

"Now, go rest and think. Here, take this book with you to pass the evening hours. Tomorrow morning, come back and tell me your choice."

He gave them each a copy of a little book of stories, kissed them both and sent them on their way.

Late that night the first boy lay in bed musing over the day's events. "Which should I take?" he wondered. "And why is our father giving us this choice?" Unable to sleep, he turned on his light and looked around for the book his father had given them both. He figured a little reading would help pass the time, and who knew, maybe he'd get sleepy.

He found the book and for the first time noticed the title embossed on the cover in simple gold lettering:

The Choice

"Hm," he muttered. "*The Choice*. Sounds mysterious. Choice between what and what?" Flipping through the book's pages, he saw that each of its many chapters was no more than a single page long, and at least at first glance their titles didn't appear to have anything to do with each other. It seemed like a random assortment of fables or children's stories. He was about to toss the book aside, but some nudge from within whispered, *Go ahead, read a little.*

He turned back to the first story, which was called "The Water Hyacinth," and began to read.

The Water Hyacinth

Once there was a little water hyacinth that grew near the edge of a big pond. It had dreams of seeing the other side of the pond, but when it murmured to itself about these dreams, the water just laughed and lapped at it dismissively. The other side indeed … for a tiny plant that couldn't even move? Impossible!

The water hyacinth can typically be found floating on the surface of ponds in warm climates around the world, and it is a beautiful plant, with delicate six-petaled flowers that range from purplish blue to lavender to pink. This particular plant was a perfect specimen: very beautiful, very small, and very delicate.

However—and this was something the water didn't know—the water hyacinth is also one of the most productive plants on earth, with a reproductive rate that astonishes botanists and ecologists. A single plant can produce as many as five thousand seeds, but its preferred method for colonizing a new area is not to cast its seeds to the vagaries of wind and water, but instead to grow by doubling itself, sending out short runner stems that become "daughter plants."

The first day this little water hyacinth appeared, nobody but the water even noticed it was there. Nobody noticed it on the second day either, as it doubled, nor on the third or the fourth, as it doubled again and then once more. It was so insignificant, in fact, that for the first two weeks, even though it doubled in size every day, you would have had to search hard to see it at all.

By day 15 it had reproduced to cover barely one square foot of water, a tiny dollop of lavender-pink dotting the pond's glassy green surface. On day 20, two-thirds of the way through the month, one person passing by the pond noticed the little patch of foliage floating off to the side, but mistook it for a lost bath towel or perhaps a discarded piece of wrapping paper.

More than a week later, on day 29, half the pond's surface was still open water. And on day 30, just twenty-four hours later, the water's surface had totally disappeared. The entire pond had been overtaken by a rich blanket of purple-pink water hyacinth.

The boy imagined the pond, covered with the lush, gorgeous plant. "Not sure what that has to do with a 'choice,'" he said out loud. He stretched and yawned. "That's enough reading for one night." He turned off the light and settled against the pillow.

A minute later he was sitting up again, switching on the light. Something prodded him to keep going and take in more of this book.

Turning the page, he came to the next story, this one entitled "In the Pail." Once again, he began to read.

In the Pail

Two frogs left the safety of their swamp one day and ventured into a nearby farm to explore. Soon they found themselves in a dairy, where they found a large milk pail. Hopping into the pail, they found it was half filled with fresh cream.

The two little frogs were absolutely thrilled. They had never tasted anything so delicious! Soon their bellies were full. Feeling sleepy, they decided it was time to leave—and that's when they realized they were in trouble.

They'd had no trouble hopping in. But how were they going to get out? The inside of the pail was too slippery to climb. And because they couldn't reach the bottom and there was nothing for them to step on for traction, hopping to safety was out of the question, too. They were trapped.

Frantic, they began thrashing about, their feet scrabbling for a foothold on the elusive, slippery curve of the pail's sides.

Finally one frog cried out, "It's no use. We're doomed!"

"No," the other frog gasped, "we can't give up. When we were tadpoles, could we have dreamed that some day we would emerge from the water and hop about on land? Swim on, brother, and pray for a miracle!"

But the first frog only eyed his brother sadly. "There are no miracles in the life of a frog," he croaked. "Farewell." And he sank slowly out of sight.

The second frog refused to give up. He continued paddling in the same tiny circle, over and over, hoping against hope for a miracle. An hour later, he was still paddling in his futile little circle. He no longer even knew why. His brother's dying words clutched at his thoughts as fatigue tugged at his tiny muscles. "Was my brother right?" he thought desperately. "Are there no miracles in the life of a frog?" Finally he could swim no more. With a whimper of anguish, he stopped paddling and let go, ready to face his fate ...

But by this time the boy was no longer reading. Unable to keep his eyes open any longer, he had fallen fast asleep as the frog paddled in his desperate circle, refusing to give up. Somewhere in the back of his mind, though, the boy had already guessed how the tale of the two frogs would turn out, and his guess was pretty much the way the story's last paragraph did in fact read:

Yet to his surprise, unlike his brother, the second frog did not sink. In fact, he stayed right where he was, as if suspended in midair. He stretched out a foot tentatively—and felt it touch *something solid*. He heaved a big sigh, said a silent farewell to his poor departed brother frog, then scrambled up onto the top of the big lump of butter he had just churned, hopped out of the pail and off toward his home in the swamp.

That night, the boy dreamed of frogs paddling on a bed of flowers, floating on a pond of pennies.

The wealthy man's other son lay awake that night, too, but he never opened his copy of the storybook their father had given them. He was too busy thinking to sleep or read. He'd made his decision the moment his father had held out that sheaf of thousand-dollar bills. He was already making big plans for his next thirty-one days.

When morning came, he sprang into action.

After notifying his father of his choice, he opened his million-dollar line of credit at his father's bank. Next, he hired an executive director to help him execute his ambitious plan, and the two rented out a hotel suite in the center of town, where they conducted interviews for the next six days. By week's end they had hired a staff of the sharpest financial advisors, market analysts, and investment experts available.

The group spent the second week researching, brainstorming, and drafting strategies to help the wealthy man's son transform his million-dollar windfall into a genuine fortune. By the beginning of week 3, they were locked and loaded and ready to rumble, and off they marched into the battlefields of commerce and speculation to turn the boy's million into billions.

A few days later, the boy decided to pay a visit to his brother, to see what he was doing with *his* million—but when he arrived, he found to his astonishment that his brother had turned down the million and taken the penny instead.

"I went to see Father again the day after we all met," the first boy told his brother, "and his butler gave me a peek into the purse: my lone penny had been joined by a companion. On the third day, I went back, peeked in again and now saw four pennies. On the fourth day, there were eight." The brother listened in disbelief as the boy continued describing his insignificant little pile of pennies. On day 5, there had been sixteen pennies; on day 6, thirty-two; and by week's end the boy had amassed a whopping nest egg of sixty-four cents. By the end of the second week, the cache of pennies was just shy of ninety dollars ($81.92, to be precise)—not even enough to pay for a decent dinner for two at the hotel where his brother's ace financial team had their base of operations. Now, a few days into the third week, the purse had grown to $655.35, barely enough to sustain the boy on his own for a week.

"You poor sap!" cried his brother. "I can't believe you went for the penny! But it's not too late—visit our father, see if he'll let you change your mind. Even if he gives you only half your million, it's certainly better than scraping by on what you've got now. Or at least let me help; I can't stand the idea of you venturing out into the world with scarcely enough to feed yourself for a week."

But the first boy wouldn't hear of it.

That night, the old man died peacefully in his sleep.

Toward the end of the month, the second boy's executive director brought him some worrisome news. The markets had gone a bit soft, and the team's earlier rosy projections would need to be revised downward. The boy thanked him and waited anxiously for the next report.

On the morning of day 31, the day on which the boys were to visit the butler and finally receive their purses, the executive director came back with his final report. He shuffled his feet and cleared his throat for a minute, asked for a glass of water, and then began his report by saying that the news was mixed. Some investments had performed quite well, others had suffered. All in all, the boy had made a modest gain: the team had succeeded in parlaying his one million into nearly one and a half million, an appreciation of 50 percent. That was the good news.

"And the bad news?" The boy held his breath.

"Well, ah," continued his executive director, "expenses, including the team's commissions, taxes, broker fees, interest on the credit line, the bill for the hotel suite," he cleared his throat again, took a sip of water, and continued, "and of course, ah, my salary for the month, come to just over one-point-seven-five million."

The boy was $250,000 in the red. Not only was he *not* rich, he actually *owed* a fortune. He was ruined. In a panic, he rushed across town to see his brother, and this time he received an even larger shock than the first time he'd gone to visit.

On day 28, the first boy's purse of pennies had passed the million-dollar mark, and on day 29, the two-and-a-half-million mark. Yesterday, on day 30, it had exceeded five million, and today, when the butler handed his purse over to his own care, it had topped out at $10,737,418 … and twenty-four cents.

The boy who chose to wait for the penny had discovered the extraordinary power that some call "the eighth wonder of the world," the remarkable creative force of *compound interest*—the very same force that blanketed the pond's surface with water hyacinth and churned the frog's cream into butter.

The boy who chose the million was broke and deeply in debt.

The boy who chose the penny was worth more than *ten million dollars*.

The Millionaire's Mom

I know, I know: the story of the two sons is only a fable. Over here in real life, there's no butler doubling your money every day for a month. Over here in real life, though, things work out that way a lot more than you might think. I'll give you a true-life example: Rosemary Olson, my mom.

My mom worked as administrative assistant in our church for

thirty-five years. Pay was minimal, and the job didn't exactly come with a lot of benefits. And if life was hard, it got a lot harder when my father died.

My dad served in World War II and came home with some health problems that never fully resolved. After twenty years or so working for the Veterans Administration, he ended up getting to know the VA hospital from the customer's point of view. He lost a lung to emphysema and eventually succumbed to a heart attack—at the ripe old age of forty-one. At the military ceremony, they did that thing you've probably seen on television, where they fold an American flag down into a neatly creased triangle, walk solemnly over and hand it to the oldest son. In this case, that happened to be me. I was eleven years old.

From that point on my mother was a single mom, raising a family of three kids. She worked, she came home, she cooked, she took care of us. She never drank, never cussed, never complained, not once, not ever. And she was always there for me, no matter what. She was so consistent that later on in life I took to calling her "Matter-of-fact Rose."

For my part, I have to admit that I more or less took all this for granted. I knew that my mom had grown up with little money, and that's how my siblings and I grew up: in a little house with little but the bare essentials. In my mind, that's just how things were. And it's easy to assume that "just how things are" is how they're always going to be.

Fast-forward to many years later, after I had built some success in my life.

In 1996 a book appeared titled *The Millionaire Next Door*, by Thomas J. Stanley and William D. Danko. A classic today, Stanley and Danko's book is still the best description I've ever read of how real-life people have become wealthy by following slight edge principles. The millionaires featured in their book don't inherit their wealth, or strike it rich by making outrageously lucky gambles. They don't "live large," drive flashy cars, or live in ostentatious homes. They live below their means and make sensible, smart choices in how they conduct their everyday lives.

After that book came out my friends would tell me, "Hey, Jeff, have you seen this book? It's about *you*. It describes exactly what you do and how you act. You're the millionaire next door guy!" Sure enough, the book described exactly how I approached my finances. For years I kept our family living on $4,000 a month, no matter how much my income increased, and I wouldn't let us raise that monthly threshold until I had a million dollars (after taxes) in the bank. Then I raised it to $5,000.

Some years later, I was sitting with my mom one day and happened to tell her about the book and about what my friends were saying about me being the steady-as-she-goes, one-foot-in-front-of-the-other, nothing-flashy millionaire next door guy.

She nodded, and then said, "You know why that is?"

"No," I replied, not sure where she was going with this. "Why?"

She looked at me and said, "Well, I'm a millionaire, too."

"What do you mean?" I said. "You mean, the house, or ...?" There was no way her house could be worth a million, not even at inflated 1996 market values, and I knew that. But I couldn't imagine what else she could possibly mean.

"No," she said. "No, I have a couple million dollars. Salted away. You know, in savings."

What? I just stared at her.

"I have a couple million dollars, too," she repeated. Seeing my astonished expression, she shrugged and added, "It's not something you'd want to brag about."

For all these years of going to work every day, going about her life, taking care of her kids, living in that little house, she had been quietly saving. Consistently and persistently. Without anyone else noticing, she had quietly made herself into a millionaire—literally.

The power that covered the pond with water hyacinth, that churned the frog's cream into butter, that turned the first son's penny into millions, is the same power that turned my mom's hard-earned paychecks into millions. That power is what this book is about.

Although completely unaware of it, I'd been living with a picture-perfect example of the slight edge my whole life.

The Cost of Waiting

I'm sure you've heard about the power of compounding interest before. In fact, you've probably heard about it many times. What makes this time different?

Nothing—unless you act on it.

The single most important thing I can tell you about the slight edge is this: it's already working, *right now*, either for you or against you. So don't wait. My hope for you—my *request* for you—is that before you reach the last page of this book you will have put in place a slight edge financial plan for yourself so that you are consistently building your equity. Some simple daily, weekly, or monthly discipline that over time will buy your financial freedom.

Easy to do? Surprisingly so. Easy not to do? Tragically so. To give you a sense of the cost of waiting, look at the following example.

Let's say you and your best friend have both just graduated from college at the ripe young age of twenty-three. You both read *The Slight Edge* and decide you'd like to start putting away enough savings so you can retire at the age of sixty-seven with over a million dollars in the bank. You friend starts doing it right now, setting up an automatic deduction from her paycheck so $250 a month goes into an IRA account.

But you figure, hey, there's plenty of time, and you put it off. You don't get around to it this year, or next, or the next. In fact, you keep procrastinating until you are thirty-nine. Then with forty staring you in the face, you decide maybe it's time to get going.

At that point, you ask your friend how her IRA is doing—and are stunned when she tells you that she's finished! After investing $250 a month for eighteen years at eight percent, she's all set. She can stop investing and just let the account accumulate interest on its own, and by the time she turns sixty-seven, that little financial snowball she started rolling will have grown into more than $1 million—even if she never puts in another penny!

That's it, you say, it's time for action. You start immediately putting in your $250 each month. How many years will it take before you've caught up to your friend? The unfortunate answer is: you won't. By starting early, your friend was able to invest for eighteen years and then turn off the spigot of new investment, and the momentum of what she'd started had time to build to her million at sixty-five. But since you're starting so much later, you won't have that luxury: by the time you both reach sixty-five, you'll have invested $81,000 over twenty-seven years (compared to her $54,000 over eighteen years), and you'll *still* be putting in that monthly $250—yet you'll have ended up with just over a quarter of the million she has stashed away.

"But what if I'm not twenty-three—what if I'm forty-three? Or sixty-three? Does that mean I've missed the boat—are you saying it's too late for me?"

Not at all. You're never too old, and it's never too late, to start applying slight edge tactics to achieve your dreams, financial and otherwise. In fact, best-selling author David Bach has written an excellent book titled *Start Late, Finish Rich*, addressing exactly that issue. Like all the other books I list in the Appendix, it's a great companion to *The Slight Edge*. My point is simply that there is a cost to waiting.

It's never too late to start.

It's always too late to wait.

The Other Side of the Slight Edge

Your friend's IRA turning into a million-plus at retirement … my mom's savings slowly compounding like the boy's penny doubling … the tiny water hyacinth blossom multiplying … the frog's little paddling movements that eventually churned cream into butter—these are all examples of how the slight edge can over time yield wonderfully positive results in our lives. But that's not the whole story. Because it works the other way, too.

Doing those simple daily disciplines was exactly the reason, and the *only* reason, that I had graduated from business school at the top of my class and had that early success in management. But then there was the other half of the roller coaster equation.

During those times when I was slipping from survival back toward failure, I had stopped doing those simple daily disciplines. That was the reason—and the *only* reason—that I kept slipping back into failure. I was making little everyday choices that seemed harmless and innocent enough, but without my realizing it they were pulling me back down toward failure. That's why my life had felt like that agonizing lament from *The Godfather, Part III*, when the Al Pacino character says, "Just when I thought I was out, they pull me back in!"

This diagram shows the two different kinds of impact the slight edge can have on your life, depending on whether you understand and apply it, or you don't. If you'll notice, these two paths are exactly the same as the two different directions of the roller-coaster diagram. That is, this is the earlier sine wave chart, only with the two pieces broken out and extended out over time.

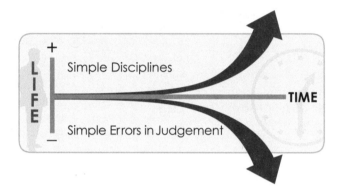

The slight edge is relentless, and it cuts both ways. Used productively, it carries you up toward success. Used carelessly, it pulls you down toward failure.

Simple productive actions, repeated consistently over time.

Simple errors in judgment, repeated consistently over time.

The choice is that simple.

You can start with a million dollars, but if you don't understand the slight edge, you'll lose it all. You can start with nothing but a penny, yet if you understand the slight edge, you can go anywhere in the world you want to go.

My mom understood that. For the first few decades of my life, I didn't. Most people don't.

Most people are like the son who went for the million—and drew down more than a million's worth of credit. Or the fatalistic frog, who couldn't see that his insignificant little paddling motions might actually churn cream into butter, if he just kept at it long enough. Most people don't stick with the simple daily disciplines it takes to get where they want to go, because they don't know how to look ahead far enough along the curve to see the results they are creating. But see it or not, those results are coming, as surely as a million dollars in the bank—or a train coming down the tracks heading our way.

The Father's Gift

When the wealthy man told his sons he was giving them a gift, the second boy thought the gift was *money*. The first boy listened more carefully. He understood that the gift was not money: it was *wisdom*. The old man wasn't simply passing on his fortune to his sons, because he knew that without that wisdom the fortune would soon be gone. Instead, he was passing on his *philosophy*.

The father's gift held a lesson. About money, yes, but it was really a lesson about leverage, growth, and geometric progression. About the fact that the simple little actions you take today can look very different when you see how they play out over time. About the tremendous potential of something as seemingly powerless as a water hyacinth or insignificant as a penny.

About patience and the understanding that little steps, compounded, do make a difference. That the things you do every single day, the things that don't look dramatic, that don't even look like they matter, do matter. That they not only make a difference—they make *all* the difference.

About having faith in the process of simple, positive actions repeated over time—the faith that miracles *do* happen, if you know when to trust the process and keep churning the cream.

It was a lesson about the slight edge and how it can transform your life.

The choice the wealthy man offered his two sons is the same choice the world offers every one of us at every moment of our lives. A rich and growing circle of friends, or deepening loneliness and alienation. Vibrant and abundant vitality, or progressively declining health. Success or failure, happiness or misery, fulfillment or despair. Millionaire or beach bum.

You are making that choice, every day, every hour, and the impact of those choices—for better *or* for worse—will spread out over the surface of your life like a thick blanket of water hyacinth.

The Slight Edge is your guide to the wealthy man's gift. It will help you learn habits of thought and action that will allow you to choose wisely—to choose the penny doubled, every time, and not be swayed by the allure of the easy-million credit line. It will keep you paddling until your cream becomes butter. It will give you the power to choose whatever hyacinths you want to plant in your life—be they pennies and dollars, smiles and encouraging words, friendships and relationships, careers and accomplishments—so that you may blanket the surface of your life's pond with the blossoms of your choice.

Personal Stories from
The Slight Edge Readers

I grew up in a middle class family where I was taught to go to school, get good grades and get a good job. Unfortunately my plan was derailed by some family medical circumstances that I could not control. At the age of twenty-one I found myself making $4.25 per hour working six days a week, pursuing the philosophies I'd learned growing up.

When I read *The Slight Edge*, it opened my mind to new horizons. I realized that my past did not have to equal my future, and that with a slight change in activity and consistency, it was only a matter of time before I would reach my true destiny.

Sure enough, by the age of thirty I had created a six-figure income. Today I am not only a millionaire but I also have five wonderful children and a beautiful wife to spend the rest of my life with.

No matter what circumstances you find yourself in, by applying the slight edge principles over time you can positively change the trajectory of your life.

—*Dave Hall, Highland, Utah*

After reading *The Slight Edge*, I decided to apply it to my job. I didn't do anything drastic or make any major changes. I simply began to read ten pages of a good book per day—and I also started to think before I made every decision. I would ask myself, "Is this decision going to help me or hurt me?" It was those day-to-day decisions that transformed *everything*. About a year and a half after putting this habit in place, I got the position I had always wanted at work, along with a significant salary increase.

I had worked for the company six years before putting in place the principles I read in *The Slight Edge.* The greatest joy was when my boss called me into his office, and said that I had changed over the last two years. I told him that I hadn't noticed, and he said, "Well everyone else has!"

—*Jerry Sanchez, El Paso, Texas*

I have applied the slight edge principles in so many areas of life. Chunking every project into annual goals, monthly outcomes, weekly agendas and daily disciplines has helped me accomplish massive improvements in every area of life from health to relationships, to communication skills, to finances. By identifying the daily disciplines in every area of life, I was able to move from cancer to outstanding health; from non-communication with siblings to best friends; from struggling as a single mom to creating a net worth of over $1 million. The slight edge principles, compounded over time, will make a massive shift in any area you choose.

—*Linda Kedy, Destin, Florida*

Essential Points from Chapter 3

 Simple daily disciplines—little productive actions, repeated consistently over time—add up to the difference between failure and success.

The slight edge is relentless and cuts both ways: simple daily disciplines or simple errors in judgment, repeated consistently over time, make you or break you.

Without the slight edge, you can start with a million and lose it all. With the slight edge, you can start with a penny and accomplish anything you want.

4. Master the Mundane

> **"An apple a day keeps the doctor away."**
> —*Benjamin Franklin (attrib.) in* Poor Richard's Almanack

I arrived at the Phoenix airport at about 6:30 in the morning. Having ample time before my plane left, I strolled around looking to see if there was anywhere I could get my shoes shined. The place was practically empty at that time of the morning, but before long I succeeded in finding a shoeshine stand. A woman in her mid- to late forties sat alone in one of the customer chairs, absorbed in a paperback. As I approached the stand she looked up, smiled, and greeted me warmly, asking if I was looking for a shine.

I told her I was. She got up from her seat and set her book down, first carefully folding over the corner of the page she'd been reading, then took up the tools of her trade and cheerfully ushered me into the chair.

As she went to work on my shoes, we started talking. She'd been shining shoes in this same spot, day in and day out, for five years now, she said. Back when she'd started her teenage daughter was in junior high. Now she was an accomplished high school cheerleader, the woman told me proudly. In fact, she'd just won a high school cheerleading contest and was hoping to go to a cheerleading camp in Dallas that summer. "Don't know how in the world I'm going to find the money to buy her the uniform and plane ticket," she confided quietly, "let alone the camp tuition."

Her stand was located right next to a service door, from which a stream of maintenance,men and janitors began to come and go, no doubt trading night shift for day. Every one of them stopped in passing to exchange greetings and bits of personal news with the shoeshine woman, who knew each one by name. It was clear they were all friends.

In the few minutes I sat with her I learned a good deal about the shoeshine woman and her life. She loved her family and liked people in general. She made friends easily and was outgoing and articulate: a natural-born communicator. She was a hard worker too, and it was clear that she enjoyed her work.

As I sat there, getting an excellent shine on my shoes and enjoying the woman's sparkling conversation, I couldn't help thinking: *What if...?*

I'd noticed the title on her paperback; it was a popular romance novel, the kind of book people carry to pass the time and survive the stretches of occupational boredom by living vicariously in someone else's fictional life. There was a small stack of them sitting dog-eared by the wall next to her stand. She obviously had a great appetite for reading.

What if, rather than sinking into the pages of those forgettable novels during the fifteen- and twenty-minute gaps tucked in between customers, she had spent the last five years reading books that were genuinely life-changing? What if that little stack of books had included Napoleon Hill's *Think and Grow Rich*, Stephen Covey's *The 7 Habits of Highly Effective People*, or Martin Seligman's *Authentic Happiness?*

What would her life be like today if five years earlier she had changed just that one simple thing? Would she still be shining shoes for tips— or be managing her own chain of shoeshine stands?

Please understand, I'm not making a value judgment on modest incomes or simple occupations. I know people who work the humblest of jobs and whose lives are rich in relationships and joy—and I've known extremely wealthy people who were also extremely unhappy. And I'm not criticizing popular novels, either. But it was clear that this woman loved her little girl more than anything else in the world, and that it pained her not to be able to give her all those things she wanted and deserved. And it was equally clear that she had all the talent, personality, and life skills it would have taken to be able to accomplish that and much more. But something was missing.

Could that something be as simple as ten pages a day? Could something so minor, so seemingly insubstantial, cause someone's life over time to take an entirely different trajectory?

Yes, it *absolutely* could do that. I knew this to be true. I knew it because I'd seen the difference those ten pages a day could make, in my own life and in the lives of so many others. Yet the world was chock full of people exactly like this delightful shoeshine woman—people with their private hopes and dreams, and with all the marvelous personalities and attributes and inborn abilities they needed to realize those dreams, yet whose pathways forward failed to take them where they were hoping to go. People who already had *so much* going for them.

As my new friend continued shining my shoes, I pictured her on a plane to Texas surrounded by giggling, excited, happy teenagers, on their way to cheerleading camp … a journey I was pretty sure would not be happening in this woman's reality. Feelings welled up in me, a mix of frustration and sadness, and for a moment I felt powerfully moved by my mental image of what might be.

That day on the plane, I started writing this book.

What Do the 5 Percent Do Differently?

How many people do you know whom you would call successful? I don't necessarily mean financially successful, although that certainly counts as one aspect of success. But I mean successful in every aspect of their lives. People who have vibrant health, plenty of good friends, people who are full of energy and curiosity, always learning new things and excited about life. *Successful* as in people whose lives are clearly working for them.

You know exactly who I'm talking about: that person who makes you smile and feel instantly at ease, even as you stand in awe of her accomplishments. The guy who is so genuinely engaged and plugged in to life that he somehow makes you feel better about yourself just being in his presence. People who seem to breathe success, to fill the space around them with it. Not that they don't have problems, or face challenges, or suffer setbacks and hurdles like everyone else. But they always land on their feet. Things just seem to go right for them. They are winners in the game of life.

How many people do you know who are like that?

My guess is: not many.

Let's be honest: most people are struggling to keep their heads above water. And I don't mean only financially. Struggling to keep from digging deeper and deeper into debt; struggling to keep their health from slipping; struggling to manage everything in their busy lives without stressing out; struggling to juggle their friendships and relationships with everything else tugging away at them. Life often feels like a race—with someone constantly moving the finish line further away.

Not for everyone, of course. There are those for whom life somehow just seems to work. But they sure aren't the majority. I've been looking at this for a few decades now, and my observation is that about 1 person in 20 is achieving a significant measure of his or her goals in life: financial, professional, personal, in terms of relationships, in terms of health, in whatever terms you want to look at.

1 in 20. Or about 5 percent.

Which means that 95 percent are either failing or falling short.

Which prompts a question: What's the difference between the 5 percent and the 95 percent? What are the 5 percent doing that the other 95 percent are not?

I'll tell you what it's *not*.

It is not heredity, education, looks, talent or inheritance. It isn't chance, blind fate, or dumb luck, and it isn't "preparedness meeting opportunity," either. It isn't karma. And it isn't an abundance of sincere wanting and wishing.

The 5 percent don't *want* success more than everyone else. They don't wish for it more, pray for it more, envision it more, or hope for it more. And it isn't that they deserve it more. Hey, we *all* want our lives to be successful. We all hope for it and wish for it, and you know what? We all deserve it, too.

But the 5 percent get it, and the 95 percent don't. Why is that?

There is only one difference: the slight edge.

The 5 percent all understand the power of the slight edge and how it is working for or against them. They may not use the words *slight edge* to describe it. They may not even see what they do as being guided by a "philosophy." But that's exactly what it is.

I'll give you an example: a teenager named Steve.

On his first day of high school, Steve filed into the auditorium along with all the other students for their first assembly. Sitting there in the middle of all those rows of seats, looking up at the brightly lit stage, he was struck by a compelling desire: he wanted to be a performer. There was a problem, though: he couldn't sing, couldn't dance, and couldn't act. "Thankfully," he says now as he looks back on those early days, "perseverance is a great substitute for talent."

Despite the fact that he didn't seem to have any special skills or talent for performing and was absolutely no good at being on stage, he set about doing it anyway. Hour after hour, day after day, he studied magic tricks, taught himself the banjo, tried out lines on anyone who would listen (and quite a few who wouldn't), and worked at turning his quirky sense of humor into bits that would hopefully not completely fall flat in front of an audience. He did that for years, with little evidence (at least not at first) that he was really getting anywhere. And fifteen years later, Steve Martin was the single biggest audience draw in the history of standup comedy.

He may have started out as a teenager with no skills at all. But he had the slight edge working for him.

The slight edge is what turned teenage Steve's sincere but awkward efforts into a box office phenomenon. The slight edge is the force behind the amazing power of compound interest. It is the force that allowed the delicate water hyacinth to conquer the pond, that allowed the persevering frog to escape with his life while his brother did not, that turned the wealthy man's first son's penny into ten million dollars. It is the steady, repeated action of water that can wear even the hardest rock to a smooth surface. Whatever you're after, whatever you want to create in your life or whatever kind of life you most passionately want to live, the slight edge is the way to get it.

That is the difference between the 5 percent and everyone else. They know how to use the slight edge to get what they want in life. No, let's amend that slightly: they know how to use the slight edge to get what they want in life—and they *do* it. They do the thing, and gain the power.

If you will learn to understand and apply the slight edge, I will guarantee you that in time—and chances are, less time than you would imagine—you will have what you desire. You will be among the 5 percent. You will be successful. And when I say "guarantee" I mean that literally: if you genuinely apply this simple principle in your own life and don't see significant improvement, we will refund every penny you paid for this book.

The $10 Million Question

Here's the most amazing thing about Steve Martin's story: the things he did to develop his stage skills were not complicated or difficult. They just took practice.

They also weren't very exciting. The idea of being up on stage in front of millions may sound terrifying and exhilarating, but when you're standing up in front of a nearly empty coffee shop, and nobody's paying any attention, and you're trying out a line you've tried thirty times already with maybe a few tiny tweaks to see if it works any better ... not so terrifying, not so exhilarating, not so exciting.

In fact, the things Steve had to do to refine his craft were often downright mundane.

The same thing holds true for success in *any* dimension, from health to relationships to career success to financial success. Remember *The Millionaire Next Door*? The big secret that Stanley and Danko revealed was that the millionaires they studied had developed the habit of doing ordinary little insignificant everyday things with their money. It would make an exciting story if they had gambled their last dollars and amazingly hit it big in the stock market with a little stock that came from behind and stunned the financial world. But, nope. It wasn't like that. The first of the book's seven rules is, "Always live below your means." Nothing too exciting about that, is there?

Downright mundane.

And the rest is like that, too. Nothing these "ordinary millionaires" did to build their riches were complicated, difficult to understand, or hard to do. None of them took sophisticated knowledge or special skills. What these millionaires did was simple: they *mastered the mundane*.

As I said above, if you apply the slight edge consistently in your life, you will find yourself among the 5 percent and see the goals and aspiration in your life coming to pass—and you will achieve those aims, goals, and dreams by doing mundane, everyday, simple things.

That sounds outrageously oversimplified, I know. But it's the truth. I've seen it happen again and again. If you learn to understand and apply the slight edge, your life will become filled with hundreds of thousands of small, seemingly insignificant actions—all of them genuinely simple, none of them mysterious or complex. In other words, you have to master the mundane. And those actions will create your success.

And here's the truly amazing thing about it. Those simple things, the things that spell success? They are not only simple, they are also easy to do. So simple and so easy, in fact, that anyone could do them.

So by now you've probably got a question burning in your brain. If these things are so simple and so easy to do, how come only 5 percent do them? Why don't more people do them?

In fact, why doesn't everyone do them?

The world of finances is one of the easiest places to see the power of the slight edge in action. Everyone knows about the power of compound interest, right? Wrong. Everyone *thinks* they know about the power of compound interest. But most people don't, not really. If they did, they'd be using it. And clearly, most people are not.

There's a principle called Parkinson's Law, after the man who coined it, Professor Cyril Northcote Parkinson. Parkinson's Law goes like this: "Work expands to fill the time available for its completion." Here's how that looks when you apply it to the world of personal finances: *Whatever I have, I spend.* Actually, in today's world it usually means something more like this: *Whatever I have, I spend that—plus a little more.*

How hard is it to put aside a few dollars a day, or a little each week? Ridiculously easy. Yet most of us don't do it. The United States has one of the highest per capita income rates in the world—and one of the lowest savings rates.

Why is that?

Or take food and health as an example. Eating offers one of the best everyday examples of the slight edge there is, simply because eating is something we all do every day throughout our lives. And there is no big mystery to what healthy eating looks like. Yet overweight and obesity continues to be a huge and growing problem in the United States. Two in every three Americans is overweight, and almost one in three qualifies for the definition of obese. In the past thirty years, obesity in kids has *tripled*.

This isn't news; Americans know they're overweight. In fact, we spend huge amounts of money on diet books and diet programs to help us lose that burdensome extra weight. There are more than 30,000 fitness clubs in the United States, all aimed at serving the national desire to lose weight and be fit. And it's not just a question of being a little too heavy, or of how we look. Nutrition is one of the most significant factors in society's major killers, like heart disease, cancer, and diabetes. Most of us are literally digging our graves with our teeth. And we *know* all this—yet clearly the majority of us aren't doing anything about it. Why not?

If slight edge habits are so easy to do, and will lead to phenomenal success, why doesn't everyone do them? That is literally the $10 million question. And it has a few answers.

Reason #1: They're Easy to Do

The first answer is one I learned from Jim Rohn: The simple things that lead to success are all easy to do. But they're also just as easy *not to do*.

It's easy to save a few bucks a day. And easy not to.

It's easy to do fifteen minutes of cardio a day. Walk a brisk mile or two. Truly easy to do. Or not.

It may not be easy to get into graduate school and pour yourself into Ph.D. studies for eighty hours a week for a few years straight. But here's something that *is* easy: pick up an inspiring, educational, life-changing book like *The Millionaire Next Door*, or *Think and Grow Rich*, or *The Magic of Thinking Big*, and read ten pages a day. Just ten pages a day. So easy to do ... and so easy not to do.

Remembering to tell your wife or husband that you love them, and do that every day. What could be easier than that? To do—or not to do.

So while anyone *could* do these successful actions, most *won't*, simply because it's so easy to skip them. And the tragic irony of it is, that doesn't actually end up making their lives any easier. We're all doing simple things anyway. Unsuccessful people just choose what they think is the path of least resistance. But it really isn't.

Fundamentally, we all take pretty much the same actions every day. We eat, sleep, think, feel, talk, and listen. We have relationships and friendships. We each have twenty-four hours a day, 168 hours a week, and we each fill these hours one way or the other with a sequence of mundane little actions and tasks.

Gold medal marathon runners eat and sleep. So do people who are thirty pounds overweight. Successful entrepreneurs think and feel and have relationships with other people. So do those who are broke or living on the streets. People who make lots of money read books. People who are broke read books, too—they just choose different books.

The successful and unsuccessful both do the same basic things in their lives, day in and day out. Yet the things successful people do take them to the top, while the things unsuccessful people do take them down and out. So what's the difference? The difference is their awareness, understanding, and application of the slight edge in their life and work.

Successful winners understand the power of the slight edge.

Unsuccessful people do not.

The difference that will make *all* the difference between success and failure, between achieving the quality of life you want and settling for less than you desire and deserve, lies not in whether you take those actions or not (because we all do), but 100 percent in *which* of those mundane actions you choose to do. This is why we are all capable of doing what it takes to be successful. We are all capable of being winners in life. And yes, that includes you. Because the slight edge is *always* working. Whether for you or against you, the slight edge is already at work in your life and always will be, every day, every moment. The purpose of this book is to help you become aware of it—how it is working in your life, every day, every hour, every moment, in every step you take and every choice you make.

Everything you need to do to transform your life is easy to do. It's easy to become healthy, fit and vibrant. It's easy to become financially independent. It's easy to have a happy family and a life rich with meaningful friendships. It's just a matter of mastering the mundane—of repeating simple little disciplines that, done consistently over time, will add up to the very biggest accomplishments.

Of course, it's just as easy not to. But that simple, seemingly insignificant error in judgment, compounded over time, will ruin your chances for success. You can count on it. That's the choice you face every day, every hour: A simple, positive action, repeated over time. A simple error in judgment, repeated over time.

So easy to do. So easy not to do.

Reason #2: The Results Are Invisible

The second reason people don't do the little things that add up to success is that at first, they *don't* add up to success. The doomed frog quit paddling in the cream because he'd been doing it as hard as he could, and it obviously wasn't having any effect. At least, not one he could see.

And that's the problem. The things that create success in the long run don't look like they're having any impact at all in the short run. A penny doubled is two cents. Big deal. Take two bucks a day and stick it into savings instead of into an expensive coffee drink, and at the end of a week you've got … fourteen dollars. Big deal.

Of course, that was exactly how my mother became a millionaire. But most people wouldn't do that—because you don't see the million in front of you when you do the saving. The results are too far in the future. They're invisible. That is, unless you know how to look through the lenses of the slight edge.

Do you know anyone who would eat a quart of Crisco or a pound of butter a day? Does anyone say, "Hmm, my cholesterol's down to 239, I need to get it up over 400. There are still a few arteries flowing— better make sure I get those clogged, too"? Of course not. Then why do we act like we do?

You know what you're supposed to eat. We all do. Fresh fruits and vegetables, complex carbs, salads, whole grains, lean meats, more fish and poultry and less beef…. You know it, I know it, we all know it. So why do so many of us still go out and chow down cheeseburgers and fries every day?

I'll tell you why: because it won't kill us. Not today.

If you ate a cheeseburger and immediately suffered a near-fatal heart attack, would you ever go near a cheeseburger again? I doubt it. It may take twenty or thirty years, but when you add up the compounded interest on all that high-fat, artery-clogging dietary mayhem, eventually your poor overworked heart just quits, stops dead. And so do you.

It's easy to eat well. But it's also easy not to, and to go on eating the food that will eventually kill us, because it won't kill us *today*. It's not the one junk-food meal; it's the thousands, over time. Eating the burger is just a simple error in judgment. Not eating it, a simple positive action.

The thing is, eating it won't kill you … today. Compounded over time, it can and will—but not at first. And *not* eating it won't transform your health and save your life, at least not today. Compounded over time, it can and will. But that's an event that's tucked invisibly over the horizon of the future, so we don't see it.

Why do you walk past the exercise bike? Because it's easy. If you don't exercise today, will that kill you? No, of course not. You know what you need to do to stay healthy and feel fit and live a long life. Get your heart rate up, a little over normal, for twenty minutes, three times a week. You know it, I know it, everyone knows it. And it's easy to do.

But it's also easy not to do. And if you don't do it today, or tomorrow, or the next day, you won't suddenly drop dead, and you won't suddenly put on twenty pounds, and you won't suddenly lose all your muscle tone. That simple error in judgment, compounded over time, will ruin your health—but not immediately.

It is the same with your health, your diet, your exercise, your financial habits, your knowledge, your relationships, your marriage, your spiritual health. With anything and everything.

Here's a slight edge action guaranteed to change your life: read just ten pages of a good book, a book aimed at improving your life, every day. If you read ten pages of a good book today, will your life change? Of course not. If you *don't* read ten pages of a good book today, will your life fall apart? Obviously not.

I could tell you that if you would agree to read ten pages of one of these good books every single day, over time, you could not help but accumulate all the knowledge you'd ever need to be as successful as you could ever want to be. Like a penny over time, reading ten pages a day would compound, just like that, and create inside you a ten-million-dollar bank of knowledge. If you kept this up for a year, you would have read 3,650 pages—the equivalent of one or two dozen books of life-transforming material. Would your life have changed? Absolutely. No question.

But here's the problem: back here in the present, on day 1 of week 1, all of that is way in the future.

When you make the right choice, you don't see the results, at least not today. And that is a problem in our push-button, mouse-click, 24-hour-news world. We expect to see results, and we expect to see them now.

But that's not how success is built. *Success is the progressive realization of a worthy ideal.* "Progressive" means success is a process, not a destination. It's something you experience gradually, over time. Failure is just as gradual. In fact, the difference between success and failure is so subtle, you can't even see it or recognize it during the process. And here's how real success is built: *by the time you get the feedback, the real work's already done.* When you get to the point where everyone else can see your results, tell you what good choices you've made, notice your good fortune, slap you on the back and tell you how lucky you are, the critical slight edge choices you made are ancient history. And chances are, at the time you actually made those choices, nobody noticed but you. And even you wouldn't have noticed—unless you understood the power of the slight edge.

Reason #3: They Seem Insignificant

The third reason most people live out their entire lives without ever grasping how the slight edge is working in their lives it that is just seems like those little things don't really matter.

So I skipped a day at the gym. What's a day? Hey, it's just a cheeseburger. What's the fuss?

The difference between success and failure is not dramatic. In fact, the difference between success and failure is so subtle, so mundane, that most people miss it. They may not realize they have a philosophy, but they do, and it goes like this: *What I do right now doesn't really matter.*

It's not hard to see how people come to this understanding of life. I don't blame them. It's completely understandable. It's just not the truth. The truth is, what you do matters.

What you do *today* matters.

What you do *every day* matters.

Successful people are those who understand that the little choices they make *matter*, and because of that they choose to do things that seem to make no difference at all in the act of doing them, and they do them over and over and over until the compound effect kicks in.

Those little things that will make you successful in life, that will secure your health, your happiness, your fulfillment, your dreams, are simple, subtle, mundane things that nobody will see, nobody will applaud, nobody will even notice. They are those things that, at the time you do them, often feel like they make absolutely no difference.

Things that are ridiculously easy to do—but just as easy not to do.

Things that don't seem to bring you any visible results—at first.

Things that seem so insignificant, they couldn't possibly matter. But they do. Things that, when you look at them as single occurrences, don't seem like they'd have any impact at all—yet when compounded over time they add up to outrageous success.

I'll give you an example from my own experience.

A Triumph of the Mundane

I told you a little about The People's Network, that personal development company I started many years ago. Let me tell you the next chapter of that story. We eventually ended up merging that company, including its entire sales force, into another, larger company that had been around for more than a quarter of a century.

This merger offered a fascinating situation of two very different cultures colliding.

First of all, the product line was completely different (legal services versus personal development materials and training). Even more significant than that, though, was the difference in cultures between the two groups.

The sales force of the company we merged into was a very large group who were quite established, successful, and very good at what they did (#1 in their space), but pretty well set in their ways. The "old guard," you could say. Many of these folks had been there with the company ten, fifteen, twenty years or more, and they represented about 80 percent of the newly merged company. The other 20 percent was us: the newcomers.

The culture in our group was completely different. Not only were our people *not* established and successful with this type of product, they had basically no experience in it at all. But we did have one thing the old guard didn't have. We had the slight edge philosophy.

We quickly developed something we called The Ten Core Commitments, which was a list of basic actions people could take to move their business forward. Little things that were easy to do and just as easy not to do. Things that wouldn't really seem to make any difference if you did them or didn't do them. Things that, if you did them, nobody would even notice.

Things that were, in a word, *mundane*.

If you'd asked anyone observing the situation right after the merger what was likely to happen, here's what they would have said: "Sure, they're different, but give it a little time: before long, the new guys will adapt, learn how to fit in, and catch on to the way things are done here." And that would have been a very reasonable prediction. The old guard controlled all the meetings and all the training. In essence, they controlled everything about how the business ran.

But that wasn't what happened. Because, while our group was four times smaller than the other group, and we had no control over the company-wide training or meetings, and we had no experience with the product line, and we were complete newcomers, we had something they didn't have: we had our simple daily disciplines—our Ten Core Commitments.

Within five years the numbers had flip-flopped: now 80 percent of the company's sales force had adopted those simple daily disciplines as they watched the inexperienced underdogs having success by putting them into action. During that same period, as its sales force realized the power of those repeated daily actions, the company grew from about $70 million in annual sales to over $400 million in annual sales. It didn't double; it didn't triple. It more than *quintupled*.

Personal Stories from
The Slight Edge Readers

My daughter had health complications a few years back, which left her on six or seven different medications that created severe weight gain. After reading *The Slight Edge*, I suggested that she ride her stationary bike every day to help her drop some of that excess weight.

At first she could do only three minutes, which seemed like so little that it would hardly have made any difference whether she did it or not. But she kept doing it, and soon three minutes became five, then eight, and over time she progressed to the point where she could do fifteen to twenty minutes on that stationary bike.

A full year after she started, my daughter "suddenly" lost twenty-five pounds—or at least it *seemed* like it was all of a sudden. But it wasn't sudden at all: it was the power of the slight edge, just fifteen minutes a day.

—*Valerie Thomas, Yeadon, Pennsylvania*

I was in my second week of a new workout program when I started reading *The Slight Edge*. Up till then I had been inconsistent in my workout routines and had never stuck with any one program for more than a couple of weeks. They bored me.

One night, soon after starting to read the book, I went to bed late and told myself that I'd just skip my workout the next morning. Then suddenly a thought went through my head—that it's the easy choices I make every day that create the difference in my success. With that thought, I got up and worked out the next morning, and every morning after that. I'm now in the sixth week and instead of being bored by my morning workouts, I'm *loving* them. I actually look forward to them.

I've never gotten this far before, and it is truly amazing how different I feel.

—*Laura Jo Richins, Mesa, Arizona*

Essential Points from Chapter 4

⌁ Only 5 percent—1 in 20—achieve the level of success and fulfillment they hope for. The other 95 percent either fail or fall short. The only difference is the slight edge.

⌁ The secret to the 5 percent's success is always in mundane, easy things that anyone could do.

⌁ People don't consistently do those simple things for three reasons: 1) while they're easy to do, they are also easy not to do; 2) you don't see any results at first; 3) they seem insignificant, like they don't matter. But they do.

5. Slow Down to Go Fast

> "Rome ne s'est pas faite en un jour.
> (Rome wasn't built in a day.)"
>
> —*ancient French proverb*

So you walk a little today, get your heart rate up a bit, you lift a few weights, you eat a little differently, then tomorrow morning you wake up and look in the mirror ... and see the same old flubber. You'll have to be pretty well along the path to see any significant results, and right now, you're not. These simple things are just as easy not to do, and right now not doing them is tempting.

So what does it take to keep you doing this simple thing, day after day?

"Will power! It's like my dad (mom, teacher, boss, older brother, minister, self) always told me—I just need more *will power*."

Really? I don't think so.

Will power is vastly overrated. (A friend of mine used to say that people on diets who complain that they lack will power are usually suffering more from a lack of *won't* power.) For most people, will power ends up looking and feeling like some sort of grim self-tyranny propped up by an arbitrary, artificial reward-and-punishment system. Besides, in most of us there is a natural tendency to resist an applied force—even when it's applied by ourselves. Will power will take you only so far before you feel yourself rebelling.

No, will power won't do it.

If you want to keep yourself on the upward path, the path of the building, growing, improving, *positively compounding* effect of the slight edge, rather than the deteriorating, disintegrating, draining, *negatively compounding* effect of the slight edge, then there's something you need.

You need an ally.

If you want to direct your life on a path of continual positive change, then you need to tap into the most powerful force for change in the universe. Fortunately for you, that force is always with you, ready to lend a hand if you just ask.

That force is *time*.

The Power of Time

Have you ever been to the Grand Canyon? Maybe you've flown over it and seen it from above (it's just east of Las Vegas) or seen it in documentaries or books. It's an amazing sight. Postcards do *not* do justice to the full breadth and scope of this geological wonder. This phenomenally beautiful trench cuts a swath through Arizona nearly three hundred miles in length and up to eighteen miles in width, and it reaches down a full mile into the earth, exposing two billion years' worth of sedimentary history in its craggy landscape.

Can you picture it?

Now hold that image for a moment—and think back to the last time you were out in the rain and saw a rivulet of rainwater running along the side of a road, or in your own backyard. Now consider this gigantic natural monument over here on the one hand, and that little trickle of rainwater over here on the other, and realize this: there is only one significant difference between the two.

Time.

The rivulet is the result of water running along the ground for, what, a few minutes? An hour? The Grand Canyon is the result of the same substance running along the ground in the same way, only for some *six million years*.

One of the amazing things about the slight edge is that it's a very generous process. It requires only a minuscule contribution from you, and yet it offers you a gigantic return. It demands of you only a penny, and gives you back a million dollars. Starting with a penny is your part of the deal. The universe around you supplies the rest of the equation. And the force it uses to do that is *time*.

You don't need millions of years to see the impact of time. It took only thirty-one days for the water hyacinth to cover the pond and the boy's penny to grow into a fortune. And only an hour or so to save the little frog's life by turning cream into butter.

The moral of the frog's survival through his ordeal in the cream bucket is not about the little creature's perseverance, determination, or will power. It certainly isn't about his strength: the force of those little paddling legs was minuscule. The point of the story is the power of *time*. His weak little efforts weren't having any real impact on the cream (which was why his brother gave up). Not, that is, until an ally came to his side. The point of the story is that one of those two frogs kept his efforts going long enough for the power of time to kick in and join him.

The secret of time is simply this: time is the force that magnifies those little, almost imperceptible, seemingly insignificant things you do every day into something titanic and unstoppable.

consistently repeated daily actions + time = inconquerable results.

You supply the actions; the universe will supply the time. The trick is to choose the actions that, when multiplied by this universal amplifier, will yield the result you want. To position your everyday actions so time works *for* you, and not against you.

There Is No Instant Life

If you were offered the same choice the wealthy man gave his sons, would you choose the million dollars or the penny? Most people would make the second boy's choice, the right-now money. Wouldn't you? After all, a million dollars, in cash—*right now*?

And of course you'd be making the wrong choice, and you would have been fooled, as millions of people around the globe are fooled every minute of every hour of every day, by those two seductive little words:

Right now.

I once watched a guy standing in front of a microwave, fidgeting impatiently as he peered through the little window at his lunch being cooked, muttering, "C'monnnn … c'monnnn…." It blew my mind. Sixty seconds wasn't fast enough?

It's become axiomatic to say we live in a push-button, instant-access, fast-food world where we want and expect everything yesterday. It isn't that we have more impatient temperaments than our great-grandparents did. It's that as a culture we have adopted an entirely different way of thinking—an entirely different philosophy.

There is a natural progression in life: you plant, then you cultivate, and finally you harvest. In the days when we were an agrarian society, everyone knew this. It wasn't something anyone had to think about, it was self-evident: just the way things were. Plant, cultivate, harvest. But that's changed. Today, we have to *learn* it.

In today's world, everyone wants to go directly from plant to harvest. We plant the seed by joining the gym, and then get frustrated when a few days go by and there's no fitness harvest. Hey, we joined the gym, right? We put in the hours, right? (All three or four of them.) Why shouldn't we be looking more buff? But that's the logic of the lottery: Why should I have to build the skills, relationships, and experience it takes to *earn* the money? Why can't I just buy a ticket and *have* it?

The step we've lost touch with, the one where the real (though invisible) power lies, is the step of cultivating. And that step, unlike planting and harvesting, takes place only through the patient dimension of time.

Because we are a culture steeped in generations of movies and television, we've gotten a little confused about the reality time. We don't understand time anymore. I'm not criticizing television and films. Film is an amazing art form, television is a powerful medium, and in the hands of true artists they can both teach us valuable lessons about life.

Just not about time.

Through a great film, you can experience the triumph of the human soul over adversity, the drama of a struggle between doing what's right and succumbing to the temptations of the world, a moving encounter between generations, the flowering of a powerful romance, the struggle and birth of a nation….

But it all has to be finished in *two hours*.

Can you imagine a nation being born in two hours? Meeting the person who will become the love of your life—the dating, courtship, romance, struggle, triumph, wedding, and happy life thereafter—in two hours? Of course not. We expect to put out the effort of a thirty-second falling-in-love sequence, or fighter-in-training sequence, or crazy-idea-turns-into-million-dollar-business sequence, and get that same heroic ending. In a world filled with instant coffee, instant breakfast, instant credit, instant shopping, instant information, and 24/7 news, we have come dangerously close to losing touch with reality and believing we have access to *instant life*.

But life is not a clickable link.

Thousands of years ago, Lao Tzu wrote, "The highest good is like water. It gives life to the ten thousand things [that's ancient Chinese for "everything in the universe"], yet does not compete with them. It flows in places that the mass of people detest—and therefore it is close to the Tao."

I like that: "It flows in places the mass of people detest…"—in other words, most people don't get it. They don't grasp the power of the quiet thing. Water, which the scientists call the "universal solvent," is a time-honored metaphor for time. And you could plug the word *time* into that verse and it would work just as well: "*Time* is like water: it gives life to everything, and flows in places most people just don't get."

You could also plug in the phrase, *the slight edge*.

Where's the Drama?

There's a reason movies and television condense those lengthy transformations, the kind that take months or years in real life, into thirty-second montages set to great music. And it's not just that they don't have enough time to show how those things really unfold in real life. Even if they *did* have enough time, they still wouldn't do it. Because it's boring.

The slight edge is boring. There, I said it.

Of course, I only said it for dramatic effect—because it's actually incredibly exciting, once you know where it leads. But it *looks* boring at first, when you're oblivious to the results that are coming down the road apiece. (There's nothing boring about the Grand Canyon, but if you'd been sitting watching it during its first few hundred years, you might have seen it differently.)

Grasping the slight edge would be a whole lot simpler matter if making the right choices were a big deal. If it were a dramatic, huge, difficult thing. Why? Because then it would be obvious. You wouldn't need this book. The challenge is that making the right choices is *not* dramatic. As we saw last chapter, it's a mundane choice, and that doesn't feel very heroic.

Deciding whether or not to take that death-defying leap off the top of an exploding building to catch onto the runner of the bad guy's helicopter so you can pull yourself up and disarm the bomb and save the city … that's a dramatic choice. Deciding whether or not to fasten your seat belt is an undramatic, boring, mundane little choice that nobody will even witness. But guess which choice has the real-life power to take a few hundred thousand lives each year? Hint: it's not the leap off the building. When the hero makes the right choice in a movie, it's dramatic. The problem is, your life is not a movie. It's real life.

If making the right slight edge choices were a dramatic thing, you'd get immediate feedback. An entire movie theater audience applauding, cheering, or screaming. But that doesn't happen. And that's the big challenge of it: *no immediate feedback.*

The thing is, it *is* dramatic, it *is* amazing, it *is* breathtaking. Remember the change in our company I mentioned last chapter? It went from $70 million to $400 million in five years. Now *that* was dramatic. In the big scheme of things, five years isn't very long.

But it's not five minutes.

And if you'd been following us around with a movie camera for the first few months, even the first year, shooting a documentary, I guarantee it wouldn't have been a very gripping experience. You couldn't have seen the drama of it—because there hadn't been enough time yet for time to kick in.

The slight edge can carve the Grand Canyon. It can do *anything.* But you have to give it enough time for the power of time to kick in.

The right choices and wrong choices you make at the moment will have little or no noticeable impact on how your day goes for you. Nor tomorrow, nor the next day. No applause, no cheers, no screams, no life-or-death results played out on the big screen. But it is exactly those same undramatic, seemingly insignificant actions that, when compounded over time, will dramatically affect how your life turns out.

So, where's the drama? It comes at the end of the story, when the credits start to roll, and that happens not two hours from now, but maybe two years from now. Or, depending on what particular story we're talking about, maybe twelve years, or twenty-two.

Making the right choices, taking the right actions. It's truly easy to do. Ridiculously easy. But it's just as easy *not* to do. And if you don't do them, there won't be any big drama about it. It won't kill you; it won't hurt you; in fact, it won't make any difference at all … not today, anyway. Not tomorrow. But over time?

Seeing with the Eyes of Time

Another good image for the slight edge is Lady Justice, the blindfolded statue. The statue itself, of the woman holding the scales and sword to represent the idea of justice, has been around since the days of ancient Rome, but in those days it didn't wear a blindfold. That part wasn't added until the sixteenth century, during the renaissance in thinking that eventually gave birth to our modern ideas of representative democracy and universal human rights. The blindfold doesn't imply that justice is "blind," as people sometimes assume; its point is that true justice is impervious to external influence.

That's exactly how you have to hold the slight edge philosophy.

If you want to understand and apply the slight edge to create the life of your dreams, you can't make your everyday choices based on the evidence of your eyes. You need to make them based on what you know. You have to see through *the eyes of time*.

Picture success and failure as the two sides of a pair of balance scales, like the one held by Lady Justice.

Let's say you're in a tough place in your life. The scales are tipped badly, the negative side tilted way down. Whether it's your health, or your finances, or your marriage, or your career … whatever it is, you've reached a place where many years of simple errors in judgment have compounded over time, and you're feeling it. You're behind the eight ball. It sure would be nice if, somehow, you could do something dramatic. If you just wake up tomorrow and have it all turned around— snap your fingers and change it.

That might happen, in a movie. But this is your life. What can you do?

What happens if you add one small, simple, positive action to the success side? Nothing you can see. What happens if you add one more? Nothing you can see. What happens if you keep adding one more, and one more, and one more, and one more …

Before too long, you see the scales shift, ever so slightly. And then again. And eventually, that heavy "failure" side starts to lift, and lift, and lift … and the scales start swinging your way. No matter how much negative weight from the past is on the other side, just by adding those little grams of success, one at a time (and by *not* adding more weight to the failure side), you will eventually and inevitably begin to shift the scales in your favor.

Way back in the beginning, when you add the first few tiny, insignificant bits of positive action, you won't see the scales move at all and that will frustrate you—if you judge your choices by the evidence of your eyes. It frustrates nineteen out of twenty people so much, they quit.

No matter what you have done in your life up until today, no matter where you are and how far down you may have slid on the failure curve, you can start fresh, building a positive pattern of success, at any time. Including right now. But you need to have faith in the process, because *you won't see it happening at first.*

If you base your choices on the evidence, on what you can see, you're sunk. You need to base your choices on your philosophy—on what you *know*, not what you see.

The Power of Compounding Effort

There is a passage in Jim Collins' classic business book, *Good to Great*, that beautifully describes the way the slight edge is so often invisible and can seem so insignificant—that is, until they build to the point of escape velocity.

> Picture a huge, heavy flywheel—a massive metal disk mounted horizontally on an axle, about thirty feet in diameter, two feet thick, and weighing about 5,000 pounds. Now imagine that your task is to get the flywheel rotating on the axle as fast and for as long as possible.
>
> Pushing with great effort, you get the flywheel to inch forward, moving almost imperceptibly at first. You keep pushing and, after two or three hours of persistent effort, you get the flywheel to complete one entire turn.

You keep pushing, and the flywheel begins to move a bit faster, and with continued great effort, you move it through a second rotation. You keep pushing in a consistent direction. Three turns … four … five … six … the flywheel builds up speed … seven … eight … you keep pushing … nine … ten … it builds momentum … eleven … twelve … moving faster with each turn … twenty … thirty … fifty … a hundred.

Then at some point—breakthrough! The momentum of the thing kicks in your favor, hurling the flywheel forward, turn after turn … whoosh! … its own heavy weight working for you. You're pushing no harder than the first rotation, but the flywheel goes faster and faster. Each turn of the flywheel builds upon work done earlier, compounding your investment of effort. A thousand times faster, then ten thousand, then a hundred thousand. The huge heavy disk flies forward with almost unstoppable momentum.

Now suppose someone came along and asked, "What was the one big push that caused this thing to go so fast?"

You wouldn't be able to answer; it's a nonsensical question. Was it the first push? The second? The fifth? The hundredth? No! It was *all* of them added together in an overall accumulation of effort applied in a consistent direction. Some pushes may have been bigger than others, but any single heave—no matter how large—reflects a small fraction of the entire cumulative effect upon the flywheel.

— *From Good to Great: Why Some Companies Make the Leap … and Others Don't*, by Jim Collins, HarperBusiness, N.Y. (2001); 165–6.

Successful people do whatever it takes to get the job done, whether or not they feel like it. They understand that it is not any one single push on the flywheel but the cumulative total of all their sequential, unfailingly consistent pushes that eventually creates movement of such astonishing momentum in their lives.

Successful people form habits that feed their success, instead of habits that feed their failure. They choose to have the slight edge working for them, not against them. They build their own dreams, rather than spend their lives building other people's dreams, and they achieve these dramatic results in their lives through making choices that are the very antithesis of drama—mundane, simple, seemingly insignificant choices.

Every decision you make is a slight edge decision. What you're going to do, how you're going to act, what you're going to read, who you're going to chat with on the phone, what you're going to eat for lunch, who you're going to associate with. How you're going to treat your fellow workers. What you're going to get done today.

Simply by making those right decisions, or making more of them— one at a time, over and over again—you will have enlisted the awesome power of the slight edge on your behalf. The unwanted circumstances, the poor results you've produced in the past, and the evidence of failures in your life, may all continue for a time. There may be no light at the end of the tunnel, or at least none you can see today. But by putting time on your side, you've marshaled the forces of the slight edge. Your success becomes inevitable. You just need to stay in the process long enough to give it a chance to win.

It starts with a choice.

Cultivating Patience

Patience is a challenge for people who do not understand the slight edge.

Often, in the beginning, the success path can be uncomfortable, even scary. Especially if you're the only one around who's on it. And with only one out of twenty people ever achieving their goals, it's quite likely that you *will* be the only one around on the path—at least for a while.

Sometimes the path of success is inconvenient, and therefore not just easy not to do but actually *easier* not to do. For most people, it's easier to stay in bed. Getting on the path and staying on the path requires faith in the process—especially at the start. That makes you a pioneer.

Pioneers don't know what's out there, but out there, they go anyway.

That's why being a pioneer takes such courage. *Courage* means to have a purpose and to have heart. Once you are aware of and understand how to use the slight edge, you will naturally have both—purpose and the strength of heart to stay on that purpose. The important point is to start on the path and to remember that no matter what has gone on before, you can begin fresh and new anytime you choose. You can start with a clean slate.

How long will it take? How long before you will actually see and feel (and smell and touch and be able to spend and enjoy and appreciate) the results? How long before you will have the experience of the success you're seeking?

Obviously, it's impossible for either of us to say exactly how long. But in my experience, in three to five years you can put virtually anything in your life solidly onto the right track. Think of what you were doing three years ago: it seems like yesterday, doesn't it? Well, three years from now, the things you're doing right now will seem like only yesterday, too. Yet this brief little period of time can change your life. How long will it take? Chances are it will take longer than you want it to—and that when the time arrives, you'll be astonished at how quick it seemed.

Patience is not an issue for the water hyacinth. It simply goes about its business, calmly, quietly doubling, until it covers the pond. You can do the same.

> Serene, I fold my hands and wait,
> Nor care for wind, nor tide, nor sea;
> I rave no more 'gainst time or fate,
> For lo! my own shall come to me.
> —John Burroughs, *Waiting*

The slight edge guarantees that *your own shall come to you*, like the water hyacinth covering the pond. The way *your own* shows up, good or bad, failure or success, win or lose, is, moment by moment, up to you. You need not "care for wind, nor tide, nor sea," but you do need to care for those simple little actions which, compounded over time, will make the difference between your success or failure.

The problem is that most of us live with one foot planted firmly in the past and the other tucked timidly in the future—never in the moment. In relation to everything—our kids, our health, our home, our career—we tick through the hours in constant regret and Monday-morning-quarterbacking about what's behind us, and with worry, anxiety, and dread about what lies ahead.

The Slight Edge is all about living in the moment. For me, this is perhaps the hardest lesson to learn about the slight edge: you can't find it in the past or the future, only right here, right now.

The reason Ekhart Tolle's modest little 1997 book on enlightenment, *The Power of Now*, took the marketplace by storm, selling over five million copies in thirty-three languages, is that his core message is one that everyone knows they need to hear: *your life exists only in the moment.* But you can't really absorb or live that truth through reading a book; you absorb and live that truth simply by being fully in the process of living your life—not regretting the past, not dreading the future.

The Slight Edge is about your awareness. It is about you making the right choices, the choices that serve you and empower you, starting right now and continuing for the rest of your life, and learning to make them effortlessly.

What feeds your patience and keeps you on the path is a philosophy (and remember, your philosophy is simply your view of *how things are*) that includes an understanding of the secret of time. Knowing the secret of time, you say, "If I stay on this road long enough, I'll get the result I'm seeking." It's not a question of your mood or your feelings. And it's not a question of will power. It's a question of simply *knowing*.

When you enter a darkened room, why does your hand reach out for the light switch? Because you know that when you hit the switch, the light will go on. You don't have to give yourself positive self-talk about how you really ought to hit that light switch, or set up a system of rewards and punishments for yourself around whether you follow through or not with hitting the light switch. You don't need any rigmarole; you just hit the switch. Why? Because you know what will happen.

You *know*.

It's the exact same thing here: you walk a little every day, lift a few weights, eat a little better, and leave the penny in the purse (hit the light switch) because you *know* it will make you healthy and wealthy (the light will turn on).

It's the exact same thing, no different—except for one thing, and that is time.

How to Achieve the Impossible

The Norwegian explorer Fritjof Nansen was awarded the Nobel Peace Prize in 1922 for an extraordinary record of heroism: he personally repatriated more than 400,000 prisoners of war after World War I, helping to save millions of Russians from starvation.

Here's what Nansen had to say on the subject of *impossible*:

> *The difficult is what takes a little time;*
> *the impossible is what takes a little longer.*

Nansen was someone who grasped the slight edge at the core of his being, and that's a fantastic way of expressing it: *Impossible just takes a little longer.*

Here's the part I love most about that: the word *little*.

Because in our lives, unlike the Grand Canyon example, remarkable change doesn't take *that* long. Success takes time, yes, more time than most people are willing to wait. But not as much as you'd think. And once the momentum of the slight edge starts to kick in it becomes unstoppable, and you reach a point where results do indeed start to happen very fast indeed.

Let me give you an example, again, from an experience in business.

Last chapter I told you about the merger we went through, bringing our TPN sales force into that larger company. Now let me tell what happened next.

After some successful years with that company, I came to a point where I wanted to do more. I was hungry for a challenge, something where I could stretch, grow, and really make a mark on the world. So I did something some people (okay, a lot of people) might think was flat-out crazy: I let go of that successful business, struck out on my own, and launched a brand-new marketing company, in an industry where it's really easy to launch a new business—and flop.

Launching and having it *work*? Not so easy.

There are a million moving parts that have to all work together. An independent sales force is a 100 percent volunteer army. You don't *hire* these folks, they have to join you voluntarily ... and *stay* with you voluntarily. Which means you have to do a lot and get it all right, because if they aren't happy they just pick up and wander off. If they double sales in six months, for example, you need to be fully prepared to support that increase—you can't be a day late on an order or a bonus check, or the word will spread and they'll start leaving. But if sales hardly grows at all in those six months, you also have to be prepared for *that*, and have the capacity to hold tight without your unsold inventory ripping through your capital.

Let me put it this way: starting a company like this is not something for the faint of heart.

In order to do everything possible to make that initial plunge and get your new company into profit and established right away, here's the common strategy: you launch your new company with the biggest fanfare you possibly can. A widely publicized pre-launch, a grand opening with as much noise as possible, major promotion of the "big leaders" you've brought in, a celebrity endorsement or two, if you have the budget for it, and so forth. Make a splash. Turn heads. Do whatever it takes to get people's attention—as many people as possible.

So we decided to do the exact opposite of that.

We decided to see what would happen if we launched a company in a completely organic way, using the slight edge. We spent a huge chunk of time and resources building the company's marketing, support, and the rest of its infrastructure, going slow so we made sure we had built a solid company before we even opened our doors. And then one day we were done building, so we invited a few friends and family over and declared ourselves open for business.

We also made it a point to teach our sales force to build the business the same way: slow but steady. Before launching we codified the slight edge into a set of simple ideas we called our Ten Core Values. These included things like *be real, be determined, pursue constant self-development*, and *dream big—and act on it daily*. Among the ten, the principal value was this: *Slow down to go fast*. In other words: you want big results? Good— then do the little things. Just do them consistently and persistently.

We based our entire business model on slight edge principles, following them and teaching them to everyone involved from the very first day.

Sales grew steadily, month by month, without any huge quantum leap—until the compounded effect of all those months of steady growth began to kick in.

In our first year, we went to over $100 million in sales.

What's more, we reached that sales figure faster than any company had ever done before in the history of our industry—in fact, we were given an award by an industry trade journal for being the first company in our field to blow past that milestone. We became a giant in the shortest time anyone had ever done. How? By going slow.

Sometimes you need to slow down to go fast.

Personal Stories from
The Slight Edge Readers

To me, *The Slight Edge* is a lifestyle, a way of living that most fail to discover—especially today in this instant gratification world we live in. *The Slight Edge* is about doing key things that are easy to do and easy not to do.

Reading and applying *The Slight Edge* daily has helped me lose more than sixty pounds over twenty-four months, attract relationships with highly successful people who are now my mentors, develop self-confidence that grows every day, and so much more. Most of all, *The Slight Edge* has helped me clearly understand that investing just a few minutes a day to improve my life has a compounding effect. I now wake up every day knowing I am on the upward track to achieving my dream goals in all areas of my life!

—*Jim Hageman, Dallas, Texas*

For many years I wanted to be my own boss, and when the opportunity presented itself I started my first business. Unfortunately, after a few years that business failed and I lost everything. It was a demoralizing experience and one for which I tended to deny responsibility.

Shortly after this happened, I was given a copy of *The Slight Edge* and my eyes were opened. I realized that although it *seemed* like my business had failed overnight, nothing could have been further from the truth. What had really happened was that I had been applying the slight edge *in reverse* for a long time, and what I was now seeing was the devastating cumulative effect of all those years.

I'm happy to say that since then I have been applying slight edge principles in constructive way, and although it has taken a while, things are now moving forward in a very positive direction. I have a beautiful wife, a lovely family, and my first children's book is being published this month, with a series of twelve planned over the next two years. The future for our family looks extremely bright, and I know from the bottom of my heart that this is down to consistent application of *The Slight Edge*.

—Mark Hibbitts, author of
Alfie Potts™ the Schoolboy Entrepreneur

At twenty-four I was ambitious but a little frustrated. I already owned my own gym, but success just couldn't come fast enough for me. It wasn't until I read *The Slight Edge* that I realized success would need to be slow and steady and come as a result of being consistent over time. I needed to take inventory and understand the exact steps it would take to become successful, and then apply those steps consistently.

Within two years after I started doing that, my business had quadrupled. I have since opened two additional gyms and an online media company, and we're on track to quadruple our revenue once again.

Since reading *The Slight Edge* I am no longer looking into the unknown, but instead looking to the present possibilities that are ingrained in my daily habits. The book gave me a paradigm shift. I have faith that my daily habits will lead to either success or failure, and that the choice is mine. Pay attention to your daily habits and it will pay off.

— Jeremy T., Marysville, Washington

Essential Points from Chapter 5

- Time is the force that magnifies those simple daily disciplines into massive success.

- There is a natural progression to success: plant, cultivate, harvest—and the central step, *cultivate,* can only happen over the course of time.

- No genuine success in life is instant. Life is not a clickable link.

- To grasp how the slight edge works, you have to view your actions through the eyes of time.

- Difficult takes a little time; impossible takes just a little longer.

6. Don't Fall for the Quantum Leap

> "I am a great believer in luck. The harder I work, the more of it I seem to have."
>
> —*Coleman Cox*

During The People's Network's (TPN) time, I sat at the center of the personal development universe working with the world's top experts and thought leaders. While the information I learned from them was brilliant, the philosophy they sold it under was wrong. They sold it as "buy this and you will fix yourself in thirty to ninety days." In other words, "In a quantum leap!" To my dismay I saw many people strive for the quantum leap results they were taught as achievable over the next one to three months with little to no results. They, too, got dismayed. More regrettably, I witnessed many of these people not just losing their belief in being able to seek a change in their life, but actually regressing to an earlier state in which they simply didn't want to make any changes! It was then that I realized that instead of teaching a quantum leap philosophy, we needed a philosophy that provided help over the interim period before they achieved their goals. It was then that I wrote *The Slight Edge* as the "anti-Quantum Leap" book.

Someday Never Comes

"Some day my prince will come…." Good old Walt Disney. Well, that may have worked out for Snow White. Back here on Earth, it's a recipe for disappointment. In flesh-and-blood life, waiting for "some day" is no strategy for success, it's a cop-out. What's more, it's one that the majority follow their whole lives.

Someday, when my ship comes in ...

Someday, when I have the money ...

Someday, when I have the time ...

Someday, when I have the skill ...

Someday, when I have the confidence ...

How many of those statements have you said to yourself? Have I got some sobering news for you: "some day" doesn't exist, never has, and never will. There is no "some day." There's only today. When tomorrow comes, it will be another today; so will the next day. They all will. There is never anything but today.

And some more shocking news: your ship's not coming—it's already here. Docked and waiting. You already have the money. You already have the time. You already have the skill, the confidence. You already have everything you need to achieve everything you want.

You just can't see it.

Why not? Because you're looking in the wrong place. You're looking for the breakthrough, the quantum leap. You're looking for the winning lottery ticket in a game that isn't a lottery.

Why Bank Presidents Never Win the Lottery

Have you ever noticed that when you read stories about lottery winners, they are hardly ever bank presidents, successful entrepreneurs, or corporate executives? That they never seem to be people who were *already* financially successful before they bought that winning ticket? Have you ever wondered why? It's because successful people never win the lottery. You know why?

Because they don't buy lottery tickets.

Successful people have already grasped the truth that lottery players have not: success is not a random accident. Life is not a lottery.

There's a popular expression you've probably heard, "Luck is preparedness meeting opportunity." It's a handy idea, but it's not quite accurate. People who live by the slight edge understand how luck really works. It's not preparedness meeting opportunity: it's preparedness, *period*. Preparedness created by doing those simple, little, constructive,

positive actions, over and over. Luck is when that constancy of preparedness eventually *creates* opportunity.

One reason the slight edge is so widely ignored, unnoticed, and un-
dervalued is that our culture tends to worship the idea of the "big
break." We celebrate that dramatic discovery, the big breakthrough that
catapults the hero into a new place. In other words, we buy lottery
tickets.

The truth of breakthroughs and lucky breaks is that, yes, they *do*
happen—but they don't happen out of thin air. They are grown, like a
crop: planted, cultivated, and ultimately harvested. The problem is, as
I mentioned last chapter, that in our culture we're trained to think we
can skip over the middle step and leap directly from plant to harvest.
We even have a term for it. We call it a *quantum leap*.

And it's a complete, utter myth.

Fictional Gods and Actual Heroes

In ancient Greek theater, characters generally got themselves into
as much of a mess as the playwright could possibly dream up. Everything would be headed for an absolutely impossible disaster when, in
the last few minutes of the play, an actor playing a "god" would come
floating down from the sky to make everything right—banishing this
character and reinstating that one, punishing another and granting divine clemency to still another, explaining the inexplicable and solving
the insoluble.

Things would be in such a mess, there'd be no way a human being
could sort the stuff out. Obviously, it would have to take a being with
divine powers. And just like in a stage production of *Peter Pan*, the actor
would be suspended by ropes and a system of pulleys, a mechanical
contrivance they termed a "machine," or *machina*.

Today, thousands of years later, people still refer to a last-minute
"cheat" solution for an impossible problem coming out of thin air as a
deus ex machina, or "god dropping in out of nowhere by a machine"—
the supernatural, breakthrough force that drops down from the heav-
ens at the eleventh hour, just in time to make all things right. And by
the way, when critics say a play, novel or film uses a "deus ex machina,"
it's not a compliment. It's their way of saying, "Couldn't come up with
a believable solution, eh? So you had to trot out some completely im-
plausible, fantasy-land hack ending. Thumbs down."

Give me a break.

In fact, that's exactly what it is people are hoping for: a break. The big break. The lucky break. The breakthrough. A break in the routine—a break with reality. A deus ex machina. They want to say, like Captain Kirk, "Warp speed, Scottie"—and suddenly zip from point A to point Z. In my decades in the personal development field, I've seen it a thousand times, a hundred thousand times. People want to walk over coals, break boards, scream primally, and have their entire lives change because they wrote down a "vision statement" on a piece of paper at a weekend seminar. But that's not how things really work.

Let's look for a moment at how things *do* really work. Let's consider some real-world problems that would have made Peter Pan or Captain Kirk or any other fictional hero pull his hair out.

For example, let's look at the history of slavery and emancipation.

Here we were, a brand-new nation, beacon of the Enlightenment, a bold experiment in idealism and the proposition that all human beings are created equal … and meanwhile we were keeping a few million human beings in chains to do our work for us. How was *that* supposed to add up? And we weren't the only ones. In fact, we learned it from the English and brought the idea with us across the Atlantic on the Mayflower.

In the mid-eighteenth century, as the new nation on this side of the pond was just still going through its teething years under President Washington, a Parliamentary politician named William Wilberforce decided the world had had enough of slavery, and he meant to see it stopped. In terms of the vested economic interests and psychological resistance this idea faced, accomplishing it would be something like cutting a new Grand Canyon—with a fork. But Wilberforce had an innate appreciation of the slight edge.

Year after year, bill after bill, Wilberforce spent his entire career introducing an endless series of legislative proposals to his colleagues in the British Parliament in his efforts to end slavery, only to have them defeated, one after the other. From 1788 to 1806, he introduced a new anti-slavery motion and watched it fail every single year, for eighteen years in a row. Finally the water wore down the rock: three days before Wilberforce's death in 1833, Parliament passed a bill to abolish slavery not only in England but also throughout its colonies. Three decades later, a similar bill passed in the United States, spearheaded by another man of conscience who had also spent much of his life failing, a patient Illinois lawyer named Abraham.

Deus ex machina? Far from it. These weren't solutions that dropped out of the blue sky. They were the "sudden" result of long patient years of tireless repeated effort. There was no fictional *deus ex machina* happening here; these were human problems, and they had human solutions. But the only access to them was through the slight edge.

Of course Wilberforce and Lincoln were not the sole figures in this heroic struggle, and even after their bills were passed into law on both sides of the Atlantic, the evils of slavery and racism were far from over. Rome wasn't rehabilitated in a day, or even a century. But their efforts—like Mother Teresa's efforts to end poverty, Gandhi's to end colonial oppression, or Martin Luther King's and Nelson Mandela's to end racism—are classic examples of what "breakthrough" looks like in the real world.

All of these real-life heroes understood the slight edge. None of them were hypnotized by the allure of the "big break." If they had been, they would never have continued taking the actions they took—and what would the world look like today?

One Small Step

Our cultural mythology, the philosophy our society subscribes to as a group, worships the quantum leap breakthrough even when we don't realize that's what we're doing.

"One small step for a man …"—wait a second! That wasn't one small step. This guy was walking *on the moon*, for crying out loud, and we were all watching it on television, with Walter Cronkite narrating. (I know, I'm revealing my age.) That wasn't a small anything—it was one *gigantic* step for man, a genuine breakthrough.

The small step was when some guy, someone you and I never heard of, and probably never will, first started tinkering with design ideas for how a rocket ship might withstand the intense conditions of space flight. There were thousands, hundreds of thousands, millions of "one small steps" for years and years beforehand that all went into that epic 1969 leap of Neil Armstrong's that was televised throughout the world (and is still played over and over in our culture as one of the most deeply ingrained news bites of history).

But we don't celebrate any of those real *small steps*. We don't even know what they are, or who made them.

The myth of our culture is the giant step, the larger-than life leap, the heroic effort. "Faster than a speeding bullet, able to…." Wait, how does that go again? Is it, "able to take small, insignificant, incremental steps, consistently, over time?" No, it's "able to leap tall buildings in a single bound!" I mean, what kind of Superman would take tiny steps?

The kind who wins. Like Edison and his light bulb.

Have you ever suddenly understood something in a "flash of recognition"? Have you ever known of someone who became an "overnight success"? Here is a great secret that holds the key to great accomplishment: both that "sudden flash" and that "overnight success" were the final, breakthrough results of a long, patient process of edge upon edge upon edge. Any time you see what looks like a breakthrough, it is *always* the end result of a long series of little things, done consistently over time. No success is immediate or instantaneous; no collapse is sudden or precipitous. They are both products of the slight edge.

Now, I'm not saying that quantum leaps are a myth because they don't really happen. As a matter of fact, they *do* happen. Just not the way people think they do. The term comes from particle physics, and here's what it means in reality: a true quantum leap is what happens when a subatomic particle suddenly jumps to a higher level of energy. But it happens as a result of the gradual buildup of potential caused by energy being applied to that particle over time.

In other words, it doesn't "just suddenly happen." An actual quantum leap is something that *finally* happens after a lengthy accumulation of slight-edge effort. Exactly the way the water hyacinth moves from day twenty-nine to day thirty. Exactly the way the frog's certain death by drowning was "suddenly" transformed into salvation by butter.

A real-life quantum leap is not Superman leaping a tall building. A real quantum leap is Edison perfecting the electric light bulb after a thousand patient efforts—and then transforming the world with it.

The Winning Edge

The slight edge is the process every winner has used to succeed since the dawn of time. Winning is *always* a matter of the slight edge.

One of the most highly anticipated events at the summer Olympics is men's swimming. Going into the 2008 Beijing games there was a lot of hype surrounding Michael Phelps, who would be gunning for Mark Spitz's thirty-six-year-old record of seven gold medals. The first seven medals came rather easily, but his eighth medal was one for the ages. When he came down the final stretch of the 100-meter butterfly, it looked like he was going to fall inches short. But moments after Phelps touched the wall, the world was stunned when the clock showed that he had edged out Milorad Cavic by *one one-hundredth* of a second. Not even a second, but *1 percent* of one second.

Yes, that's a *very* slight edge. But it's all he needed to secure a record eighth gold medal and earn the reputation as the greatest Olympic athlete ever.

Do you know what makes the difference between a .300-hitting baseball star with a multimillion-dollar contract and a .260-plus player making only an average salary? Less than one additional hit per week over the course of the season. And you know what makes the difference between getting that hit and striking out? About one quarter-inch up or down the bat.

No golf fan who watched the 2004 Masters tournament will ever forget how it ended: Phil Mickelson, winner of more tournaments over the previous ten years than anyone else but Tiger Woods, was left with a twenty-foot putt on the eighteenth hole of the final round. Miss it, even by one inch, and he would head into a playoff with the number two player in the world, Ernie Els. Make it, and he would finally silence the critics and win his first major. The putt rolled in and Mickelson had his green jacket. Over the course of the tournament's four days, Mickelson shot a 279, six strokes better than two-time Masters champion Bernhard Langer.

The difference? One and a half strokes per day better.

The slight edge.

And it's not just in sports. It's in everything. No matter in what arena, in life or work or play, the difference between winning and losing, the gap that separates success and failure, is so slight, so subtle, that most never see it. Superman may leap tall buildings at a single bound. Here on earth, we win through the slight edge.

Magic Bullets and Miracles

Every January in every gym across America, hundreds of thousands of people start over in a process that they will soon quit. And the only reason they're going to quit is that they haven't set themselves up with the right expectation. They aren't looking for incremental progress; they're looking for results they can feel *right now*. They're looking for a breakthrough. They don't have a whisper of a chance.

Easy to do, easy not to do ... and in that tiny, seemingly insignificant little choice *not to do*, so many people quit the effort and then go on to live out lives of quiet desperation.

Believing in the "big break" is worse than simply being futile. It's actually dangerous, because it can keep you from taking the actions you need to take to create the results you want. It can even be lethal. Think of the poor frog that gave up and let himself drown because he couldn't see a breakthrough on the horizon. He was wrong, of course: there *are* miracles, even in the life of a frog. It's just that the break-through didn't come down out of the clouds; it came at the end of a series of consistent, determined, compounding-interest foot-pad-dlings.

What's the greatest gift you can give to an inner-city kid? An under-standing of the slight edge. Because that's not the answer he's getting from the world around him. He believes that the only way out of his world of poverty, violence, oppression, and fear is to become a sports superstar—because that's what we tell him. That's the quantum leap answer. The truth, of course, is that very, very few individuals will have the talent to break out of that world by becoming sports superstars. And deep down, every one of these kids knows that, or soon finds out. So they give up. Why bother? And they become victims of the quantum leap myth.

Can you imagine if every first grader was required to start read-ing ten pages of a good book a day? How would their finances, their health, their relationships change as adults?

Over the past few decades it's been amazing to me how many people I've been close to have persisted in making fun of my dietary choices, exercise habits, and personal development goals. The "insignificant" little things I've been doing every day for years have always struck them as funny, because they couldn't see the point. They couldn't see the results coming further on down the path.

Today I see these friends and ache for them: many now have failing health, are languishing in poor financial conditions, and seem to have lost their hopes for the future. What they have a hard time seeing is that my good health isn't an accident, and their poor health isn't a stroke of bad luck. They don't see that we all, beach bums and million-aires alike, have gotten to where we are today the exact same way: the slight edge. They are victims of the quantum leap myth.

Our society is sliding rapidly into an ever-increasing economic crisis of poor health stemming from an epidemic of adult-onset diabetes, heart disease, obesity, and a score of other chronic illnesses that have steadily fed a monstrously overgrown health care system, tax system, and social security system. The cause of all this is no mystery, and neither is the solution—not to those who know how to recognize the slight edge at work. Our entire health crisis is nothing but one set of little decisions, made daily and compounded daily, winning out over another set of little decisions, made daily and compounded daily.

We look for the cure, the breakthrough, the magic pill—the med-ical-scientific quantum leap miracle our press has dubbed the "magic bullet." But the solution already exists. It always did. Is it magic? Yes—the same magic that caused the problem: the power of daily actions, compounded over time. The magic of the slight edge.

There's a great line in the movie *Bruce Almighty*, when God, played by Morgan Freeman, is leaving the all-too-human Jim Carrey character to solve things on his own. (Notice: this isn't some Greek god, this is capital-G *God* we're talking about—and *he* refuses to be used as a *deus ex machina*). He says, "You want a miracle, Bruce? *Be* the miracle."

Once you absorb the slight edge way of being, you'll stop looking for that quantum leap—and start building it. You'll stop looking for the miracle, and start *being* the miracle.

Personal Stories from
The Slight Edge Readers

I grew up as the seventh of eight kids. We did not have a lot of money, and nobody in my family had a college degree, but I had big dreams for my future. How would I make them become a reality without the advantages of the wealthy and successful showing me the way? How could I start with nothing and truly live the American Dream? I had a close relative who was always pursuing the next gold mine, investing in the "just discovered" oil well, the "next big thing." I thought, was that the way to pursue my dreams? I didn't think so.

When I discovered the slight edge principles, I started channeling my burning desire for success into daily habits that I knew would eventually build momentum and over time help me to reach my goals. I knew that by consistently working toward my goals with a positive attitude, I would see my dreams become a reality. And boy, was I right. While my relative continues to pursue "the next big thing," I've since had the privilege to travel the world, raise a great family, and do things I've never dreamed of, all because of these principles!

—*Dennis Windsor, author,* Financially Free!

After reading *The Slight Edge* I realized how I had ended up where I was in life. I was like a ship without a rudder, a wandering generality. I have always known I wanted to be successful; however, I never realized that it was not some big chance or huge deal that was going to do it. Finally, I understood that it was the day-to-day events, the things I did—or decided not to do—that would make the true difference.

As I looked back over my life I got a clear picture, and from that day forward I began applying the slight edge to everything I did, from business to relationships. It was hard at first, but once I got used to the habit of choosing the right "little things" to do every day, it made all the difference in the world. I now have a wonderful woman in my life, a thriving business, and time to reflect on what is most important to me.

—*Adam Russell, CEO, Global Resource Broker LLC, Miami, Florida*

Essential Points from Chapter 6

➤ Quantum leaps do happen, but only as the end result of a lengthy, gradual buildup of consistently applied effort.

➤ No success is immediate, no collapse is sudden. They are both the result of the slight edge accruing momentum over time.

➤ Hoping for "the big break"—the breakthrough, the magic bullet—is not only futile, it's dangerous, because it keeps you from taking the actions you need to create the results you want.

7. The Secret of Happiness

> "Success is not the key to happiness.
> Happiness is the key to success."
> —*Albert Schweitzer*

S everal years after we first published the original edition of *The Slight Edge*, I made a discovery that rocked my world and took my understanding of the slight edge to a whole new level. Up to that point I had studied, applied, and taught the slight edge mainly as it applied to four big areas of life: health, wealth, personal development, and relationships. Then, starting in the late 2000s, I began learning about a fascinating new frontier of science called positive psychology.

In plain terms, the science of happiness.

A graduate assistant of Marty Seligman, the father of the science of positive psychology, shared with me a funny story about the massive shift in psychology that occurred over the past 20 years. He said, "The difference between positive psychology and traditional psychology is that with traditional psychology the ambulance is at the bottom of the cliff and with positive psychology the ambulance is at the top of the cliff."

What Science Has Learned About Happiness

Let me take a moment to tell you how this science happened, because it is itself a great example of the slight edge at work.

For most of the last hundred-plus years, the modern study of psychology has focused mainly on what goes wrong with people: emotional disturbances, psychological illness, trauma, neurosis, psychosis, mania, obsession, insanity … call it what you will, it's mainly been about examining humanity's darker side. There has been startlingly little attention paid to what habits, practices, or influences build up our nobler instincts and better nature.

Until the turn of the twenty-first century.

In the late nineties a Philadelphia psychologist named Martin Seligman had a thought: What if happiness is more than simply the absence of sadness? What if there's more to humanity's nobler nature than simply treating illness? What if we could have a kind of psychology that focused on the positive, instead of the negative?

Call this idea a water hyacinth.

Seligman shared the idea with a colleague, and they shared it with a few more. The small group then invited nearly two dozen of the best and brightest young researchers in the country to join their cause. They began generating a stream of research cash to pursue their idea. Six months later Seligman presented the idea to a convention of thousands of psychologists drawn from around the country. By the early 2000s millions of dollars were funding an avalanche of new research, international associations and journals were founded, and an entirely new branch of psychology had been born.

By the middle of the decade, the public caught on to what was happening. In January 2005 *Time* magazine ran a cover story titled "The Science of Happiness." The following year a Harvard professor offered a lecture course in positive psychology and 855 students showed up, making it the largest class at Harvard. The press went nuts, calling it "Happiness 101." School systems, *Fortune* 100 corporations, and the U.S. military all got involved. Governments floated proposals to begin measuring GNH—"gross national happiness"—along with GNP and GDP as yardsticks of their countries' health. In 2010, when Zappos CEO Tony Hsieh published his business memoir, *Delivering Happiness*, it debuted on the *New York Times* bestseller list at No. 1 and stayed on the list for twenty-seven consecutive weeks.

The water hyacinth had covered the lake.

And the Pursuit ... Make That the *Realization* of Happiness

In a way, the happiness revolution was not entirely new. In a way, all that science echoed and built upon another revolution that happened a few hundred years earlier.

Thomas Jefferson and Benjamin Franklin really nailed it in the American Declaration of Independence when they identified humanity's "three inalienable rights." They wrote that every one of us, by virtue of our showing up on this planet as a human being, has the right to life, liberty, and the pursuit of happiness.

Here's how you might express those three inalienable rights in modern-day terms.

Life means your health. The healthier you are, the more life you experience. Better health not only lets you live out all the days of a longer life, it also lets you live *more life* in each and every one of those days. Poor health is like a cloudy, smoggy day: it cuts off the sunlight. Let your health get bad enough, and you lose your life altogether.

Liberty in the modern world (assuming you don't live in North Korea or some other pocket of political oppression) means finances. If you don't have money handled, you don't live free. Financial health gives you freedom; freedom to follow your passions, chase your pursuits, develop your skills and talents and gifts, to fulfill the promises of life itself.

And the pursuit of happiness? Now that's a great question.

The founders of the American experiment wanted to frame a context, an environment where individuals could go about pursuing happiness, whatever that meant for them, in relative peace and freedom. They didn't try to guarantee happiness itself, just a place where you stood a better chance of chasing it down without being clapped in irons.

What Seligman's happiness revolution has done is worked out the precise steps that it takes to do that. And what the positive psychologists have found is that happiness isn't some big thing you *pursue*, not something you chase after. It's not something "out there" that you have to go way out of your way to hunt down, like some sort of psychological or emotional safari. It's right in front of our noses.

It's not something you *pursue*, it's something you *do*.

Or to be more accurate, it's a lot of somethings you do. A lot of *little* somethings. Simple things you do every day, in fact. Or, as the case may be, *don't* do every day.

In the past fifteen years, science has learned:

> → Happiness doesn't come from genetics, luck, or chance.
>
> → Happiness has a lot less to do with circumstances than we think it does.
>
> → Happiness isn't the result of some big, out-of-reach event or attainment.
>
> → Happiness is created by simple, easy things we do every day.
>
> → And *unhappiness* is created by *not* doing those simple, easy, everyday things.

So, at the risk of getting historical purists all bent out of shape because we're fiddling with such a venerated document, let's make a one-word update to that Declaration: let's frame our definition of success as: life (health), liberty (financial freedom), and the *realization* of happiness.

And how you realize happiness is not by winning the lottery, not by buying a mansion or a Lamborghini, not by moving to the Riviera, not by becoming rich and famous or marrying a movie star. Not by gigantic achievements and accolades. Not by having a fairy godmother or fate or phenomenal good luck somehow make everything in your life perfect.

How you realize happiness is by doing some simple things, and doing them every day.

Learning from My Mom, Revisited

Remember that day when I was sitting talking with my mom and learned that she was a millionaire? I thought a lot about that over the years, and now I realized that when we had that conversation, there was something about it that had struck me, something even more stunning than her revelation about money. It wasn't that my mom was literally a millionaire that hit me like a hurricane. (Although to be honest, that one *did* hit me like, say, a good-sized sledge hammer.) It was something else, something that occurred to me only years later. Something so obvious, so dirt simple, that I'd never really looked at it before.

She was not only rich, she was *happy*.

Now I started wondering about that. Just why was that? Sure, she had all this money stashed away, and I'm sure that gave her a sense of security. But she still lived an incredibly simple lifestyle. Wherever she had that money on deposit, it was pretty much invisible in her everyday life. And besides, it had taken her many decades to accumulate that fortune, and as I reflected back I realized that even when I was a young boy, even when we had so little, she was happy way back then, too.

She had *always* been happy.

How could that be? Her life sure wasn't easy in those early days. I was a handful, and then there were my siblings. Her husband was gone, snatched from life long before his fiftieth birthday. Her circumstances certainly didn't seem to warrant her being happy.

Yet she was.

It wasn't until years later, well into the twenty-first century, that I began to understand the secret to my mom's happiness—and another crucial element to the slight edge.

Growing up, I never heard her say a negative word, not about anything or anyone. No matter how bad things were, she always somehow found something positive to see in the situation. No matter how obnoxious or annoying or mean someone was, she found a way to see them in a positive light. All of which turns out to be one of those everyday behaviors that the researchers tell us are what create happiness.

In fact, as I began collating all the key points I was learning from all the happiness research, I realized that my mom had been following every one of them for my whole life. She never talked in negative terms. She always found the good in everything. She made a regular practice of counting her blessings. She did kind things for people. She probably never used the words "practice positive perspective" in her life, but that's what she did, every moment of every day.

She exemplifies the principles of everyday happiness. Even when things were tough, even when money was tight (which was *always*) or when problems happened (which sure *felt* like always), she always seemed happy and content. What I now realized was that she didn't just seem that way, she *was* that way. And the reason she was that way was that she did a number of those simple, everyday things that science has now informed us are what creates genuine, lasting happiness.

It wasn't until years later that I realized what it was she had showed me, what it was I had learned from her: Success doesn't lead to happiness—it's the other way around.

Happiness Comes First

One of the most radical and remarkable things about the happiness research is the discovery that doing things that make you happy doesn't just make you happier. It also makes your life work better.

There's a reason this chapter is called The Secret *of* Happiness, and not The Secret *to* Happiness. There are certainly secrets *to* happiness, that is, things that will lead to happiness, and given the last fifteen years of positive psychology research they're not secrets anymore, if they ever truly were. Most of them are actually commonsense things.

But we called it The Secret *of* Happiness because happiness itself is a secret ingredient to something else. To what else? Practically everything. Extensive research since 2000 has shown that people who are happier also:

> have fewer strokes and heart attacks
> have less pain and inflammation
> have greater immune function and more resistance to viruses
> develop more resilient personalities and handle adversity better
> have better work performance and more professional success
> have more fulfilling and longer-lasting marriages
> have larger and more active social spheres
> are more involved in their communities
> are more altruistic and have a greater net positive impact on society
> are more financially successful
> live longer

And here's the truly radical thing about it: it isn't that people who have greater success, more money, and better marriages are happier as a result of those things. The research is very clear on this: the greater states of happiness *precede* all these outcomes.

This is one of the central findings in the entire movement of happiness research: when it comes to understanding how to achieve happiness, most of us have it backward. We believe, "Once I become successful, then I'll be happy." Or, "Once I become healthier … once I find that relationship … once I'm living where I want to live … once my income is high enough to manage my life without stress … *then* I'll be happy."

But that's not how it works. Oh, we *think* it does. We all *assume* that's the way things work. If I do this, and I do it long enough, then I'll be happy. That makes sense. But it's just not what happens. In fact, says the research, it works exactly the opposite way. Once you do what it takes to raise your everyday level of happiness, *then* you will become more successful, *then* you'll become healthier, *then* you'll find that relationship. The more you raise your own happiness level, the more likely you'll start achieving all those things you want to achieve.

Happiness is *not* the brass ring at the end of the merry-go-round ride. It isn't the *result* of getting all the other stuff right, but something you can do right now, and that then *leads to* getting the other stuff right. The other day I saw a piece of graffiti that I thought put it perfectly: "Be happy, and the reason will appear." I *love* that.

Happiness doesn't come at the end. Happiness comes first. Albert Schweitzer put it beautifully: "Success is not the key to happiness. Happiness is the key to success."

The Words You Use May Predict How Long You'll Live

In June 2013 I attended the Third World Congress on Positive Psychology and heard Dr. Seligman present some amazing evidence that showed a direct correlation between attitude and health.

He showed the audience a map showing incidence of atherosclerotic disease, county by county, throughout the northeastern United States, as reported by the CDC. Then he put up on the screen a second map, right next to the first, this one showing the incidence of atherosclerotic disease, county by county, throughout the northeastern United States—only this time, as predicted by analysis of the words people in those counties used on Twitter.

The two maps were practically identical.

It was stunning. The study had analyzed some 40,000 words in over 80 million tweets, and when the results were overlaid with a county-by-county analysis of heart attacks, it was a nearly exact correlation.

What kind of language patterns were so predictive of illness? Overall, they were expressions of anger, hostility, and aggression, as well as disengagement and lack of social support, including "mad, alone, annoying, can't, mood, bored, tired"—and a slew of words that I can't repeat here.

He next showed charts displaying the correlation of *positive* attitude and *lower* risk of heart attacks, and they were just as dramatic. The slide of words that correlated with low incidence of atherosclerotic disease included: "morning, fabulous, helpful, share, running, forward, great, interesting, lunch, discussion, seems."

I had the honor and great pleasure of spending significant time meeting privately and developing a friendship with Dr. Seligman. We talk regularly about well-being and real-world applications of the ideas of personal development and positive psychology. What an incredible man.

Personal Development and Happiness

When I started reading material from the happiness movement a few years ago, I got excited about it and started getting other people to read it. As they did, I noticed that something peculiar happened: they got way more excited about this stuff than they ever had gotten about personal development.

That really made me stop and think.

When you spend time in the personal development world, as I did for several decades, it's pretty easy to get frustrated by how readily people turn their back on it or don't give it the credence it deserves. "Oh, right, personal development…" they say, like it's not a "real" subject worthy of serious attention.

But for some reason, that doesn't happen with happiness. Or maybe it's for *several* reasons.

For one thing, positive psychology has the built-in credibility of serious academic research behind it. The personal development movement has been driven largely by individual people's personal experience and the teachings of compelling teachers, people like Napoleon Hill, Norman Vincent Peale, Denis Waitley, Brian Tracy, and Jim Rohn. The happiness movement has a completely different genesis: it has been driven largely by scientific research. When you show up with the intellectual weight and credibility of academia and all this well-documented research in your back pocket, it opens doors you never could get through with personal development.

There's a second reason, though, and it may be even more compelling than the first: people really want to be happy.

Far more people have a strong desire to be happy than a strong desire to develop themselves to a fuller potential. "Personal development" sounds to most people like work, and who wants to work harder than they are already working? But "happiness" doesn't sound like work. It sounds like … well, it sounds like being happier.

From what I've observed, within the general population only about 10 percent of people (10 percent *at most*) are genuinely open to working on personal development. When you bring the dimension of happiness into it, when you show them what has been happening in the last fifteen years in happiness research, then suddenly that 10 percent becomes more like 50 percent.

If you take a pair of average, loving parents and tell them, "I can make your child more personally developed, or I can make your child rich—which would you prefer?" most likely they would say, "Rich." But if you say, "I can make your child either rich, or happy," then nine times out of ten they'd immediately choose happiness.

What parent doesn't want their kid to be happy? What person doesn't want to be happy?

And here's the fascinating thing: comparing happiness, which virtually everyone wants, and personal development, which only 1 out of 10 at best are really interested in, at the heart of it we're really talking about *the same thing*. When you read all the research about what it takes to raise your level of happiness, you begin to realize that these scientists are describing exactly the same kinds of behaviors that all the personal development teachers have been advocating for decades, just applied in a slightly different context.

And positive psychology, as it turns out, is the perfect mate to positive *philosophy*. In other words, the slight edge.

The Key to Making the Slight Edge Work

Since the first edition of *The Slight Edge* came out in 2005, I'd seen the impact it had in people's lives. A *lot* of people's lives. Over those eight years I was inundated with letters and calls from people talking about how *The Slight Edge* had changed their lives. Later on in these pages, I'll share a few stories of how entire companies have transformed using the slight edge philosophy.

So was the slight edge working? It sure was, for thousands and thousands of people. Was it changing lives? You bet it was. But I knew it could do more. I knew it could be working for more people, and that for those people who *were* applying it in their lives, it could be doing more for *them*. Having the right philosophy (that is, the slight edge) didn't always translate into the right actions. And I needed to understand why.

I knew there was still a missing piece.

For years I'd taught that your philosophy determines your attitude, which determines your actions. And those actions are what produce your results. For people to get the results they wanted, they simply needed to do the right actions. That's the how-to's. But you're not going to do the right actions, day in and day out, unless you have the right philosophy, in other words, unless you fully grasp the importance and the power of simple daily actions: the slight edge philosophy. Once you have the slight edge philosophy, then you have the key to how to do the hows.

I knew how the equation worked:

$$\textit{the right philosophy} \longrightarrow \textit{the right attitude} \longrightarrow \textit{the right actions}$$

But there was this in-between step, this stepping stone from philosophy to action. This thing called *attitude*. Your attitude is the thing that translates your abstract understanding (philosophy) into your concrete actions. It's like a gigantic synapse, where a nerve impulse has to make a biochemical leap from one nerve ending to another—and your attitude is what determines the quality of that leap.

Another word for attitude is *emotions*, that is, how you feel. And even with a solid philosophy, feelings can be fickle. You can greatly improve your control over your attitude by a genuine commitment to personal development … but as I'd learned, barely one person in ten is even open to the idea of serious, focused personal development. And over the years of working with the slight edge I'd seen that, even though a *lot* of people got a *lot* of results, I knew there were still far too many times when people's poor attitude got in the way and gummed up the works, even with a decent grasp of the slight edge philosophy.

What we needed was some sort of key to managing attitude.

And I'd just found it.

What I realized was that while the slight edge was the missing ingredient people need to make their lives work, happiness was the missing ingredient that quite a few people needed to make the *slight edge* work.

Happiness. The perfect workout partner for the slight edge.

Happy Habits

So you're probably wondering, what exactly *are* the everyday actions that will you happier?

What all the positive psychology research and writing tells us is that you can reprogram your brain through some very simple exercises that are both simple and easy to do. Not any kind of huge, massive effort or difficult personal transformation, not some breakthrough, nothing dramatic or heroic or titanic—just simple, fairly mundane, repetitive tasks that are easy to do, and to do again, day after day. Simple tasks that, if you do them consistently and persistently over a long enough period of time, will get the results you are looking for. In other words, that will make you happier.

Which sounds a lot like the slight edge. In fact, it *is* the slight edge. It's just the slight edge as applied specifically to creating more happiness in your life.

I call these *happy habits*.

But wait, it gets better. Happy habits don't just make you happier. They also create exactly the attitude you need to make that synaptic leap from the slight edge philosophy to slight edge actions. In other words, now those actions start *working* for you. In every aspect of your life.

Put the slight edge philosophy together with happy habits, and before long all the other how-to's start working in your life, too. The better eating habits, the workout schedule, the attention to smarter financial habits, the greater learning and personal development, the stronger, healthier relationships, the progressive development of a life of powerful, positive impact—all of it.

Here's the equation:

slight edge + happy habits = success

It's that simple.

Shawn Achor, author of *The Happiness Advantage*, is the happiness researcher and author I've worked with most. I have brought him into my company to conduct three-hour workshops on how to be happy as I am committed to spreading happiness! Shawn teaches a set of five simple things you can do every day that, if you do them consistently over time, will make you significantly, noticeably, measurably happier. They are slight edge actions for happiness: happy habits.

1. **Each morning, write down three things you're grateful for.** Not the same three every day; find three *new* things to write about. That trains your brain to search your circumstances and hunt for the positive.
2. **Journal for two minutes a day about one positive experience you've had over the past twenty-four hours.** Write down every detail you can remember; this causes your brain to literally reexperience the experience, which doubles its positive impact.
3. **Meditate daily.** Nothing fancy; just stop all activity, relax, and watch your breath go in and out for two minutes. This trains your brain to focus where you want it to, and not get distracted by negativity in your environment.
4. **Do a random act of kindness over the course of each day.** To make this simple, Shawn often recommends a specific act of kindness: at the start of each day, take two minutes to write an email to someone you know praising them or thanking them for something they did.
5. **Exercise for fifteen minutes daily.** Simple cardio, even a brisk walk, has a powerful antidepressant impact, in many cases stronger (and more long-lasting) than an actual antidepressant!

According to Shawn, if you do any one of these things faithfully for just three weeks, twenty-one days in a row, it will start to become a habit—a happy habit. You will have literally begun to rewire your brain to see the world in a different way, and as a result, to be happier on an everyday basis.

An interesting thing is that you don't have to do all five at once—in fact, Shawn actually recommends that you don't even try to do that, but instead start with just one and keep repeating it until it becomes a habit, then add another, and so on.

There is fascinating logic and powerful research behind all five, but these are not the only happy habits that the research supports; these are just five good examples. Other happiness researchers have different lists, including things like:

> Make more time for friends.
> Practice savoring the moment.
> Practice having a positive perspective.
> Put more energy into cultivating your relationships.
> Practice forgiveness.
> Engage in meaningful activities.
> Practice simple acts of giving.

They all share similarities, and they are all drawn from the same body of research. Because I place a high value on personal development and learning, my list would include:

> Read at least ten pages of a good book daily.

And you would probably have your own especially favored happy habits, too, that might be slightly different from mine. We're including a few of the best happiness books at the end of this book, and you can feel free to read through those, choose your favorites, and make your own list.

But I'll tell you one thing they all have in common: *they work*. Do these simple things consistently, every day, and in time—a lot less time than you might expect—you will become a significantly happier version of you.

And that will make everything else in your life work better, too.

Personal Stories from *The Slight Edge* Readers

For me, my most important slight edge habit is looking for and finding something positive in every situation, no matter what. Life experiences train us to see the negative, our shortcomings, and react to situations. To look for what we did wrong. It is just as easy to look for what we did well and build on that. Life gives us numerous opportunities to grow, if we just see them for what they can mean.

—*Jim Hageman, Dallas, Texas*

I'm a reader. There wasn't much else to do in Poland before the fall of Communism. We had a black-and-white TV with only two channels, and I didn't see my first PC until I was eleven. So I read, and this habit stuck with me. I've read several thousand books in my life.

In August 2012 I read *The Slight Edge*, by Jeff Olson. It took me a month to start implementing some ideas from this book.

I had not really thought seriously about my life for years. I was overweight, stressed, constantly worried about my finances, and quietly desperate about my relationship with God. I was aimless, with no plans as to how my life would be in two, five, ten years.

Soon I changed the type of books I was reading, and started reading more books on personal development. By the middle of November I had created a personal mission statement, which was the real starting point of my progress. Over the next several months I applied plenty of different slight edge disciplines—and started seeing results:

I rejuvenated a few old friendships and made several new ones with people from all over the world. I overcame my shyness (partially). I started two blogs. I learned WordPress and built a website with a hundred of useful tips. I stopped playing computer games (which was my vice) and wrote a fantasy short story. I read Homer's *Iliad* and I'm halfway through the *Odyssey*. I read ten books written by saints and listened to more than 100 hours of educational and motivational audio materials.

Things in my life started changing. I lost fifteen pounds (and my wife lost thirteen). My savings doubled and my donations to charities grew by 75 percent. I found I now read 50 percent faster—and my ten-year-old son reads 250 percent faster (no exaggeration!) and his grades improved. As a birthday present, I gave my wife a gratitude diary about her. She was amused—and amazed.

I can track a slight edge discipline behind each and every one of these accomplishments—and this list is not even complete.

I became a self-published author. I had been dreaming about writing since I was a child, but had never done anything about it. Since November I've written about 100,000 words, mostly in English (which is not my native language). Now I've finished my second booklet (a guide on how to use ten-minute disciplines in weight loss) and plan to write four more books in the series.

Most of all, I'm happy. I feel alive. I keep three different gratitude journals: one about my wife, one about my kids, and one about my life. Every day I produce three pieces of paper full of my gratitude. I feel I have discovered what my life is about. My dreams are coming true. I'm fulfilling my destiny. And I'm doing it by following dozens of simple disciplines incorporated into my days.

—*Michal Stawicki, Warsaw, Poland*

Essential Points from Chapter 7

↗   Happiness is created by doing some simple, easy things, and doing them every day.

↗   Success does not lead to happiness, it's the other way around: more happiness creates more success.

↗   Elevated levels of happiness create elevated levels of health, performance, social involvement, marital fulfillment, financial and career success, and longevity.

↗   Greater happiness is key to making the slight edge work in your life.

↗   Shawn Achor's five happy habits:

1.   Every morning write down three new things you're grateful for.

2.   Journal for two minutes a day about a positive experience from the past 24 hours.

3.   Meditate daily for a few minutes.

4.   At the start of every day, write an email to someone praising or thanking them.

5.   Get fifteen minutes of simple cardio exercise a day.

Sharing Your Gratitudes

One of the keys to happiness is sharing your gratitudes. Tweet your three daily gratitudes and include #SlightEdge or post them on our Facebook wall www.facebook.com/yourslightedge.

8. The Ripple Effect

> "Strange, isn't it? Each man's life touches
> so many other lives."
>
> —*Clarence the Angel, in* It's a Wonderful Life

After discovering the slight edge and experiencing how it works in the four basic areas of health, finances, relationships, and personal development, it's been amazing to see this whole fifth area of happiness open up as well. But that wasn't the end of it.

The more I thought about the slight edge and the way it was operating in so many people's lives, the clearer it became that there was something bigger going on here, too. There was a larger dimension to the slight edge that went well beyond the way it could improve our own lives.

As wide a range of benefits as health, finances, relationships, personal development, and happiness are, they all have one thing in common. They are all essentially about *me*: *my* health, *my* happiness, *my* finances. But what happens after I'm gone? And for that matter, what happens while I'm still here? What difference does my life make in what's happening beyond the doors of my home?

When I grasp the power of the slight edge and put it into practice, it has a huge impact on my life. But what about my impact on the rest of the world?

I also soon realized that I wasn't the only person this question mattered to. In fact, whether we realize it consciously or not, it matters to *everyone*.

Everyone likes a good meal and a warm bed. Everyone wants the companionship of someone they love, and who loves them. Everyone wants to be happy in their lives. But once those basics are taken care of, we all want something more, too. One of the most compelling, universal human drives is the desire to feel that we make a difference—that because we were here, the world is a better place. Human beings are social animals, and there's something hardwired into us that needs to know that we've had an impact on the world. That we *matter*.

But I may not be the best person to tell you about this one. This part of the slight edge story may be better told by someone else. Someone who has a genuine passion for how the slight edge creates a legacy in the world, and someone who knows the slight edge from the inside out—because she grew up with it.

Among all the achievements in my life, my daughter Amber is one of the things I'm proudest of. She has grown up with the slight edge and knows the importance of getting this information into the hands of young people to help them understand that the choices they make today will affect the rest of their lives.

So I'll stop writing here, and let Amber take up the pen for the rest of this chapter…

Amber Olson Rourke: Growing Up with the Slight Edge

People ask me, "What was it like growing up with the slight edge?" To tell you the truth, for most of my childhood growing up in the Olson household, it wasn't something I was really aware of. It was just the way my family lived.

Growing up, I always had the perception that *anything* was attainable, as long as I was consistent about working on it every day. I saw other people my age who would get intimidated by big goals and say, "That's so unattainable, why even try?" I was fortunate in that I never saw things that way. I can't remember ever feeling really overwhelmed by anything I wanted to do, because I always knew that all it took was to break up that bigger goal up into pieces and then consistently work on those little chunks. And that helped me sort out the idea that all things were possible, that I could do anything I set my mind to do.

I heard Will Smith once talking about his upbringing. He described how, one summer when he was twelve years old, his father tore down a brick wall and told Will and his brother (then nine) to rebuild it.

"That's impossible," said Will. It took them a year and a half to do it, and when it was finished their dad said, "Now don't you *ever* tell me that there's something you can't do."

"You don't set out to build a wall," as Will later explained it. "You set out to lay that first brick as perfectly as a brick can be laid. And you do that every single day … and soon you have a wall."

He never used the phrase, but I knew exactly what he was talking about.

The slight edge.

Another big influence on my childhood was that in our house, there was no separation between work and home. If either of my parents had a business call, they wouldn't go off into another room, they would have it right in front of me. They took me to meetings. My parents both loved their work, and I guess I absorbed that love of work by osmosis. For me, "work" never had the connotation of being drudgery or something you *had* to do. It was something we loved, something we always looked forward to doing.

In high school I worked as office manager for a chiropractic office. I was able to get into a work program, where I spent half my day at school and the other half-day working, so that by the time I graduated I already had some good experience at the management level.

College was the first time I started to become consciously aware of how the slight edge works. Here I was, surrounded by other kids who all had 4.0 grade point averages and really high SAT scores. I knew I wasn't necessarily the smartest person in the room, or the most talented, or the most intuitive. But even if I was surrounded by people who were more talented than I was, I knew I could surpass them just by consistently showing up and doing the work.

I started seeing the kinds of choices my classmates would make, and began to understand the philosophy behind those choices. I'd always had a lot of discipline—not a stern, forcing-yourself kind of discipline, but the kind that comes from understanding that this is just how life works. The kind, as my dad says, that grows naturally out of your philosophy.

After four years of college I got a job working as a marketing account manager at a big financial services firm, which I loved doing. About a year into it, my dad called and asked if I wanted to go into business with him. My parents owned a medical spa that wasn't being run that well, so I moved back home to Texas and took over management of the spa for a while. This, too, was a great experience, but it wasn't long before I was drawn to a career path that would allow me to have a much greater impact.

Impact of *The Slight Edge*

While I was managing the medical spa, I also began working on another family project that fascinated me and absorbed my attention: I started gathering stories to include in the second edition of *The Slight Edge*.

The original edition of the book had come out while I was in college, and it had played a big role in my starting to become more consciously aware of the life philosophy I'd always followed, but more or less without thinking about it. During the next few years, as I worked my way through college, the book and its message were working their way into thousands of people's lives. People would share their personal stories with my dad, about how the slight edge was working in their lives. Thinking it would be great to get back in touch with these people and get their stories down on paper, he would take their business card, then bring it home and stick it in a drawer. By the time I moved back home to manage the spa, that drawer was spilling over with business cards.

I decided it was time to start contacting these people and collecting their stories. When I did, the experience just knocked me over. I ended up collecting hundreds, thousands of stories from people about how the slight edge was working in their lives.

Up to that point, I'd understood how the slight edge worked in the context of business, how it helped to get things done, to develop skills and get ahead in life. But now I was reading about people's relationships, and how doing little things every day had transformed their marriage, taking it from a bad place to a really great place ... or seeing how it had helped someone through a painful and difficult rehabilitation after they'd been in a car accident ... or how they'd been struggling with depression and didn't know how to get out of it, and now they were able to take little steps in the right direction and see the impact in their lives and in how they felt every day.

I'd never really thought about the *magnitude* of what the slight edge could truly mean, and I found this incredibly exciting. Doing better in business is great—but your business is only a fraction of you as a whole person. I started seeing that the slight edge could literally change people's *lives*.

I was really enjoying my work managing the spa—but I wanted to do something else, something of my own, something really big. I was totally inspired by all the slight edge stories I'd read, and I wanted to do something that would make a bigger difference.

The Price of Success

I've always felt that the reason you seek out personal development is so you can do more, so you can live a bigger life, touch more people, and leave a bigger legacy.

I've seen people who have really taken personal development far, who are very developed, but have never moved beyond that. To me, that's just a waste of that knowledge.

I believe we are all, each and every one of us, graced with a unique mix of talent, passion, and vision, and that we were put here to live that out on a grand stage. The purpose of the slight edge is to allow us to live out those talents, passions, and visions to their fullest potential. I believe we are here to learn and grow, and to become so abundant in belief in ourselves that we finally tap into the full potential of the greatness that is within us and share that greatness with the world.

But that greatness comes with a price.

Growth creates abundance, and that abundance in turn creates responsibility. The more success we have, the more greatness we step into and the more abundance we experience, the more responsibility we have to the world around us. Achieving greatness—in anything—isn't simply a matter of taking the steps that get you there. It's also a matter of being willing to pay the price. And that price is responsibility.

I mentioned Will Smith before, and I'll quote him again here. He said something that I often repeat in speeches these days, because it goes right to the heart of this whole idea:

I want the world to be better because I was here. I want my life, my work, my family to mean something. If you are not making someone else's life better you are wasting your time. Your life will only become better by helping make other lives better.

He says he learned this from his grandmother, who told him, "If you're going to be here, there's a necessity to make a difference."

I began finding I had a passion for the question of how we pay all that forward—that knowledge, that mentorship, that personal growth and development, and that success. Helping people understand not only the value of their own personal development, but also how that in turn creates ripples that touch all the people around us in our everyday lives. And then beyond that: how are we collectively changing the world?

You have probably heard the famous quote from anthropologist Margaret Mead, "Never doubt that a small group of thoughtful, committed citizens can change the world." It's a wonderful insight. But knowing the slight edge lets us take her statement one step further: never doubt that *a single thoughtful, committed person* can change the world.

Because one person, by his or her committed, consistent, persistent actions, will have a ripple effect that will in time created a thoughtful, committed group of thousands.

Of millions.

MyRipple

I wanted to put these ideas together in a practical way, to create some kind of business or structure that would take the kinds of powerfully positive slight edge experiences people were having in their own lives and leverage them so that they could touch the lives of others. Eventually I came up with a concept for a new social network that would be all about people's own personal development and the ripple effect it could have on the world.

I took the idea to my dad and asked if he would work on it with me, and he agreed. We decided to call it MyRipple.

Soon we were moving fast and furious, building all the components of what it would take to launch this new social network. I put together a comprehensive business plan for creating a whole movement, centering on the social media platform but also building out live events and more. We even got to the point where we were hiring developers to build the social media platform and doing technical layouts for all the pages. The network had a tagline: "Individually taking responsibility, collectively changing the world."

And then something happened that took the whole concept in a new direction: a whole new business venture showed up at our door. (The one he told you about in chapter 5, the "Slow Down to Go Fast" chapter.)

At that point, I had to do a lot of soul-searching. I really wanted to work at this new company, but I also knew it would completely absorb all my energy and focus, and I still really wanted to realize my vision for MyRipple. I didn't want to let go of the idea of creating a way for people to come together around their vision of changing the world.

And then I realized that everything I'd wanted to do in MyRipple, I could do within our new company.

And that's exactly what we did. About six months into the company's new life, as it was becoming established, we started asking, "How can we integrate that ripple concept into our business?" Before long, we had made The Ripple Effect a central theme of the entire company. Since that time I've been blessed to see that MyRipple vision come to pass—not exactly in the form I'd first imagined it, but in many ways in an even better context. It's given me a platform where I can reach out to thousands and potentially millions of people.

Especially young people.

Toward a Slight Edge Generation

I love talking about the slight edge philosophy with the next generation—teens through late twenties—because the most abundant resource available to them is *time*. It may be a cliché to say, "You have your whole life ahead of you," but for young people it really is the truth. And because they have so many years still in front of them, they have a unique opportunity to put the slight edge into effect in their lives and, through the ripple effect of their impact on others, to change the world.

With my ten-year high school reunion around the corner, it saddens me to see where some of my high school acquaintances have ended up. These were young men and women who had everything going for them, everything in place for them. They were smart, popular, and outgoing, had loving families and great opportunities—yet somehow they never grasped the true implications of their own everyday choices. They never saw the slight edge working in their lives—and never realized it was working against them. Small errors in judgment, repeated daily over time, had landed them far from where they wanted to be.

It made me realize once again how fortunate I was. Because I grew up surrounded by slight edge thinking, it wasn't that difficult for me to make the kinds of day-in, day-out choices that have propelled my life forward in so many positive ways. And one of my driving desires is to help support other young people in learning to make those kinds of slight edge choices, too. It is my deepest desire for the next generation to grasp the slight edge philosophy, and to become true champions of it in their lives and in the lives of those around them.

A few years before we produced the second edition of *The Slight Edge*, I collaborated with my dad and the SUCCESS Foundation in a version of the book aimed specifically at teens, called *SUCCESS for Teens: Real Teens Talk about Living the Slight Edge*. This revision presented the same basic information as the original *Slight Edge*, but organized in an especially easy-to-read format and sprinkled with engaging exercises, action steps, and stories from real teens.

The idea was to reach out to teens, to help them clarify their goals, learn how to practice the simple, slight edge efforts necessary for success, and accept responsibility for their own destiny and shape the futures that they want. Through the SUCCESS Foundation's efforts, copies of the book have been placed in the hands of literally millions of teens.

It's been an amazing experience to see how quickly and eagerly teenagers and young adults grasp the ideas of the slight edge and the ripple effect. In the course of producing the teen book, our new company, and its ripple effect programs, we're seeing more and more of this next generation contributing to society and becoming champions for change. Charitable organizations founded by young adults are on the rise, as is the amount of time they are contributing to serve others. Young adults are now heading up many of today's environmental awareness efforts. I think it's safe to say that most of the next generation understands the problems that face our nation more than our politicians do. They know that the status quo isn't an option, and that we can't keep doing what we have been doing and expect it to go away.

Beyond the fabulous humanitarian and charitable efforts they are contributing, the next generation is going to change the world one individual at a time, one choice at a time, one day at a time. They are going to take responsibility for the life they lead and leave the blame game to generations past. They are not going to look to others to provide for their financial security—they will do it *themselves*. They are going to be conscious about their health and vitality by treating their bodies like the precious gifts they are. They will value the biggest resource they have—*time*, and will make correct daily decisions that will improve every facet of their lives.

How do I know this? Because they're already showing us!

The Ripple Effect

When you create positive improvements in your life, you create positive ripples that spread out all around you, like a pebble of positivity dropped in a pond. Those ripples may not all be visible; in fact, they may be mostly invisible. But just because you or others may not see them doesn't mean they're not there. They are, and their impact can be enormous. When you reach out and positively affect one other person through your interactions and words you create a slight change in that person, who is then more likely to reach out and positively affect someone else. Simply put, one touches another, who touches another, who touches another.

Through your everyday attention to those simple positive actions, your happy habits and daily disciplines, you don't only have an impact on yourself, you are also having a powerful impact on everyone around you. You become a better relative, a better friend, a better business associate. A better father, mother, son, daughter, brother, sister, aunt, uncle. You become a more positively contributing community member and a more influential thought leader, which in turn creates a spreading positive impact on the world around you and society at large.

We are all having a ripple effect of some sort already, whether or not we realize it. But if our moods go up and down and our actions are inconsistent, if we smile at people sometimes and walk past them stony-faced at others because we're "having a bad day," then our positive and negative impact may just cancel each other out, and the net effect may not add up to much. Worse, if we more consistently lean to the negative—always complaining, typically looking at the problems rather than the solutions, playing the role of critic and cynic—then we may be having a *net negative* ripple effect, bringing the world down.

We all have the capacity to have a powerful ripple effect. The question is, what kind do you want to have? The choice is always yours.

I want you to hear from Renee Olson, my mother, because she consistently applies the slight edge to relationships and exemplifies the ripple effect perhaps better than anyone else I know.

Here's Renee:

My first slight edge experience began as a child, watching my own mother interact with everyone around her. She made a difference every day, with friends and strangers alike. We didn't know what it was at the time, but it was the slight edge in action.

I didn't inherit my mother's gregarious personality, but I did inherit her heart for people. I have made it a habit to be present with whomever I happen to be with. To take an interest in them and what is going on in their world, to ask questions, and most importantly to give encouragement for a job well done, to notice and comment on what is right, and not what is wrong. I do this even with strangers, sales clerks, waitstaff, and other people whom I come across during my daily activities. I'll share a kind word or a smile with someone at the checkout line at the grocery store, and the next thing I know they are spilling out their hearts and telling me all about their personal lives—simply because I took an interest in them, even if just for a moment.

I may never see these people again, and often have no way of knowing how these little encounters affect them. But I know it matters. The truth is, we *never* know what people may need at any given point. But so often a smile, a caring gesture, a sincere question about their lives, or someone just to listen, may be just exactly what that person needs at that moment. And it would be so easy not to do—to just stay caught up in our own thoughts and not make the little effort it takes to not take an active interest in what's going on around us, outside of ourselves. But if we do it, if we cultivate this slight edge habit of creating positive moments for all those who cross our paths, I believe it will in time create a shift in the negativity and indifference that so often greets us in the world.

I try to do the same thing with my friends and family, but on a much bigger scale. When Amber was born I felt I had begun the most important job of my lifetime. I have made the effort to practice the slight edge with her in every way I could think of, and have practiced my habitual positive, encouraging, you-can-do-anything attitude more on her than on anyone else in my life, starting from the time she was born. (She is an only child, so no one got left out!)

With children it is often so much easier to take the path of least resistance—to let them eat that fast food they love rather than cook something healthy, to let them watch TV rather than read to them, to let them play video games rather than interact with them. But making the extra effort is so worth it. I worked hard to make the slight edge decision with her every day and in every way I could, and it has paid off in a big way. She has grown up to be a woman who knows she can do anything she sets her mind to. I can no longer make her slight edge decisions for her, but that's okay, because now she is making her own slight edge decisions for herself—and I have no doubt sure she will pass those on to her children, too.

Closing Thought from Jeff

There's nothing I can really add to what Amber already said, because she already said it perfectly. I just wanted to close out the chapter sharing a few thoughts about what it all means.

Amber has two titles in our company: she serves as vice president of marketing, and she does a fantastic job at that. But she also serves in another role: vice president of culture. In that position she heads up our whole ripple movement, which includes work with organizations like Big Brothers Big Sisters and the SUCCESS Foundation. It's been amazing to watch her spread her wings and fly. A few chapters back, in our discussion of the power of time, I mentioned the Ten Core Values that drove our company from zero to $100 million in the course of a single year. The person responsible for driving those Ten Core Values and making them an organic, integral part of the company's culture, at every level, has been Amber.

To me, Amber is the greatest evidence in my life of what the slight edge can do.

I'm deeply grateful for everything the slight edge has done in my life—the financial rewards and business success, good health and great friendships, continuous learning and personal development. But there's nothing that comes close to a father's joy at seeing his daughter flourish and spread light in the world the way Amber has.

Of all the ways you might define success, happiness, and fulfillment—of all the ways you might demonstrate the ripple effect—I can't think of a better example.

Positive Improvements

What positive improvements are you creating in your life? Create a #RippleEffect by tweeting the positive difference you're making. Be sure to include #SlightEdge. Or post them to our Facebook wall at www.facebook.com/yourslightedge. I would love to hear the positive difference you're making!

Personal Stories from
The Slight Edge Readers

Growing up as a youth in Mahwah, New Jersey, the two constants in my life were my mom and football. I was fortunate to have a mother who always told me that there was something special about her baby boy. Football, my other constant, was an activity in which I had success from the very first day I stepped on the field.

Football brought me acceptance by others, which made me feel worthy. As time went on I became very dedicated to the sport. Like many boys my age, I dreamed of playing in the NFL. In high school I worked my way up through the ranks to become one of the top college recruits in the Northeast. I attended the University of Iowa and became an All Big Ten and All-American lineman. In 1989 I was drafted in the third round by the New York Giants. The pinnacle of my career came early in my second season, when I played in Super Bowl XXV against the Buffalo Bills, and won.

I was on top of the world and everything was in my favor—but the problem about to hit me like a freight train was that I had become comfortable.

Satisfied with my success, I struggled the following season, and actually lost a game when William "The Refrigerator" Perry pushed me back and blocked a game-winning field goal. It was the lowest moment of my career. I had personally lost an NFL game. The media crucified me, and so did the coaches. I was benched and feared I would be released from the Giants.

I decided to rededicate myself and put all fear aside. Hard work paid off. I kept my position on the team and two years later became one of the top free agents in the NFL. Though I did not know it yet,

I was practicing the slight edge. I signed a very lucrative contract and was now one of the highest-paid guards in the league.

Then comfort set in, once again. I had received my payday, but had not truly met my personal goals.

Retiring from football, I started my own retail store and began raising a family. Life was good. No more hard training camps. I was living my dream owning my own business. Then, in 2008, the economy collapsed, and life became very stressful. And it wasn't just the economy. For thirteen years since retiring from the NFL, I had let my weight get out of control. I was now 340 pounds, my business was failing, and my body ached from years of football and neglect. Toxic people filled my life. I became depressed and emotionally spent.

Finally my wife Kristi decided to go back to work to help with the family finances. She found a job in sales, and part of her training included some inspirational audios and a book called *The Slight Edge*. She began to encourage me to read it, too, which I resisted at first, but seeing the changes in her, I became inspired to pick up the book.

I really don't like reading books—but *The Slight Edge* caught my attention right away. Though no one would have suspected it, I was at a very low point. I started applying the basic principles of *The Slight Edge* in my life. And sure enough, simple, positive actions repeated over time soon began having a compounding effect—an effect that has changed my life forever.

The slight edge philosophies and ideas seem so simple, but when you apply them consistently, the results are amazing.

My health and spirit turned around. I began to eat nutritional foods, and exercise became a daily activity. Not only did I start to lose weight, but my whole perspective on why my eating was out of control changed. At a restaurant I would find myself saying, "Well, it's easy to order that big juicy cheeseburger—but it's just as easy to order that fresh grilled chicken salad!"

In the course of one year I lost more than 70 pounds, and my cholesterol went from 289 down to 179 in just nine months! I now read or listen to personal development material every day. Having grasped the benefits of simple disciplines, practiced over time, I know I will never go back to living an unhealthy lifestyle.

But the best thing of all has been to see the impact these changes have had on others.

Once I found myself in the rhythm of The Slight Edge, I was amazed and, honestly, at times emotionally moved by the changes in my life. I had not realized that the true gift of my slight edge awakening would be the effect it would have on the people in my life. The value I finally started seeing in myself has begun to have a ripple effect on the people who mean the most to me.

Now my children have read *The Slight Edge* and are implementing its principles in their lives, too! Friends and coworkers have noticed a major shift in my attitude, patience, and follow-through, and seen my newfound happiness. They see that I have found new ambitions and goals to attain, including becoming the husband and father I was meant to be. I wish this book had been written when I was playing football—but then again, it was published at just the right time for me: I'm now in the second half of my life, and it's the most important half!

I would encourage anyone who reads this to apply these principles in your own life, as well. Not only will it change you, but it will positively change everyone you care about.

— *Robert Kratch, Minneapolis, Minnesota*

Essential Points from Chapter 8

↗ Everyone wants to know that they make a difference in the world—that their lives matter.

↗ Greater success also creates a greater responsibility to share that success with others.

↗ A single thoughtful, committed person can change the world.

↗ We are all having a ripple effect on others; the question is, what kind of ripple effect, negative or positive, do we want to have?

9. But You Have to Start with a Penny

> "The journey of a thousand miles starts with a single step."
>
> —*Chinese proverb*

I've presented the story of the penny doubled every day to hundreds and hundreds of audiences, and people often come up to me afterward and say something like, "Wow, that's amazing—to think that you could start with nothing and build a fortune!"

But that's not quite what the story says. The wealthy man's son didn't start with nothing. He started with a penny.

"Yeah, but no big deal, right? Of course he started with a penny. But that's basically the same thing as starting with nothing."

No, it's not: it's starting with a penny. It may seem like an insignificant difference—but then, by now you're probably starting to have a different perspective on that word "insignificant," aren't you. Because the truth is, while that penny might be small, it's far from insignificant.

In fact, it makes *all* the difference.

It All Starts Somewhere

By this point I'm sure you've grasped the central idea of this book: it doesn't take superhuman leaps to accomplish great things. Whatever success you want to create, whatever feats you want to achieve, whatever dreams you want to make real, you can, and you don't have to do impossible, extraordinary things to make that happen.

But you do have to do *something*. You have to start with a penny.

Success doesn't come out of nowhere. It can't be conjured up out of thin air, brought to you by the genie from Aladdin's lamp simply because you rubbed it and thought good thoughts. Success does come from a small beginning, often a beginning so tiny that it seems invisible and most people miss it. But there has to *be* a beginning.

Some of the largest companies in the world started out as little more than a penny. In 2003, a Harvard sophomore named Mark sitting in his dorm room cobbled together a web site that let other students compare two student photos at a time and vote on which one was better-looking. He called his little project Facemash, and it nearly got him kicked out of Harvard. Today, ten years later, it has more than a billion users, it has transformed the nature of global communications, and Mark Zuckerberg is one of the wealthiest and most influential people in the world.

Facemash may have been more a sophomoric prank than a serious business idea, when Zuckerberg first came up with it. But the point is, he came up with it. The billion-dollar phenomenon Facebook didn't come out of nowhere. It started with a penny.

Thirty years before Zuckerberg was getting into trouble at Harvard, a dead-broke young English teacher named Steve was struggling to make a living writing stories for men's magazines in his spare time. He had started a story about a troubled high-school girl, but after writing the first three pages he realized the story wasn't working, and tossed the pages in the trash. Why add yet one more to his large and growing stack of rejection notices?

The next day, as Steve's wife was doing some straightening up, she bent down to empty his trash basket and happened to notice the curled little sheaf of papers. She straightened them out, dusted off the cigarette ashes, read them, and set them back down on Steve's desk. "I think you've got something here," she told him. "Maybe something worth finishing."

She was right. He did finish it, and the paperback rights sold for nearly a half a million dollars. What's more, his story of the troubled school girl named Carrie launched his career. Propelled by the novel that was pulled from the trash, Stephen King became one of the most successful writers of the twentieth century.

What Tabitha King recognized in the trash basket may have been a tarnished penny, but still, it was a penny.

Let's go back another twenty years, to one chilly day in December 1955, when an unknown forty-two-year-old seamstress in Montgomery, Alabama, decided she'd had enough. She was tired after a long day's work. Most of all, she was tired of being treated the way she was—and tired of every other person of her color being treated that way, too. So when she was told to give up her bus seat to a white passenger, she refused—even when the bus driver threatened her with arrest.

It was no idle threat; she *was* arrested, then convicted and fined for violating a city ordinance. Her case was the catalyst for the formation of a new civil rights organization. On the same day of the woman's hearing, the newly formed Montgomery Improvement Association elected a young and relatively unknown minister named Martin Luther King, Jr., to be its spokesperson, launching a movement that over the next decade abolished legal segregation and radically transformed the face of the nation.

Rosa Parks was a penny.

Now let's do one last bit of time travel. There was a time, a certain number of years ago, when a tiny blob of gelatin began to pulse with hidden potential. It was barely more than a speck of matter, about the thickness of a dollar bill, at the very threshold of human sight: any smaller and it would have been invisible to the naked eye.

Though tiny, this insignificant little dot of matter (you could have fit about twenty of them on the head of a pin) contained chemical instructions that, if printed out, would have filled more than 500,000 pages; in fact, it was among the most organized, complex structures in the universe. Over the next nine months of slight edge compounding, this little blob of gelatin would blossom into over thirty trillion cells before being born into the open air … and letting out a wail as it took its first breath.

It would become *you*.

You started as a penny.

A Penny for Your Thoughts

Now imagine that instead of a penny doubling every day, it's your health that you're increasing by one penny's worth, and then by two pennies, and then four, then eight, and so on … up to $10 million. If you could come up with something that would make you feel one penny's worth better, could you do that every day? Of course. A little moderate exercise, a brisk one-mile walk, fifteen minutes on a treadmill. Get your heart rate up slightly, no big deal.

And your reward? When you get up the next morning, do you feel better? Not really. That is, not noticeably. Maybe just a *little*. Say, a penny's worth. Hardly seems worth the effort. And after a week, you're feeling sixty-four cents' worth better. Big deal. You've had to put up with some rainy weather, walk through a few stiff muscles, and miss your favorite news program, and after all that it's not like you're feeling like a million bucks. Hey, is this all really worth it? Maybe not. But then, what if you kept doing it anyway? Would you *eventually* feel like a million bucks?

No: *ten* million. But you need to start with the penny.

Now imagine that penny is your knowledge.

If I told you that reading Napoleon Hill's *Think and Grow Rich* would change your life, would you sit down and read it, cover to cover, today? Mind you, that's a 256-page book, and those aren't lightweight pages. Or another classic, Stephen Covey's *The 7 Habits of Highly Effective People*. That's a 358-pager, and it's not easy reading. Would you read either one in a single day? I doubt it. I wouldn't—I can't spend the entire day reading, and I'll bet you can't either.

But could you read a penny's worth, say, ten pages? (Ten pages of the Hill book would actually cost you about fifty cents, and ten pages of the Covey would run about a dime—but I'm using the penny here as a metaphor.)

I don't know how much you would get out of ten pages. Maybe a lot, maybe a little. Let's say you get hardly *anything* out of it. But if you could read ten pages today, could you read ten more tomorrow? Of course you could. Anyone who can read could do that.

If you do, will your life change on that first day you read ten pages? Probably not. And if you *don't* read those ten pages, will your life start to fall apart? Of course not. But successful people do what unsuccessful people are not willing to do—even when it doesn't look like it makes any difference. And they do it long enough for the compounding effect to start to kick in.

If you read ten pages a day of books like this and keep it up every day for a year, you will have read about a dozen powerful, amazing, life-transforming classics. Your mind will be filled with the strategies and know-how necessary to create a startling new level of success. You will have absorbed the thoughts of millionaires.

But to do that, *you have to read those ten pages*. You have to start with the penny.

The Power of One Percent

"Okay," you might be thinking about now, "it's all very well to talk about a penny doubling every day. But I don't see anyone offering to double *my* money every day, not in real life."

Fair enough. Let's change the equation. Forget about doubling for a minute, and let's forget about compound interest, too. Instead, let's talk about just *adding a penny* every day. No magical doubling, no compound interest, just the same simple action, over and over, of adding one penny a day.

And while you're adding a penny a day, let's also imagine doing one equally simple thing every day in *all* the areas of your life that matter to you. Add one penny's worth to your happiness, to your sense of self, to your friendships, your health, your studies, whatever skills and areas of knowledge you're pursuing. In every area that's important, you add *one cent* daily.

How do you add one cent's worth of happiness or knowledge? Here's how:

The word "cent" is short for *centum*, meaning one-hundredth. A penny is called a cent because it is one-hundredth, or *1 percent*, of a dollar. So let's say you add 1 percent of whatever value you want to achieve, in all these areas. By the end of a year, by adding 1 percent each day—pure addition, no compound interest—how much have you added? A total of 365 percent. In other words, times three-and-a-half.

If your little actions—your happy habits, kind words, practice or study sessions, workouts, reading times, and the rest—each represented a 1 percent improvement in that area, your level of achievement in a year's time would be not doubled but *more than tripled*.

Do you think you could improve yourself—your health, your happiness, your knowledge, your skills, your diet, your relationships, whatever area of life you want to look at—just 1 percent's worth per day?

That's so slight an edge, you might not even know quite how to measure it. But if you did that again tomorrow, and the next day, and kept it up every day for the next year?

Here's what that looks like when it's actually happening. The first day you'll improve by a factor of 0.01, so little it will probably be impossible to notice. The second day, your improvement will be 0.02; the next day, 0.03. So little, still, that it's almost invisible.

Again, this is why people quit the gym, skip their assignments, and don't bother with thank-you notes. What good is feeling 0.03 times slimmer or 0.03 times more fit? Why bother? Yet by pursuing that course and adding just one penny a day, by the end of the year you would be more than three times as fit, three times as happy, three times as knowledgeable, three times as skilled, three times the *you*, in just one year.

And how do you accomplish this? By trying twice as hard, three times as hard? No. Besides, you're already trying. We all are. It's not a matter of trying harder.

Well, maybe a little harder: just by 1 percent.

A Penny Saved …

We've been talking about just adding a penny a day. But the thing is, when you add a penny a day, you don't just add the penny, because compound interest *does* happen. Just as surely as it happens in a savings account, it happens in a relationship, a skill, your health, and anywhere else you put effort into anything. Growth compounds. That's not only the nature of the water hyacinth, it's the nature of *life*.

You've probably heard this one a thousand times:

A penny saved is a penny earned.

This is one of those things people say without really thinking it through, because it is so *not true*. If it were, then a penny would just be a penny. Big deal. But a penny saved is not a penny earned; a penny *earned* is a penny earned. How much is a penny *saved*? It's a thousand dollars, if you save it long enough at a great enough rate of interest.

But you have to start with a penny. And that's the irony of it, the sad truth about all those who tread the easy-not-to-do path in life. The billions of dollars of personal debt and colossal lack of savings in the United States come down to "the road not taken," only in this case, it's *the penny not put away*. The path that's so easy to take, yet so easy not to.

You're walking down the street, and you see a penny. It seems so insignificant, so small, so silly, why even bother to bend over and pick it up? After all, can you imagine walking into your bank to deposit a single penny into a savings account? Can you imagine looking in your savings passbook, deposit box, or piggy bank, and finding a balance of $0.01? It might as well be a balance of zero, right? I mean, we're talking about a *penny*. What can you do with a penny?

If you understand the slight edge, practically anything.

Every day, in every moment, you get to exercise choices that will determine whether or not you will become a great person, living a great life. Greatness is not something predetermined, predestined, or carved into your fate by forces beyond your control. *Greatness is always in the moment of the decision.* But you have to start with a penny.

Pennies and Butterfly Wings

Let me tell you about the man who saved millions of people's lives—very possibly including yours—by washing his hands.

Back in the middle of the nineteenth century, a time when the role that bacteria played in disease was still completely unknown, most women would rather give birth on the street than go to the clinic. They knew their chances of survival were better on the street. They knew that delivering their babies in the medical establishments of the day gave them a 1 in 10 chance of dying. At the Vienna General Hospital, where a Hungarian obstetrician named Ignaz Semmelweis worked, the mortality rate was more like 1 in 3.

Semmelweis made a radical proposal: before operating, surgeons should *wash their hands*. He was widely ridiculed. Surgeons kept delivering babies dirty-handed, and women kept dying. The medical establishment just couldn't see how something as insignificant as washing your hands could make any difference, and because of it thousands of people died unnecessary deaths.

But Semmelweis kept washing his hands anyway, and his idea eventually was accepted—which led to the saving of untold *millions* of lives. In fact, if it weren't for Semmelweis's insignificant little idea, there's a pretty decent chance you and I wouldn't be here, because our grand-mothers, or great-grandmothers, might have never made it through labor.

You've probably heard of the "butterfly effect." This is a famous proposition of chaos theory, which says that when a butterfly flaps its wings in South America, it can set off a chain of events that ends up causing a typhoon in Southeast Asia. The truth is, you create your own butterfly effect, whether you know it or not, and you do it all the time.

One of my favorite butterfly-effect stories is the film *It's a Wonderful Life*. A small-town businessman named George Bailey reaches the edge of despair, and decides his life has no meaning and makes no dif-ference. On the brink of suicide, he's visited by an angel improbably named Clarence, who walks George through an experience of what the world would look like if he had never been born. (Which is exactly why we quoted a great line of Clarence's for the epigraph of the last chapter, "The Ripple Effect.") George gets quite an eyeful. And so would you, if you had a Clarence come along and take you on the same tour of your life. But outside Hollywood, there's no Clarence to provide that clarity. It's something we need to learn to see with our own eyes.

The Smallest Things Are the Biggest Things

It seemed to George that his life was a little thing that didn't matter. But it wasn't a little thing after all, and it mattered a great deal. In fact, as he learned, if he'd never been born, the fate of the entire town he lived in would have been drastically different. (Marty McFly learned the same lesson four decades later in *Back to the Future*. The best stories always repeat themselves for each new generation.)

Sometimes even the most important things feel futile or pointless at the time, long before you can really see or feel their ultimate impact. Like the frog paddling in the cream. Like watching a penny turn into two, and then four. "Big deal ... what can you buy with four cents?" Once it turns into ten million dollars, *just about anything*.

Little things, things that might seem like they have no power at all, can make all the difference in the world. Sometimes, they can even change the course of history.

And I can tell you this for certain: they will change *your* history.

They sure have changed mine.

"But that's just movies." Perhaps, but the same thing happens in real life, too.

Think about the greatest figures of the twentieth century, the people who had the biggest positive impact on history. John F. Kennedy? Jonas Salk? Mother Teresa? Oskar Schindler? Martin Luther King, Jr.? Pick your hero—and then realize this: there is a very real chance that if Ignaz Semmelweis hadn't kept insisting on washing those hands, that person—that Jonas Salk, that Mother Teresa—*would have never existed.*

By the way, in 2006 *It's a Wonderful Life* was ranked by the American Film Institute as the #1 most inspiring film of all time—*sixty years* after it was made. After all this time, it's still a powerful message, because it's one we need to hear:

What you do matters.

Personal Stories from
The Slight Edge Readers

After suffering a stroke, my doctor's initial diagnosis was that I would probably never walk again. When I started on the long road to recovery I could barely move and had lost the ability to speak. I knew that if I wanted to get back to the life I had enjoyed before the stroke, I would have to stay focused on improving a tiny bit each day and not get bogged down in my current circumstances.

The Slight Edge taught me that if you do a little bit each day, a little bit, a little bit, you can make great progress. I applied that philosophy to my rehabilitation. I started moving my fingers, a little bit. Then my hand, and then my arm—a little bit. Today I go bike riding and spend thirty minutes a day on an elliptical trainer. I've made a full recovery, including walking and talking, and have been able to go back to doing the things I am passionate about, including playing music and speaking to audiences. My doctors tell me that half the patients who've suffered my kind of stroke don't even survive, let alone improve—yet when they look at me they can't even tell I've had a stroke.

Throughout the entire rehabilitation process, I had faith that if I could just improve a tiny bit each day, compounded over time, I would make a full recovery. And it happened, just as I knew it would. It all starts with just a little bit.

— *Al Lewis, Chicago, Illinois*

Six years ago I learned that my accountant had embezzled $2 million from our company. I ended up in bankruptcy and languished in depression for five years. Then, about six months ago, I bought a copy of *The Slight Edge*, and after reading it I was able to find the motivation to just take a small step every day toward rebuilding my life. Now I am back on TV and radio and writing again. I have rebuilt my website and have had multiple financial breakthroughs.

What I realized was that I could not change my past, but I *could* rebuild a new future by taking a small step every day in the right direction—just like the power of the penny. Now, as a result of those small steps, I am well on the way to regaining the success I had prior to losing everything.

— *Jim Paris, creator of ChristianMoney.com, Daytona Beach, Florida*

Essential Points from Chapter 9

- Great success often starts from a tiny beginning—but there has to *be* a beginning. You have to start somewhere. You have to do something.

- If you add just 1 percent of anything—skill, knowledge, effort—per day, in a year it will have more than tripled. But you have to start with the 1 percent.

- Greatness is not something predetermined, predestined, or carved into your fate by forces beyond your control. Greatness is always in the moment of the decision.

Part II

LIVING THE
SLIGHT EDGE

10. Two Life Paths

> "I took the one less traveled by
> And that has made all the difference."
>
> —*Robert Frost,* The Road Not Taken

The alarm goes off. 6:00 a.m. Without conscious thought your hand shoots out and hits SNOOZE. A ten-minute reprieve. You tentatively slip a foot out from under the covers. Brrr. You open one eye. Still dark out.

Now you face a choice.

You could sit up, switch on the light, and start grinding your brain into gear, prod your groggy gray matter to search out three new things you're grateful for so you can jot them down. You could then fire up the machinery of tired legs, hips, and back to crane yourself out of bed and go do the twenty sit-ups you promised yourself you'd do every day. When you said that, did you mean even on Saturdays? Today is Saturday. You yawn.

Or you could slip back down under the sheets and catch some more Z's. No, that's lazy. Compromise: flip on the news. Catch the follow-up on that unfolding juicy political scandal, see what's happening with the manhunt for the murderer of the week.

You reach for the remote.

And you just set the direction your life will take.

"Oh, c'mon!" you protest. "Give us a break here! It's one Saturday morning—a few *minutes* out of one Saturday morning. That hardly has life-altering consequences!"

But it does. Greatness is always in the moment of the decision, and so is fate. The wealthy man's gift to his sons, the wisdom to recognize the slight edge, shows up in the mundane little choices we make every day, not in some big dramatic moment with the orchestra swelling in crescendo behind us. And those private, unseen, everyday moments are what determine the path your life will take.

Where you end up in life isn't about whether you are a good or a bad person, or whether or not you are deserving, or your karma, or your circumstances. It's dictated by the choices you make—especially the little ones. I know it doesn't seem like it. It seems like you're just choosing how to spend the next hour, not the next forty years. But you *are* choosing how you'll spend the next forty years.

The reason this is hard to see is that it looks like your actions move in a simple straight line. You write down three gratitudes, or you get ten more minutes of snooze time, do twenty push-ups or catch the bad news on TV. Either way, you end up in the same place, on the other side of the next ten minutes, right?

Only you don't. You end up in different places. Because your actions don't move in a straight line. They curve.

Everything Curves

There was a time when the people of the world were convinced that the earth stood still, at the center of the universe. A few visionaries stubbornly refused to accept what was obvious to everyone else, and because Copernicus, Galileo, and a handful of others risked their lives to choose the road less traveled, the rest of the world eventually caught on to what is now obvious to everyone in the twenty-first century: the earth revolves around the sun. In the last hundred years, we've discovered that even space is curved, though that one's still a little hard for most people to wrap their minds around.

The truth is, *everything* is curved. There is no true straight line. Everything is always, constantly changing. Including your life. You are on a journey called your *life path*, and that path is not a straight line, but a curve. As you walk your path, it is always, every moment of every day, curving either upward or downward.

It may seem to you that today is much like yesterday. It isn't. It's different. Every day is. Appearances can be deceiving; in fact, they almost always are. There may be times when things seem to be on a steady, even keel. This is an illusion: in life, there is no such thing as staying in the same place. There are no straight lines; everything curves. If you're not increasing, you're decreasing.

Above and Below the Slight Edge

Let's take a look at what the slight edge actually looks like by going back to the wealthy man's lesson. If you make a graph of the penny doubled every day for a month, it will look something like this:

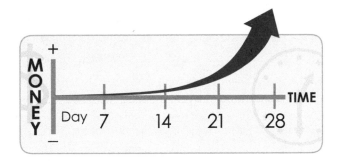

This is not only a picture of compound interest; it's also a picture of how the slight edge looks when it's working *for* you.

Now, let's get a sense of what the slight edge looks and feels like when it's working *against* you instead. It's simple: just place a mirror at the foot of the first illustration. The graph in the mirror shows you that when it's not working in your favor, the slight edge can be a very sharp and unforgiving edge indeed.

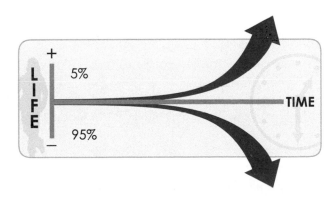

If you understand and live by the law of compound interest, your life will look like the upper half of the graph. If you don't understand and live by the law of compound interest, your life will look like the lower half of the graph. The upper curve is the formula for success: a few simple disciplines, repeated every day. The lower curve is the formula for failure: a few simple errors in judgment, repeated every day.

The upper curve represents that one person out of twenty, the 5 percent who are successful and happy at the end of their lives. The lower curve represents the twenty's other nineteen, the 95 percent who reach their "golden years" angry and bitter, and have no idea or concept of how they got there, or why. Life, it seems to them, is unfair, and that's just how it is. But you and I know that's not the case. It's not "just how it is," and it's not a matter of being fair or unfair.

It's pure geometry—the geometry of time.

Most people hold time as their enemy. They seek to avoid the passage of time and strive to have results *now*. That's a choice based on a philosophy. Successful people understand that time is their friend. In every choice I make, every course of action I take, I always have time in mind: time is my ally. That, too, is a choice based on a philosophy.

Time will be your friend or your enemy; it will promote you or expose you. It depends purely upon which side of this curve you decide to ride. It's entirely up to you. If you're doing the simple disciplines, time will promote you. If you're doing the few simple errors in judgment, time will expose you, no matter how well you appear to be doing right now.

Life is a curved construction; time is its builder, and choice its master architect.

Why People Don't Fly

Have you ever wondered why people can't fly? We have a phrase for when something difficult, painful, or tragic happens; we say, "Whoa: that's heavy." And indeed it is. Life is heavy. The predominant force on Earth is gravity, and gravity is always pulling you down. Just ask Bishop Milton Wright, the founder of Indiana's Huntingdon College, who in a sermon delivered in 1890 declaimed this self-evident truth: "If God had meant man to fly, he would have given him wings."

But some people just can't seem to accept self-evident truths. For instance, like Bishop Wright's two sons, who thirteen years later built and flew the first successful, man-powered, heavier-than-air flying machine. Their names were Wilbur and Orville.

Social science research says that as a child, you heard the word "no" about 40,000 times by the age of five, before you even started first grade. And how many times had you heard the word "yes"? About 5,000. That's eight times as many nos as yeses. Eight times the force holding you down, compared to the force lifting you up. Eight times the gravity against your desire to soar.

"Don't do that! Don't slouch. Don't touch that, it's hot. Don't talk to strangers. No, you can't stay up later. No, not till you're older. No, we don't have time right now. No no no…"

Granted, most of these nos are well intended; like the police force motto, their purpose is only to protect and serve. So I'm not criticizing the nos. But where are the yeses?

In his landmark 1994 book *Word-of-Mouth Marketing*, Fortune 500 consultant Jerry Wilson describes how he based his revolutionary "exceptional customer service" strategy on a single earthshaking statistic he'd discovered in marketing research: the average customer will tell three people about a positive experience with a business or product, but will talk about a negative experience to *thirty-three* people. Eleven bad-experience stories to one positive; eleven reasons an idea won't work to one reason it will.

As I mentioned earlier, only about one person out of twenty will ever achieve his or her goals and dreams in life. Regardless of what realm of life or work or play we're talking about, we'll see an average success rate of not more than 5 percent. Why is that? Those numbers provide the answer. When we grow up with 40,000 nos to 5,000 yeses, thirty-three negatives to every three positives, is it any wonder that 95 percent of us are failing?

Is it any wonder most people don't fly?

If you are one of those rare and special 5 percenters who decides to ignore gravity and take to the sky—one of those rare birds, like Orville and Wilbur, who chooses to break free of the downward pull of life and rise to a higher quality of accomplishment and success, to be a pioneer and risk discomfort and ridicule for the sake of your dreams—well, I've got good news and bad news.

The good news is, you're already exceptionally well oriented toward success.

The bad news is, all those 95 percenters are going to be yanking on you, sitting on you, naysaying and doomsaying on you, and doing their level best to pull you back down. Why? Because if you succeed, it reinforces the fact that they are not where they want to be. They know instinctively that there are only two ways to make their building the highest structure in town: build an even bigger one, or tear down all the others. Since the odds are against them building the big one, and since it takes just too darn long to start seeing any results, and since they are not at all aware of the slight edge, they're going to take the path of least resistance and go into the demolition business.

You can use the slight edge to break free of the downward pull of life and become the best you can possibly be. Or, the slight edge will pull you down, keep you down, and eventually take you out. It's up to you.

For things to change, *you've* got to change. For things to get better, *you've* got to get better. It's easy to do. But then, it's just as easy not to do.

Blame and Responsibility

If you want to measure where you are, if you want to know whether you're on the success curve or on the failure curve, or if you want to assess anyone else and determine which curve they're on, here's how. There is one attitude, one state of mind, which overwhelmingly predominates either side of the curve.

The predominant state of mind displayed by those people on the failure curve is *blame*. The predominant state of mind displayed by those people on the success curve is *responsibility*.

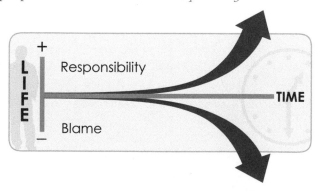

People on the success curve live a life of responsibility. They take full responsibility for who they are, where they are, and everything that happens to them.

Taking responsibility liberates you; in fact, it is perhaps the single most liberating thing there is. Even when it hurts, even when it doesn't seem fair. When you don't take responsibility, when you blame others, circumstances, fate, or chance, you give away your power. When you take and retain full responsibility—even when others are wrong or the situation is genuinely unfair—you keep your life's reins in your own hands.

Negative and difficult things happen to all of us; most of them are mostly or completely out of our control. It's how we react, how we view those circumstances and conditions, that makes the difference between success and failure—and that is completely within our control. As the American naturalist John Burroughs put it, "A man can fail many times, but he isn't a failure until he begins to blame somebody else." Don't complain about what you allow.

The 5 percenters who dwell on the upper curve know there are no excuses; they understand and accept the fact that nobody can do it to them, and nobody can do it for them. They live by the axiom, "If it's going to be, it's up to me." They set their own standards—and their standards are high. They realize that their only limitations are self-imposed. They understand that it is not what happens to them that's important, but how they respond to what happens that makes the difference between their failure and success. They are aware of the slight edge and they understand how it operates in their lives.

People on the failure curve are masters of blame; they blame everyone and everything—the economy, the government, the oil crisis, the weather, their neighbors, the rich, the poor, the young, the old, their kids, their parents, their boss, their coworkers, their employees. Life itself. The inhabitants of the lower curve are life's victims, the great mass of "done-to's."

I knew a man whose self-declared philosophy was this: "Life is an unpleasant practical joke which occurs somewhere between birth and death." On which side of the curve do you think he was living? Where was he headed? Can you imagine what results that thought, "Life is an unpleasant practical joke," would create when magnified by the water-hyacinth-like force of time?

You've heard the expression, "Be careful what you wish for—you just might get it." But it's not even a question of wishing: take care with what you *think*. Because what you think, multiplied by action plus time, will create what you get.

Don't Complain About What You Allow

People on the failure curve are oblivious to the slight edge.

Werner Erhard, the personal development author and trainer, wrote a definition of responsibility that is so relevant here, it's worth quoting in full:

> *Responsibility is declaring oneself as cause in the matter. It is a context from which to live one's life.*
>
> *Responsibility is not a burden, fault, praise, blame, credit, shame, or guilt. All these include judgments and evaluations of good and bad, right and wrong, or better and worse. They are not responsibility…*
>
> *Responsibility starts with the willingness to deal with a situation from and with the point of view, whether at the moment realized or not, that you are the source of what you are, what you do, and what you have.*
>
> *It is not "right," or even "true," to declare oneself as "cause" in the matter. It's just empowering. By standing for yourself as cause, "what happens" shifts from "happening to you" to "just happening" and, ultimately, to "happening as a result of your being cause in the matter."*

The people on the upper half of the slight edge curve are the cause of what happens in their lives. They view all the forces that brought them to this point—God, parents, teachers, childhood, circumstances, you name it—with gratitude and appreciation and without blame. And they view themselves as the cause for what comes next in their life.

Are you your own cause?

The people on the upper curve take full responsibility for all the choices they make in their lives and in their work. Do you? It's easy to do … and just as easy not to do. And if you don't take full responsibility for your thoughts and actions and circumstances right now, will that kill you today? No—*but…*

But that simple error in judgment compounded over time will absolutely, positively destroy you.

Successful people do what unsuccessful people are not willing to do: they take full responsibility for how the slight edge is working in their lives. Unsuccessful people blame the slight edge for their lives not working. Successful people know that they cannot afford that luxury.

Past and Future

Try this experiment: Take a comfortable, seated position and look down at the floor. Then, without changing position, take the next five minutes to think about your life. Anything and everything, whatever that means to you, just think about your life.

Go ahead and do that now …

Now, clear your mind, walk around a minute, then come back and do the second half: Take the same comfortable, seated position, only this time tilt your head up so you're looking at the ceiling. Spend the next five minutes thinking about your life. Anything and everything, whatever that means to you, just think about your life.

Go ahead and do that now …

I don't know what results you had, but here's what most people find: when looking down, it's pretty hard not to start thinking about the past. When gazing upward, it's pretty hard not to start thinking about the future.

People on the failure curve tend to focus on their past—and it pulls them down. People on the success curve focus on their future. And you can guess what happens: it pulls them up.

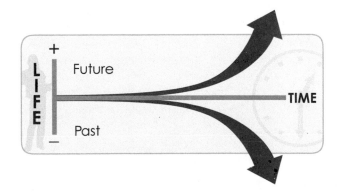

People on the success curve don't ignore the past, but they use it as a tool, one of many with which they build their futures. People who live on the failure curve use the past as a weapon with which they bludgeon themselves and the people around them. Regrets, recriminations, remorse, and retribution.

It seems most people live with one foot in the past, saying, "If only things had been different, I would be successful." And the other foot in the future saying, "When this or that happens, I will be happy and successful." And they completely ignore the present—which is the only place where life actually occurs.

A friend of mine says that people make two lists about their spouses and carry these lists around in their heads. The long list is a detailed accounting of what's wrong with their spouse, and the short list is a summary of what's right. The long list they consult every day. And the short list? That's the one they read at the funeral.

People on the success curve don't wait for the eulogy. They rip the long list to shreds, scatter its pieces to the wind, and spend every day reading from the short list. They make themselves experts in "what's right," and let go of "what's wrong." They never hold a grudge—not because it's morally wrong (although they may agree with that reason, too), but because it simply gets in the way of the curve their life is taking. It slows them down. They're too busy moving toward the future to be gazing into the rearview mirror.

One of the quickest and most direct routes to getting yourself up and onto the success curve is to get out of the past. Review the past, but only for the purpose of making a better plan. Review it, understand and take responsibility for the errors you've made, and use it as a tool to do differently in the future. And don't spend a great deal of time doing even that—the future is a far better tool than the past.

The future is your most powerful tool and your best friend. Devote some serious, focused time and effort into designing a crystal-clear picture of where you're going. Toward the end of this book we'll take some time to help you do exactly that. For now, I'll just say this: when you do have a clear picture of the future and consciously put time every day into letting yourself be drawn forward by that future, it will pull you through whatever friction and static you encounter in the present—and whatever tugging and clutching you may feel from the past.

One last thing about past and future—and I *have* saved the best for last.

You can't change the past. You *can* change the future. Would you rather be influenced by something you can't change, or by something you can?

Where Are You Headed?

On which side of the slight edge curve are you standing right now? Which way are you headed? Are you one of the 5 percenters, one of those individuals living on the success curve and going up—or are you among the resigned majority, the 95 percenters on the failure curve and sliding down?

Not sure? Perhaps, in the middle, you say?

Sorry, there is no middle. You are either going up or going down.

The early part of both curves is fairly flat, so it can certainly *look* like you're moving along on a nice, even keel, heading neither up nor down. But appearances can be deceiving. (And usually are.) In a constantly and rapidly changing world like ours, you simply cannot remain the same as you were yesterday. You are in motion—you have no choice in that. But motion in which direction? You have *total* choice in that.

You are either improving or diminishing in personal and professional value. You are building toward greater happiness and fulfillment, or deeper unhappiness and dissatisfaction. Your relationships are growing deeper and richer, or growing more stale and distant. You are learning more and more about the truths of life, or slipping deeper and deeper into denial about the truths of life. You are building your long-term security and financial freedom, or dismantling it. And your health is building day by day … or ebbing slowly away.

So before we go on, let's take a moment for some honest self-assessment. Looking at each of these seven areas of your life, one at a time, ask yourself, "Right now, in my [health, happiness, etc.], am I on the success curve, or the failure curve?" It's an either/or, thumbs-up or thumbs-down question.

Let's take an honest look at your health.

Are you building it every day? The way you eat, the way you exercise, the kind of schedule you keep, the ways in which you take care of yourself—are all these building a greater feeling of health and vibrancy every day? Or does it feel like you're making more and more withdrawals from your life-energy bank account, and the balance is steadily decreasing? Is your health on the success curve or failure curve?

Let's take an honest look at your level of happiness.

Do you take time every day to notice those things you're grateful for? Do you make a habit of looking at things in a positive light, rather than a negative light? Do you practice savoring the moment and regularly expressing your appreciation of others? Do you engage regularly in activities that are meaningful to you, things you do not because you *have* to but because you *want* to? Are you building greater happiness every day, or is day-to-day happiness drifting further away?

Let's take an honest look at your friendships and close relationships.

Is the number of friends in your life, people with whom you stay in touch, with whom you share meaningful exchanges and mutually enriching experiences, growing larger every year? If you are married, and you were to describe your marriage as a plant, would it be a plant that is growing taller, riper, fuller, and richer with each passing year? What about your family—children, parents, brothers, sisters, and others? Are those relationships growing deeper and richer or more distant and shallower?

Let's take an honest look at your personal development.

Are you learning more about yourself, about the world around you, and about how life works every day? Are you learning new skills and sharpening old ones? Are you becoming a more capable person, one more interesting to know and valuable to be around? Or is your character being gradually etched with the age-lines of disappointment, disillusionment, boredom, and bitterness?

Let's take an honest look at your finances.

Are you building assets and putting money into a long-term plan that will create true financial freedom? Is your net worth growing larger each year? Are you living within your means and investing a portion of your income into a program that will build equity for you over the years, growing dollar by dollar and picking up momentum through the power of compounding interest so that, like a snowball rolling down a wintry hill, it will have gathered tremendous financial mass in the years when you need it most? Or are you living on credit, on borrowed money as well as borrowed time, running your coffers empty and storing up debt instead of equity, digging yourself deeper and deeper into a hole that grows only harder to escape?

Let's take an honest look at your career.

Is your professional life growing every day? Are you moving along a path that is taking you toward greater accomplishment and fulfillment in your chosen occupation? Is your work growing not only in its financial rewards, but also in your sense of meaningful contribution, personal satisfaction, and respect among your peers?

Let's take an honest look at your positive impact on the world.

What kind of impact are you having on the people around you? How is the world different as a result of your being here? After you leave this world, what will you leave behind as a legacy and how will people remember you? When you add together your career and all your professional accomplishments, your relationships and all your personal accomplishments, your sense of connection with nature, humanity, and God, how would you describe the overall value or meaning of your life? And is that sense growing stronger, deeper, richer, more powerful every day, month, and year?

Life is not a practice session; there's no dress rehearsal. This is it. This is for real. So play it straight and be real with yourself. Take a look at your life and tell the truth about where you really are at. Do this exercise with me right now. Take a pencil (not a pen—remember, everything changes) and put a check in the up or down box next to each area of your life as listed below.

Which way are you headed right now?

	UP	DOWN
Your health	___	___
Your happiness	___	___
Your friendships and relationships	___	___
Your personal development	___	___
Your finances	___	___
Your career	___	___
Your positive impact on the world	___	___

There is no treading water in life, no running in place, because everything is in motion. If you're not improving, enriching, building, unfolding—if you're not adding assets to your personal and professional value every day—then you're headed down the curve.

In my line of work, I talk a lot about success in financial terms. But genuine success is a far greater issue than one of purely financial health. A genuinely successful life means your health, your happiness, your relationships, your personal development, your career, your spirituality, your sense of fulfillment, your legacy and the impact you have on the world... it means all these things and more.

And the best thing about genuine success is that *it spreads*. Like ripples in a pond, even small successes in any one of these areas begins to affect all the others, too. Improve your health and you improve your relationships; work on your personal development and you have an impact on your career. Everything affects everything else.

If you are having a hard time making progress in one area—say, in business—take action to make a small positive change in an unrelated area. Start taking a walk around the block, organize that junk drawer that has been haunting you. Feeling successful in one area will provide you with renewed confidence and energy to continue on your journey of attaining that other big goal. Success in one area breeds success in every area.

The key is, *start somewhere*. Wherever you can take action and begin creating little successes, *do it*. Don't wait. The rest of your life is waiting.

The Good News

The alarm goes off. 6:00 a.m. Without conscious thought your hand shoots out and hits SNOOZE. A ten-minute reprieve. You tentatively slip a foot out from under the covers. Brrr. You open one eye. Still dark out.

Now you face a choice.

And that is the good news, because in every moment you *always* face a choice. Where you are right now is poised in the present, with the past stretching behind you and the future lying ahead. At any moment in your life, you can choose to change which side of that curve you're on. You cannot change the past. You can absolutely change the future.

Are you heading upward on the success curve, or downward on the failure curve? Right at this moment, at this exact juncture in your life, with your hand on the SNOOZE button, you can answer the question either way. Where you've been heading is not necessarily where you will be heading after you turn this page, or put down this book, or wake up tomorrow morning. The past does not equal the future.

In fact, you cannot look in both directions at once. You can look down, or you can look up; you can look back, or you can look forward; you can look in the rearview mirror, or at the highway ahead. All the information you need is already there. You're already doing the actions. All you need to do is choose to have them serve and empower you—and *keep on choosing*.

Step onto the upper curve, the path of success, and in time, you will put any area of life on track—your health, your finances, your relationships, your family life, your career, your spiritual health, your sense of accomplishment and fulfillment and purpose.

And it will be less time than you might think.

Personal Stories from
The Slight Edge Readers

Before reading this book, I tended to lead a life of blame. I never accepted any responsibility; it was never my fault, always someone else's, always something other than me that prevented me from succeeding. After reading the book, I realized I had a decision to make: Continue on my path of failure, or change.

Sometimes it seems like it's too late in life to change things. I realize now that it is never too late. But you have to start *somewhere*. It's up to you to dig deep, look at things from the past, and strive to be better in the future with just a few simple changes.

—*Charleigh Vigil, Dekalb, Illinois*

As an actress, it is so easy to get overwhelmed by everything that comes with this competitive business. *The Slight Edge* helped me to understand that the small choices I make every moment of every day have a huge impact on my life. Living in a society with so much emphasis on success, I've found that *The Slight Edge* has redefined what success is for me. It helps me to take the next step forward in my everyday life and do the next right thing. I know those steps will ultimately lead to a very successful and fulfilling life—and I attribute much of my success to the simple principles outlined in this book.

—*Cara Cooley, New York City*

Being an alcoholic was taking over every ounce of goodness and skillfulness I had. Fortunately, destiny had a better plan for me. I made the decision to fight and enrolled myself in a sobriety outpatient facility. At the same time, another positive occurrence happened: I was introduced to *The Slight Edge*.

The simple principles described in the book were an absolute revelation for me. By understanding how I had let my worst enemy work the magic of the slight edge to my disadvantage, I was able to take the appropriate baby steps necessary to change the curve of my life and turn it to the positive side.

Today, I am free and happy. I wake up in the morning energized, aware of which steps are necessary to achieve my goals, and I walk a path that leads me, a day at a time, to fulfillment.

—*Michele Tremblay-Suepke, Tacoma, Washington*

Essential Points from Chapter 10

↗ Everything is always in motion. Every day, every moment, your life path is either curving upward, or curving downward.

↗ Growing up we heard five times as many nos as yeses. Life has a downward pull.

↗ People on the success curve live in responsibility. People on the failure curve live in blame.

↗ People on the success curve are pulled by the future. People on the failure curve are pulled by the past.

↗ No matter where you are, at any moment you can choose to step onto the success curve.

11. Mastering the Slight Edge

> "There is one quality which one must possess to win, and that is the definiteness of purpose, the knowledge of what one wants, and a burning desire to possess it."
>
> —*Napoleon Hill,* Think and Grow Rich

When you were still a small child, you made your way around the world crawling on your hands and knees. Everyone else was walking, and one day you got it into your little head that maybe you could give that a try, too. Once that thought appeared, there was suddenly no "maybe" about it: you *had* to give it a try. It was the next frontier, period. There was no way you were not going to attempt it, fail at it, and then keep attempting it until you mastered it.

So step by step—quite literally—you started working to develop the skills you needed to walk.

First you declared it. Maybe not in so many words (words were a whole other thing, a world you hadn't even thought about pioneering yet). Like Babe Ruth pointing to the outfield before hitting a homer, you gabbled and gooed and grunted it, declaiming in the only way you knew how, "Get ready, I'll be walking now!"

Then you grabbed onto something above you and pulled yourself upright. You stood, holding on to a playpen or chair or your biggest stuffed animal. You were wobbly and unsure. You let go, whether on purpose or by accident, and it didn't matter which, because the result was the same—*crash*. Back down you fell. And then, either right away or later that day or the next, you tried it again. And then you tried it again, and again … until eventually you stood up all by yourself. Look, Ma, no hands.

Then you took a step—and in that step you assumed the mantle of mastery.

Yes, mastery, *right then.*

No, you weren't actually walking yet, not like the practiced strider you would become. And yes, you probably fell right back down in the very next moment. But that didn't matter. You had taken the Neil Armstrong step—and you were on the path.

Baby Steps

Mastery is not some vaunted, lofty place that only the elite few ever inhabit. The pursuit of any aim, goal, or dream—personal, professional, spiritual, in any area—is a slight edge journey of continuous improvement, learning, and refinement. But mastery is not an exalted state that lies at the end of the path; it is a state of mind that lies at the very beginning. Mastery is in the act of setting your foot on the path, not in reaching its end.

You don't need to be born with exceptional abilities to enter into mastery, nor is it reserved for the super-talented. You don't even need to have gotten an early start. The upward journey of success on the slight edge curve is available to anyone who is willing to get on the path and stay on it. But it's only by being immersed in the process—the day-by-day progression—that you will come to know the road. That's how you will acquire and refine the skills and awareness you'll need to master the slight edge and, therefore, master your success and your life.

All that's required is taking the first step.

So here you are, just completing your very first step. Now, you know that the big people you've been watching go around taking one step after another. You've watched them do it: right foot, left foot, right foot, left foot … so you try. You complete that first, tentative, epic-making step and get ready to swing into the next one, and then, *crash.*

You try again. And again. And again. After days of side-stepping around the coffee table, awkwardly bringing one little foot out from behind the other while you hold onto Mom's or Dad's fingers, you eventually take your first sequence of two steps … then three, and four, and then all alone, all by yourself, and to the encouraging cheers and applause of your proud family, you take those newly assured baby steps, one at a time—*and you're walking.*

In the process of learning to walk, did you spend more time falling down or standing up? If you were anything like most babies, you failed (fell) far more than you succeeded (walked). It didn't matter: you were on the path of mastery.

Did you ever have the thought of quitting? Did you ever say to yourself, "You know, it looks like I may just not be cut out for walking. Oh well. Guess I'll have to crawl for the rest of my life. Hey, it really isn't all that bad, when you stop and think about it, won't be that hard to get used to…." Of course not. You were on the path of mastery. You were already a master. Now it was only a matter of your walking skills catching up.

Constantly falling down was really uncomfortable (it *hurt*), and you looked pretty foolish lying there on the floor like a beetle on its back. But you kept at it anyway. Why? Because successful people do what unsuccessful people are not willing to do.

And here's the fascinating part: *all infants are successful.* As infants, we are all masters. That's just the way we're designed. All newborns instinctively understand the slight edge. We only let go of our natural pull toward success, our mastery, over the course of those 40,000 nos.

Are there any situations in your life today where you've given up and decided to keep crawling for the rest of your life, rather than go for what you really want, what you truly deserve? Have you let go of the capacity to make up a goal, go for it, and get it? If so, you have to ask yourself, why is it so difficult, so impossible, to do something today that you had no trouble doing when you were less than a year old?

The answer is as simple as it is sad: somewhere along the way, you lost faith. You became too grown-up to take baby steps, too sure you would never succeed to let yourself fail a few times first. You gave up on the universal truth that simple little disciplines, done again and again over time, would move the biggest mountains. You forgot what you used to know about the slight edge.

You stepped off the path of mastery.

There is something treacherous about letting go of that childlike willingness to try and try again. Something insidiously dangerous about buying into the idea, "That'll never work for me." It is this: settling for less, giving up on the power of baby steps and embracing failure, soon becomes a habit.

The first time you give up, it's painful. The second time it's still painful but now it feels a little familiar, and there is some comfort in familiarity: it is the silent sleepy comfort of carbon monoxide. And the more you give up, the easier and easier it gets, and the sleepier and sleepier you become to the wakefulness of genuine accomplishment … and success recedes ever further from your grasp. Can you guess why? That's right: it's the slight edge—working against you.

Before you know it, life has become heavy. Welcome to the 95 percent.

And as always, all you need to do is turn over the coin to find the good news here: it is *just as easy* to step back into the habit of succeeding as it is to slip into the habit of failing. The longer you live, the easier it can get.

You can step back onto the path of mastery anytime you want.

Wanting

"There is one quality which one must possess to win," writes Napoleon Hill in his all-time classic *Think and Grow Rich*, "and that is definiteness of purpose, the knowledge of what one wants, and a burning desire to possess it."

The knowledge of what one wants. That is a powerful thing, and worth looking at for a moment. We all have visions of the way we'd like things to be that are different from the way they are. It could be something as simple as wishing we weighed ten pounds less, or something as far-reaching as wishing we could feed the millions of children around the world who go to bed hungry every night.

Have you ever wanted something so badly that it hurt? Of course you have. Everyone has. Sometimes it's a sweet sort of ache, sometimes not so sweet, but either way it is a powerful force. I call it *the ache of wanting.*

Having a dream, a goal, an aspiration, is not always a matter of all roses and sweetness; ambitions, aspirations, and desires can be uncomfortable, even painful.

The word "want" has two meanings. It can mean you desire something; it can also mean you *lack* something. (That second sense of the word, by the way, is its original and far older definition.) And in a way, those aren't really two meanings; they're two sides of the same meaning. We tend to desire what we lack, and lack what we desire.

Which is why dreams can be painful. Letting yourself become aware of what it is that you desire but do not presently have means experiencing the *lack* side of the wanting coin as well as the desire side. It means becoming more fully aware of what you don't have. It means staring at your present reality with a sober eye and refusing to kid yourself. Noticing that you're not where you want to be can be uncomfortable. When Hill says "a *burning desire* to possess it," he's not kidding. And burning is not a comfortable thing.

Wanting hurts.

Here's an interesting thing: if putting voice to your fondest dreams can make you a little uncomfortable, it can also make everyone around you uncomfortable, too, and often far more so. Tell your five closest friends about your biggest ambition, and watch how many of them squirm. Why? Because showing them *your* want (desire) also makes them more acutely aware of *their* want (lack).

This is one reason that, when you are formulating goals and creating a vision for your future, it's important to be careful whom you share them with. It's natural to share your enthusiasm with the people in your life, especially those you are closest to—and it's also useful to re-member that people often tend to respond by raining on your parade. When they do, it's not out of malice or the conscious desire to blunt your excitement. More often it's simply a form of self-defense. They'd rather not hear about the vision you have, because it reminds them of the one they've lost.

Closing the Gap

That pain of wanting, the burning desire to possess what you lack, is one of the greatest allies you have. It is a force you can harness to create whatever you want in your life.

When you took an honest look at your life back in the previous chapter and rated yourself as being either on the UP curve or the DOWN curve in seven different areas, you were painting a picture of where you *are now*. This diagram shows that as point A. Where you *could* be tomorrow, your vision of what's possible for you in your life, is point B. And to the extent that there is a "wanting" gap between points A and B, there is a natural tension between those two poles. It's like holding a magnet near a piece of iron: you can feel the pull of that magnet tugging at the iron. Wanting is exactly like that; it's magnetic. You can palpably feel your dreams (B) tugging at your present circumstances (A).

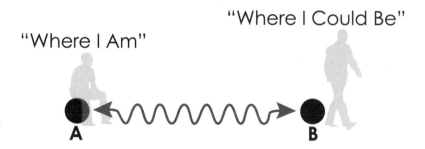

Tension is uncomfortable. That's why it sometimes makes people uncomfortable to hear about how things *could be*. One of the reasons Dr. Martin Luther King, Jr.'s famous "I have a dream" speech made such a huge impact on the world and carved such a vivid place in our cultural memory is that it made the world of August 1963 very uncomfortable. John Lennon painted his vision of a more harmonious world in the song *Imagine*. Within the decade, he was shot to death. Gandhi, Jesus, Socrates … our world can be harsh on people who talk about an improved reality. Visions and visionaries make people uncomfortable.

These are especially dramatic examples, of course, but the same principle applies to the personal dreams and goals of people we've never heard of. The same principle applies to everyone, including you and me.

Let's say you have a brother, or sister, or old friend with whom you had a falling out years ago. You wish you had a better relationship, that you talked more often, that you shared more personal experiences and conversations together. Between where you are today and where you can imagine being, there is a gap. Can you feel it?

Or let's say you are a hard worker and make a pretty good income, but have no solid retirement plan and don't know how you'll be able to live comfortably when you reach your seventies. There's how you'd *like to be* living at age seventy-two, and how you're worried you *may end up* living at age seventy-two if things go the way they're going. Between those two, there's a gap. Can you feel it?

Do you have any health or fitness goals? Career goals? Goals for your kids? Dreams of living somewhere else, of doing something else? Each of those images you have, of how things *could be* but at the moment *are not*, creates a gap with your present reality.

Most people, when confronted by problems larger than or of a different sort than they're already handling, immediately feel defeated or thrown off course. Most tend to see larger or different problems as negatives, and infect their own lives with negativity. What they don't realize is this philosophy: *The size of the problem determines the size of the person.*

You can gauge the limitations of a person's life by the size of the problems that get him or her down. You can measure the impact a person's life has by the size of the problems he or she solves. If the size of the problems you solve is, "Do I put the cans in the bottom of the bag, and then put the bread on top?" as a grocery store bagger, that's the level of your problem solving and that's the level of your pay. If you can solve big problems, you can graduate to big pay—because the size of your income will be determined by the size of the problems you solve, too.

What most people call a "problem" is simply a gap, an open space between point A and point B. And if you keep an open mind, it's an open space you can bridge.

Here is the reason I've spent this time describing and explaining this gap: *That gap can work against you or it can work for you.* The gap between A and B cannot last forever. It has to resolve, and it will, one way or the other. It's a law of nature, and there's nothing you can do to stop it. But you do have a choice in *how* it resolves.

The first way to resolve the tension is to move your point A (the way things are today) steadily closer and closer to point B. Let yourself be drawn by the magnet of your vision, pulled along by the future. Remember what pulls those who dwell in the failure curve? The past.

And what pulls people who live on the success curve? The future.

People who live with huge, vivid, clearly articulated dreams are pulled along toward those dreams with such force, they become practically unstoppable. What made people like Martin Luther King, Jr., Gandhi, or Mother Teresa, Edison or IBM's Thomas Watson, Wilberforce or Lincoln such forces of nature that nothing could stand in their way, no matter what the odds or obstacles? It was not some magic in their character, though they certainly became people of exceptional character along the way. It was the power of their dreams. The vision each of these men and women held created a magnetic force against which no opposition could stand.

Again, I'm using dramatic examples of famous people, but the exact same thing occurs with people you and I have never heard of, everyday people who are not at all famous, but simply have dreams they care about and keep alive every day. That's the force you can harness in the pursuit of your own dreams.

What about the other direction? I said there were two ways that tension can resolve, and the second way is the one that works against you. If you don't close the gap by moving your present circumstance (A) constantly toward your goals and dreams (B), how else can you let the tension resolve?

Quit dreaming. Just let go of all your dreams, goals, ambitions, and aspirations. Settle for less. Make point B disappear, just delete it, and—poof!—the tension is gone. And that, sadly, is the choice that the 95 percent who travel the failure curve eventually make.

It's not hard to understand why so many people make that second choice. After all, when you're standing here at point A, gazing off into the distance at point B, it's easy to be intimidated by how far away it looks. People don't even want to set foot on the path if they don't think they can make it to the end. "Why even try? If the mountain's that huge, why take the first step? I'll probably never make it anyway...."

When the journey seems daunting, *easy not to do* can be a lot more appealing than *easy to do*. Hey, hit the SNOOZE button. Who will know the difference, right?

But remember, you have to go one direction or the other; you can't stand still. The universe is curved, and everything is constantly changing. There are only two possibilities. Either you let go of where you are and get to where you could be, or you hang onto where you are and give up where you could be. You are either going for your dreams or giving up your dreams. Stretching for what you could be, or settling for what you are. There is simply no in-between. Remember, this is the slight edge—and doing nothing means going down.

It's your choice.

The Deceptive Majority

Those two slight edge curves, the success curve and the failure curve, typically run parallel to each other for a long time. The two paths may be so close together that it's almost impossible for most people even to see the distinction between them. Then, all of a sudden, they veer away from each other, the success curve shooting up like an eagle and the failure curve plummeting downward like a stock market crash.

The people living on top, those who take responsibility, live a life that is in some ways uncomfortable. Successful people do what unsuccessful people are not willing to do, and that often means living outside the limits of one's comfort zone. When you're one out of twenty, you're always going to be going in the opposite direction from the other nineteen.

The people on the other side are hanging with the masses, and their lives are often more comfortable during that long early stretch. But they become more uncomfortable later on. Suddenly they find they don't have the finances, don't have the health or the happiness, no longer have the relationships, and their lives become very uncomfortable. By contrast, those on the success curve end up ever more comfortable as their lives progress, because over the course of time they continue to have the finances, the health and happiness, the relationships, the successes. In fact, they have *more* of those things.

This means changing your thinking about the comfort zone. It's a change in philosophy. It means embracing living uncomfortably in order to attain a life that is genuinely comfortable—not deceptively comfortable.

"All truth passes through three stages," the great German philosophy Arthur Schopenhauer reportedly observed. "First, it is ridiculed. Second, it is violently opposed. Third, it is accepted as being self-evident." Gandhi put it this way: "First they ignore you, then they laugh at you, then they fight you, then you win."

Both quotations show a brilliant insight into the nature of the 95 percent.

The majority always let the first and second phases pass them by and wait until a truth is self-evident before signing on. The key to success is to identify those things that are eventually going to become self-evident *before* they are self-evident. Or to put it even more simply: find out what the majority is doing and do the opposite—which can be uncomfortable. At least at first, when the 95 percent are ignoring you, laughing at you, or fighting you. But in the end, you win.

When you side with the slight edge, you *always* win.

Of course you have to apply some intelligence and discernment here. You can't expect things to work out for you simply because you're moving in opposition to what the majority is doing. Being contrary for contrary's sake is just another type of conformity: you're still a slave to the majority, only expressed in oppositional terms.

The chances are excellent, though, that when you do step up onto the success curve, you will be stepping out alone. Like Wilberforce, Edison, or Lincoln.

Do what the majority won't dare to do. Risk being the one, not one of the nineteen. Will people criticize you? Of course. But have you ever seen a statue erected for a critic? We don't build statues for the 95 percent. We build them for the 5 percent.

What I Learned from Funerals

As I mentioned earlier, when I went to work for Texas Instruments I was all ready to work my way up in management, but life had other plans for me. I showed up for work—and they put me in sales. I was aghast. There was no way I could go out on sales calls and do anything but fail miserably. What I had was not fear of rejection, it was *abject terror* of rejection. I would have to quit this job, right now, and go back to graduate school with my tail between my legs....

But by this time I knew that successful people do what unsuccessful people are not willing to do. I was up against the wall: I *had* to do it, and I knew it.

For my first sales call, I pored through the customer files and found the tiniest, most insignificant account I could: a tiny little drug store in Gainesville, Florida. I figured that if I was going to make a mess, I might as well do as little damage as possible.

I drove for two and a half hours to arrive at that store, white-knuckled with fear. I parked and sat in the lot for a good half hour, leaning my face into the air conditioner vents (with the AC turned up full blast) and sweating buckets. I was terrified. Staying in that car would have been the easiest thing in the world to do right then. And on some level, even though I had not yet articulated the slight edge philosophy in my life, I knew that this simple little error, compounded over time, would rob me of all my dreams.

As I had prepared myself to go on this first sales call, I had been literally praying for help, and as so often happens when you ask a question in all sincerity, an answer came. In this case, it came in the form of an article I happened to read in a magazine a day or two earlier. An article, of all things, about funerals.

At the average funeral, I read, about ten people cry.

I couldn't believe it. I had to read the paragraph over again to make sure I'd gotten it right. "Ten people—that's *it*? You mean I go through my entire life, spend years enduring all those trials and tribulations and achievements and joys and heartbreaks—and at the end of it, there are only ten people in the world who care enough to show up and cry?"

I went on to the next paragraph. It got worse.

Once those ten (or fewer) people had yanked their hankies and honked their schnozzes and my funeral was over, the number one factor that would determine how many people would go on from the funeral to attend the actual burial would be ... the weather.

The *weather*?

Yes. If it happened to be raining, said the article's author, 50 percent of the people who attended my funeral would decide maybe they wouldn't go on to attend my burial after all, and just head home.

Now I *really* couldn't believe it. "You mean, I'm lying there dead, at the grand conclusion of everything I've ever said and done, of everything I call my life, in those final moments when my entire existence is called to account and acknowledged and memorialized by those nearest and dearest to me, those whose lives I've most deeply and profoundly touched—and half the congregation checks out halfway through *because it's starting to rain*?"

This really bummed me out ... when I first read it. But now, sitting there in my car outside that little drugstore in Gainesville, I discovered it was liberating. "You know what?" I thought. "I don't give a damn what anybody thinks of what I'm doing any more. If the odds are that iffy as to whether or not they even cry at my funeral, and chances are no better than 50/50 that they'll duck out before I'm planted if the sky happens to cry for me more than the people do … then why am I spending so much time worrying about what they're thinking now?"

Why would I be afraid of rejection? Why would I care about having a door or two slammed in my face? Why would I be concerned about what the majority thinks, or worry about what the 95 percent say, think, or do?

Facing truths about one's own death can also bring one face to face with some important truths about one's life. That article on funerals had enlarged my comfort zone and given me an edge of courage—just a tiny edge, but an edge I hadn't had before. A slight edge.

I finally mustered what courage I could, turned off the car, went inside, and gave what I am convinced to this day was the worst presentation in the history of sales. They did not buy a thing. And in that sense, it was a total failure—but when I got back into my car I was elated. I had blown the sales call and achieved a victory in my life.

A few days later, I happened to be thinking about that article once more as I sat in my car again, this time stopped in traffic. Just then I glanced out my window and saw why we were all stopped: of all things, a *funeral procession* was going by. It took less than a minute, too, because it contained only a few cars.

As traffic slowly started moving again, I thought about the person reclining there in the hearse. Had he or she lived his or her entire life worrying about what other people thought?

And it suddenly hit me. Who has long funeral processions? At whose funerals do thousands cry? For whom do the millions mourn? For those who will do what others are not willing to do. For the people for whom we erect statues. For Martin Luther King, for Gandhi, for Mother Teresa, for Lincoln. Gigantic funerals are held and great crowds, even entire nations, mourn for those who spend their lives not worrying about what others thought.

Talk about having a ripple effect.

Talk about mastery.

Personal Stories from
The Slight Edge Readers

Shortly after my baby girl was born, I reluctantly turned to a state-run WIC program that provided milk for her—milk I couldn't afford to buy myself. It was a clear and defining moment in my life. I was in my early twenties and my life was spiraling downward fast in all categories: finances, family, fitness, faith, friends, fun, and freedom.

I could see that where I was in life was based entirely on the decisions I'd made over the last five years, and nearly every one of them led me down the path of gradual decline. Deep down inside I knew I had to move from a life of entitlement to a life of responsibility.

One decision I made was critical. Every day, while I was taking care of my baby girl, I would have a TV channel called The People's Network playing in the background. Whenever I fell off track, I would hear someone on that channel share some wisdom, some insights that helped get me get back on track.

Around that time I attended an event where Jeff Olson shared the slight edge concept. He said it had served him well in life and then added, "I think it will do you well, too." He shared how it is in the last 20 percent of the time we invest in a discipline that all the rewards come. I needed something to believe in, so that day I bought into his belief in the slight edge philosophy.

Every decision I made over the next five years was a slight edge decision—only now they were decisions that fed those simple positive disciplines, instead of those simple errors in judgment. The majority of my decisions were now leading me down the path of growth.

I'll never forget those days of struggling—fall off track, get back on track, fall off track, get back on track. Realizing I was the project, I went to work on me. I read and applied what I learned. I went to work and I did my best. I applied long-term vision and delayed gratification. I knew that in order to be successful, I had to do what others were not willing do to themselves. If I became a success, it would be because of me. If I became a failure, it would be because of me. I couldn't blame anyone, I wouldn't and I didn't. Was it easy? Not at all. Was it worth it? In a *very* big way.

Over time I started to hit that magical 20 percent slight edge tipping point in my finances, and with my family, and in my fitness, faith, friends … and yes even fun and freedom followed. I became living proof that the slight edge works.

Since that time I've taught the slight edge philosophy to audiences in over twenty countries. I created a slight edge chart for myself, the same chart my daughter used to keep her on track to earning a black belt in the martial arts, the same one she used to develop the habit of reading fifteen pages of a personal growth book a day, the same one she used to develop powerful critical thinking skills.

My daughter recently turned eighteen and just left on a ninety-day trip to Italy. I'm thrilled for her, and a bit sad. I miss her. And I know she'll be fine; after all, the slight edge philosophy is now part of her DNA. She also has a three-year-old sister. And yes, thanks to *The Slight Edge*, I can afford the milk this time around.

—*Art Jonak, Houston Texas*

Essential Points from Chapter 11

↗ Mastery begins the moment you step onto the path. Failure begins the moment you step off the path.

↗ Wanting is uncomfortable, yet wanting is essential to winning.

↗ There are two ways to close the gap between where you are and where you want to be: 1) you can let go of where you are and be drawn to your goal, or 2) you can let go of your goal, hit the SNOOZE button, and stay where you are.

↗ Chances are good that when you step out onto the path of mastery, you will step out alone.

12. Invest in Yourself

> "Give me six hours to chop down a tree, and I will spend the first four hours sharpening the axe."
>
> —*Abraham Lincoln (attrib.)*

The greatest gift you could ever give yourself is also the wisest business investment you could ever make. It is also the most critical step in accomplishing any challenging task, and is the one step without which all other success strategies, no matter how brilliant or time-tested, are doomed to fail.

What is this mysterious gift? It is your own personal development. Investing in your own improvement, your own personal growth and betterment, is all these things and more.

"Give me six hours to chop down a tree," goes the quote attributed to Abraham Lincoln, "and I will spend the first four hours sharpening the axe." Which left just two hours to do the actual chopping. In other words, he would spend twice as much time working on the tools of the job as he would on the task itself. And in the task called *your life*, what are the tools of the job? They are simply you: *you* are the axe. And no one knew that better than our sixteenth president, who poured enormous effort during his half-century of life into making himself into the sharpest, strongest, truest axe he possibly could.

What do most people do? When there's a tree in the way they grab that axe, dull or not, and start whaling away at it. And if they aren't making a major dent in that tree pretty soon, they quit, probably muttering something about how it's the tree's fault.

How you swing the axe, how hard, in what arc, with what rhythm, and onto exactly which spot on the tree are all tactics that can be measured, weighed, and improved. But it all starts with the axe itself. And the axe is you.

Continuous Learning

Earlier we talked about the power of time, and how vital it is that you learn to harness the power of time in the pursuit of all your aims. And that is certainly the strategy of all strategies. Time may not heal all wounds, but it does bring about all change, sooner or later. But in terms of living and mastering the slight edge, the most important force you can harness to accelerate and amplify your path through life is the power of *continuous learning*.

When I say "learning," I don't mean simply learning from school, although schooling certainly has its place. And I don't just mean learning from books or from a teacher—though you already know that I revere the knowledge to be gained from good books, and I feel the same way about great teachers, too. I'm also not just talking here about learning from the example of others, or from advice from your friends, or from your own mistakes and the "school of hard knocks." When I say "learning," I don't mean any particular one of these things—I mean *all* of them.

Once you've grasped the philosophy of the slight edge and set foot on the path of mastery, educating yourself through any and all means available is the critical process that will keep you on that path and make the slight edge work for you.

I also don't mean "educating yourself" in the more narrowly defined sense of learning specific skills or subjects. Naturally, you need to pursue continuous learning in order to acquire the knowledge and skills involved in mastering any subject or pursuit that will contribute to your personal and professional growth and development. But it's more than simply a matter of acquiring specific knowledge. Continuous, lifelong learning is the material from which you continually build your philosophy and your understanding of how it plays out in real-life situations and circumstances, which is also critical in mastering the slight edge.

Here's a statistic that may blow your mind: among high school graduates who do not go on to college, 58 percent—more than half—never read a book again. I mean, *for the rest of their lives.* When I first read that figure I was shocked, but not all that surprised. It's just one more reason the 95 percent stop paddling, slide down the failure curve, and drown in the cream. They spend their lives building someone else's dream, not because they aren't capable of building their own but because they never gained the knowledge they need.

Illiteracy is a much greater problem today than many people realize. Of the slightly more than 7 billion people on earth, according to the United Nations, more than 1 billion cannot read. Can you imagine that? One person out of every seven—1 *billion* people. But consider this: if you are one of that 58 percent who never picks up a book once high school is behind you, what's the difference between you and the billion souls around the world who couldn't read that book even if they did pick it up? No difference at all.

And it isn't just reading. It's what you read. Among those 6 out of 7 who *can* read books, most who do accomplish little more than to entertain themselves and pass the time. Don't worry, I'm not knocking entertainment. (Who doesn't love to have fun?) I'm just saying that all the whodunits, Hollywood tell-alls, and teenage vampire novels in the world won't vault you up and over onto the upper half of the slight edge curve.

"The trouble with the world," wrote Mark Twain, "is not that people know too little, but that they know so many things that ain't so." Or as Mr. Twain might have put it in assessing the state of literacy in today's media-crazy world: the problem is not that people *read* too little, but that they fill their brains with stuff that ain't doing them no good.

But what if you add to your summer paperback pile some titles from John Maxwell, Jack Canfield, Zig Ziglar, or Jim Rohn? Or *The Happiness Advantage, The 7 Habits of Highly Effective People, Think and Grow Rich*, and any of the hundreds and thousands of other inspirational, educational, empowering books out there?

Now, that's a different story.

When was the last time you attended a seminar or took an adult-education class, not because you were required to but simply to improve yourself? When was the last time you went bowling? If your bowling average is over 200, congratulations! You're a heck of a bowler ... and you may want to rethink your priorities. If you lined up the one hundred most successful men and women in America and calculated their bowling averages, I bet they wouldn't break 70. The average American will go bowling 233 times in his or her life—and they all have something better to do. I know bowling is one of the most popular pastimes in the United States, but wouldn't you rather have success be your most popular pastime? I'm not picking on bowling or any other form of recreation. We need balance in our lives, and taking time at the bowling alley can also serve you in all sorts of ways, including your fitness, your relationships with your friends, your ability to let work go, to relax and have fun—all good things. The question is, though, are you developing yourself? Are you building your dream, or only your boss's?

If you read ten pages a day, then you'll go through an entire 300-page book in one month. Take a title like *Think and Grow Rich*, where someone has packed a lifetime of extraordinary learning about success between the covers of a book. Why *wouldn't* you want to spend a little time every day for a month learning what someone like Napoleon Hill spent a lifetime observing and putting onto paper?

Invest in yourself. Sharpen your axe. Read just one chapter of an information-rich, inspiring book every day. Listen to fifteen minutes of a life-transforming audio. Take a course or seminar every few weeks or months. Are these things easy to do? Sure. And those simple disciplines compounded over time, like a penny doubled every day for a month, will send you up to the top. Are they easy not to do? No question. And if you don't do them today, right now, will your life be destroyed? Of course not. But that simple error in judgment, compounded over time, will pull you down the curve of failure and take away everything you've hoped for and dreamed about.

Book Smarts versus Street Smarts

Here is a pop quiz. Ready?

> *Five frogs sit on a lily pad.*
> *One decides to jump off.*
> *How many are left?*

If you answered "four," then your math skills are just fine. Unfortunately, this isn't a math problem. It's a *life* problem. The correct answer is "five." Yes, all five are still sitting there on their lily pad. That one frog only *decided* to jump.

He hasn't actually done it yet.

Plenty of people invest a good amount of time and effort accumulating knowledge, but still end up living their lives on the failure curve. Why? Because mastering the slight edge and moving onto the success curve is not only a question of the quantity of your learning but also the quality of that learning—and especially whether it includes any *doing.*

There are two kinds of learning: learning by study—which includes reading, listening to audios, and attending classes and seminars—and learning by doing. As passionate as I am about improving yourself by studying with great teachers, through great books, audios, and workshops, I also know that all the study in the world won't build your business, establish your health, create a rich and fulfilling family life, and make you a happier person. That takes your getting up and out of your chair and *doing it.* Book smarts is not enough: all true success is built from a foundation of study plus street smarts. If you want to stay grounded and move ahead at the same time, you need a balance.

Life is not a spectator sport; as a matter of fact, it's a contact sport, and there are no practice sessions, and you've been in the game from day one. Life lives in the right-here, right-now. That's why Emerson, who was an exceptionally well-educated man in the traditional book-smarts sense, advised, *Do the thing, and you shall have the power.*

And note: this is not a reversible philosophy. You can't go get the power and *then* do the thing—though people certainly try to do it that way, and they spend their entire lives gathering the power and doing nothing. *Do the thing, and you shall have the power.* The only way to have the power is to do the thing. Just do it. Learn by doing.

You've heard the famous Chinese bit of wisdom that says, "The journey of a thousand miles starts with a single step." Another excellent example of traditional slight edge understanding. But note: The journey starts with a single step—not with *thinking* about taking a step.

In the course of my businesses I'm often approached by people wanting to know the secret to success, the magic formula. "What's the one thing I can do," they'll say, "to guarantee my success?" My answer is always the same: "Be here, actively immersed in the process, one year from now." That's really the only right answer. It's the slight edge

answer. You can't build your dream by what you're going to do or planning to do or intending to do. You only build your dream by building
it. You have to jump off the lily pad.

Life is *doing*. If you aren't doing, you're dying.

The Rhythm of Learning

I can read a book like James Allen's classic *As a Man Thinketh*, return
it to my bookshelf, then come back a year later to read it again—and
it feels like somebody sneaked into my room while I was sleeping and
completely rewrote the thing. In fact this happens to me all the time. I'm
constantly discovering, or rediscovering, all sorts of insights in books
that I'd already read before, even many times before. Why? Because of
the learning by doing I've gone through in the interim. My experiences
have changed my perspective. Now, when I read a particular passage
or point the author makes, I understand it in a way I could not have
possibly seen a year ago. And that in turn informs my behavior. Now,
when I go to engage in my activity of the next day, I can apply what
I've learned from Allen in a way that I would not have thought of even
twenty-four hours earlier.

"Knowledge without practice is useless," said Confucius, but he
added a second line: "And practice without knowledge is dangerous." It
isn't that street smarts are *better* than book smarts. They're both critical.
One without the other, as Confucius pointed out, is either useless or
dangerous, and either way, it sure won't put you on the success curve.

Book smarts, street smarts. Learning by study, learning by doing.
Read about it, apply it, see it in action, take that practical experience
back to your reading, deepen your understanding, take that deeper understanding back to your activity… it's a never-ending cycle, each aspect of learning feeding the other. Like climbing a ladder: right foot,
left foot, right foot, left foot. Can you imagine trying to climb a ladder
with only your right foot?

Not only do the two work better when they work together in a
rhythm, each amplifying the other, but the truth is they really cannot work separately *at all*. At least not for long. You can't excel based
purely on knowledge learned through study; and you can't excel purely
through knowledge gleaned through action. The two have to work together. You study, and then you do activity. The activity changes your

frame of reference, and now you are in a place where you can learn more. Then you learn more, and it gives you more insight into what you experienced in your activity, so now you re-approach activity with more insight. And back and forth it goes.

That back-and-forth rhythm is worth noting, because it isn't just the rhythm of learning. It is the rhythm of success. It is what you began mastering the moment you took your first baby steps. In fact, it's something you learned even before you got to the walking phase, and it's even more basic. Psychologists have found crawling is one of the most important activities we ever accomplish, because it profoundly affects the neurological wiring of the brain and its capacity to learn. The right-hand-left-leg, left-hand-right-leg rhythm of alternation acts upon our nervous systems like the surf upon the coastline, developing it, shaping it, and preparing it for all sorts of more sophisticated levels of learning and awareness later in life.

You've heard the expression, "You have to crawl before you can walk." There is a more profound truth to this than most of us ever realized.

That alternating rhythm, and your capacity to coordinate the behavior of opposites, is a critical slight edge skill. Balancing book smarts and street smarts is one aspect of that, and so is the daily success strategy that we'll look at next: course correction.

Course Correction

What's the shortest path between two points—a straight line, right? Wrong. While that might be true in theory, it's never true in reality. In the real universe, everything is curved. And reality is where you and I live, and where we succeed or fail.

Think about how you drive on a road that is perfectly straight—or that gives the illusion of being perfectly straight. Of course, it isn't really straight at all. It's filled with little bumps and imperfections and subtle shifts in elevation and tilt and torque. How do you know that? Think about how you drive. Even when you're on one of those interstates that seems like a straight shot to forever, do you hold the steering wheel perfectly still? No, you move it back and forth constantly, making minute corrections to the course you're on. That continuous moving and adjusting of the steering wheel is so familiar, so second nature, that you probably never think about it anymore.

But if you decided to hold the wheel rigidly in place, you'd be off the road within less than a minute. And life is exactly like that.

By the way, this constant-course-correction mode doesn't apply only to driving cars on imperfectly engineered asphalt roadways. It also happens in the most sophisticated types of travel we've ever invented. It happens in space flight.

On its way to landing astronauts safely on the surface of the moon, the miracle of modern engineering that was an Apollo rocket was actually on course only 2 to 3 percent of the time. Which means that for at least 97 percent of the time it took to get from the Earth to the moon, it was *off course*. In a journey of nearly a quarter of a million miles, the vehicle was actually on track for only 7,500 miles. Or to put it another way, for every half-hour the ship was in flight, it was on course for less than one minute. And it reached the moon—safely—and returned to tell the tale.

How was such a thing possible? Because modern space travel is a masterful example of slight edge course-correction in action.

If this machine, at the time one of the most sophisticated, expensive, and finely calibrated pieces of technology ever devised, was correcting its own off-course errors twenty-nine minutes out of every thirty, is it reasonable to expect that you could do better than that? Let's say you were able to match an Apollo rocket's degree of accuracy in the pursuit of your own goals: that would mean you'd be perfectly on target and on course no more than ten days in any given year. The next time you're giving yourself a hard time because you feel like you've gotten off track, think about the Apollo program, and give yourself a break.

For those who lack a grasp of the slight edge, being off course is something to be avoided at all costs. After all, if you're off course you're failing, right? But those who understand the slight edge embrace Thomas Watson's philosophy about failure. Here's the more extended version of Watson's statement:

Would you like me to give you the formula for success? It's quite simple, really. Double your rate of failure…. You're thinking of failure as the enemy of success. But it isn't at all. You can be discouraged by failure—or you can learn from it. So go ahead and make mistakes. Make all you can. Because, remember that's where you'll find success. On the other side of failure.

Remember, Armstrong and Aldrin did walk on the moon, and the only reason they did is that *the rocket got there*. And so can you. Why? Because of continuous course correction.

Your Internal Gyroscope

The device that enabled the rocket to continually make those adjustments, that allowed it to bring itself back on track every time it was off, was the rocket's computerized guidance system, the heart of which was a gyroscope. You may have played with a toy gyroscope as a child. You remember: you wind it up with a string like a top and make it spin, and no matter how you hold it or what you do to it, it remains upright as long as it's spinning. The force created by that toy gyroscope is so powerful that the thing can balance on the tip of your finger or dance upright along a string. The gyroscope at the heart of an Apollo rocket's guidance system is essentially the same thing: a spinning mass mounted in a base that retains the same orientation no matter in what direction the base itself is moving.

So the rocket starts from point A (its current position) and heads for point B (the moon). As it travels its first few miles, it gets slightly off course. Now the rocket's gyroscope shows one reading, while the rocket's instruments show that it's actually headed in a slightly different direction. But the gyroscope is always pointed in the *right* direction, the direction the ship actually wants to go.

The computer processor detects that the rocket's off course and tells it to make an adjustment. If the processor and the rocket were speaking English, the conversation might sound something like this:

> Processor: "Rocket, you're 1.27 degrees north—bring it back to 1.29."
> Rocket: "Okay... done."
> Processor: "Good... Whoa, that's too much, now you're 1.30—move it 0.01 degrees south."
> Rocket: "No problem, I'll do that, too."
> Processor: "Great—no, wait, too far west. Adjust

course 0.067 degrees."

Rocket: "Got it, consider it done."

Processor: "Whoops, too much, come back 0.012."

Rocket: "Right, 0.012... how's that?"

Processor: "Little too far north again, ease back to 1.27... "

And so it goes, from here to the moon, a constantly occurring series of adjustments turning what is predominantly a string of failures into ultimate success.

You have a gyroscope, too, and it works in much the same way, if you allow it to. Your gyroscope is your vision of where you're going—in other words, your dream. Your processor is the slight edge: a consistent series of tiny, seemingly insignificant actions, easy to do and easy not to do, and in this case, doing them leads you directly to the moon instead of shooting off into the vacuum of outer space.

You're hungry. There's a bunch of greasy junk food in a vending machine beckoning you. Your gyroscope is spinning—it's focused on your health. Your processor goes, *click, click, whirr...* and you choose a salad or a piece of fruit instead.

There's a display rack of books and magazines. You reach toward the copy of *People* because it has a juicy piece of gossip about a movie star that you'd just love to read, and it's only a few bucks, and you've got some time over lunch, and—*click, whirr, click,* and instead you decide to go back to your car for your copy of *The Happiness Advantage.* Or to take a brisk twenty-minute walk around the park.

You're having coffee with friends and they start complaining about their work, their bosses, their jobs—*click, click, whirrrrr*—and you find a way to change the subject, because you know that if the talk doesn't get onto a positive track within another sixty seconds, you'll have to find a reason to excuse yourself.

Knowing where it is you want to go, and knowing how the slight edge works to take you there, you make the adjustments automatically. You make those right choices, the ones that serve you. You do those simple, seemingly insignificant things that forward your progress up the success curve. You read good books. You listen to motivating audios. You hang around successful people who empower you. You're a 5 percenter, a winner, a success.

Once you know the slight edge, you know that in getting from point A to point B you'll be off track most of the time. And you know that it's the adjustments—those little, seemingly insignificant corrections in direction—that have the most power in your life.

John McDonald, author of the classic book *The Message of a Master*, wrote a beautiful description of this internal gyroscope and how it works:

You return again and again to take the proper course—guided by what? By the picture in mind of the place you are headed for.

You may have heard the expression, "It's not how you plan your work, it's how you work your plan." That's *almost* true. But a solid slight edge strategy means doing both at the same time—one tiny, course-correcting step at a time. The slight edge is a process. You are constantly choosing which way you go: up with the 5 percent, or down with the 95 percent. You don't just make that choice once and then say, "Ahh, I'm finished, now I'm all set." You make that choice moment to moment to moment—and keep making it, every month and every day, for the rest of your life. At first, it requires your constant awareness. In time, your internal gyroscope learns the drill so well that it becomes automatic.

And what does or doesn't become automatic will spell the different between beach bum and millionaire, misery and joy, life on the failure curve or life on the success curve.

A Penny (That Is, $10 Million) for Your Thoughts

There is a running commentary in your head, and chances are good that most of the time you're not even aware of what it's saying. Sometimes that running commentary even spills out into the things you say to yourself out loud. But most of the time, it's that silent voice whispering between your ears—and there is no voice more powerful.

There's a reason Napoleon Hill didn't title his book, *Build Sound Businesses and Grow Rich*, or *Do the Right Things and Grow Rich*, or *Take Action and Grow Rich*. Sure, doing the right things, taking action, building sound businesses, all good stuff. But Hill knew that wasn't the point. He knew the secret to how wealth actually happens. He called it *Think and Grow Rich*. He did that for the same reason James Allen titled his phenomenal little classic *As a Man Thinketh*, and not *As a Man Doeth*.

Your own thoughts are one of the most powerful examples of the slight edge there is. Your thoughts multiply themselves by the power of compounding interest and, like a mental water hyacinth, over time (often a lot less time than you might expect) they come to cover the pond of your mind.

This is true of positive thoughts. And just as true of negative thoughts.

As we saw earlier, it's not even a matter of "Be careful what you wish for, you just might get it." Forget wishing—it's a matter of what you think, period. Because what you think, multiplied by action plus time, will create what you get. You, through the power of your own thoughts, are the most influential person in your life. Which means there is nobody more effective at *undermining* your success—and nobody more effective at *supporting* your success.

The purpose of investing in yourself is not to accumulate skills or fluency in specific areas of knowledge. While those things are valuable, they are not the principal aim. The principal aim in self-investment is to train *how you think* and *what you think*.

So let's look at how thoughts actually work. Like learning (like everything), there are two kinds, and it's critical that you know how they work together.

The human brain is the most complex, powerful information-processing device known. Your brain is made up of about a hundred billion neurons, and it has the capacity to perform some ten quadrillion unique operations per second. Every second of every day, your brain is keeping track of billions of different metabolic activities going on throughout your body, without your conscious awareness—and it has been doing this every second of every day you've been alive. But there is something about the brain that most people don't realize, and that is where in the brain the real power lies.

There are two different broad types of function happening here, the conscious brain and unconscious brain. Your conscious brain is the part that does what we think of as "thinking." It focuses intensely on one thing at a time, something like a flashlight beam scanning a darkened room.

The conscious brain is incredibly powerful at what it does, but its scope is very limited. For example, most people cannot hold more than a handful of digits in their head at one time. You can prove this to yourself: open up the phone book, read any three phone numbers at random, then close the book and see if you can remember even *one* of them.

And the unconscious? It can remember *trillions* of phone numbers at the same time. If your conscious brain is like a flashlight, illuminating one object at a time, your subconscious brain is like a superfloodlight, illuminating everything at once—but only on a subconscious level.

Your conscious brain is easily distracted. The average person loses conscious focus six to ten times per minute. How often does the subconscious lose focus? Try *never*.

Who's Really Running the Store?

Here lies the key to our destiny that most people don't grasp. We think of our conscious functions—our will, our conscious decisions, our conscious thoughts—as what is "us," and our subconscious as something vaguely going on under the surface that's maybe not so important. The truth is, the subconscious runs virtually *everything*.

Try this: make a fist with your thumb sticking up, like an "all systems go!" sign, and hold that fist out at arm's length. Now, look at your thumbnail. The area of your thumbnail at that distance is about the area that your eye can focus on with its focal vision; everything else lies in your peripheral vision. That's something like your conscious and subconscious: your conscious can focus really well, but only on a tiny, minuscule part of your life at any one time. Your subconscious keeps track of *everything*.

Have you ever driven or walked a familiar route while your mind was wandering, thinking about something going on at school, or drifting back through a movie you'd seen, and suddenly you wound up at your destination? And it was almost like you didn't even know how you got there? That's an example of automatic pilot: your conscious mind had learned the route so well that it handed it over to your subconscious mind. Just like the way you tie your shoes, or the way you make your legs walk. Just like the way you answer, "Yeah?" when you hear your name called. Just like all the quadrillions of metabolic functions that you do without thinking.

The sobering fact is, you do 99.99 percent of everything you do on automatic pilot.

The sobering fact is, we all do 99.99 percent *of our lives* on automatic pilot.

In other words, in the same way you take a walk and end up at home without even thinking about it, that's how most people end up in the life they're living at age thirty, or fifty, or seventy. "How did I get here?!" On automatic pilot. What determines where you end up? It's all a question of what route you have programmed into your subconscious. And that's something that you can let others program for you (your school, parents, teachers, friends, TV, etc.)—or you can choose to program it yourself.

It's up to you.

So, how do you program that life route? How do you determine the choices and decisions that your subconscious makes for you in carving out your life path? The same way you learned to tie your shoes: you create it first with intention, with your *conscious mind*, and then repeat it over and over, in slight-edge fashion, until it is handed off to your subconscious— at which point those three magic words kick in:

It becomes automatic.

Click, click, whrrr...

Personal Stories from
The Slight Edge Readers

The Slight Edge has been especially helpful to me in the area of my personal development. I have always been around people who felt that it was a waste of time to sit and read books. Now I take the time every day to read at least ten pages. Over the past year I have read fifteen books, and the wealth of knowledge and ideas I have gained is priceless.

—*Jane Lehman, Lexington, Michigan*

I was introduced to the slight edge philosophy when I was nineteen. Before that I never really saw myself doing much with my life. I couldn't hold conversations with strangers and I truly wasn't interested in people. I wouldn't say I was a troublemaker, but I was willing to settle for mediocre. I was an average student in high school and dropped out of college my first year.

After reading *The Slight Edge*, I realized that I wanted more. I started diving into other great books, reading ten pages a day, and started transforming. I soon found that I genuinely wanted to be successful, and I began talking to other people about success. At every job I held, I shot straight up to management, ahead of people who had worked at the establishment for years. Even more importantly, successful people began being attracted to my attitude and my energy.

I'll never forget the day at the gym when a highly successful real estate developer approached me. He said he had a great location for a new business. He said if I was interested he would finance the entire project in the beginning and help me get the new company running until I could repay him through the cash flow of the business. The opportunity literally fell into my lap—and I jumped on it. The business has now been up and running successfully for a year, and in a couple of years I will begin expanding my company. I'm twenty-two years old, and if it weren't for the slight edge principles and for my learning the discipline of investing in myself by reading ten pages of a good book every day, I wouldn't be the man I am today.

—*James Fortner, New Haven, Missouri*

Essential Points from Chapter 12

↗ The wisest investment you can make is to invest in your own continuous learning and development.

↗ Learning by studying and learning by doing—book smarts and street smarts—are the two essential pistons of the engine of learning.

↗ On the path to a goal you will be off-course most of the time. Which means the only way to reach a goal is through constant and continuous course correction.

↗ Most of your life—99.99 percent—is made up of things you do an automatic pilot. Which means it's essential that you take charge of your automatic pilot's training.

13. Learn from Mentors

> "You must hold your head high and keep those fists down. No matter what anyone else says to you, don't let 'em get your goat. Try fightin' with your head for a change."
> —*Atticus Finch, in* To Kill a Mockingbird *by Harper Lee*

In the previous chapter we explored the idea that there are two principal types of learning: learning through study and learning through doing. But there is a third type of learning, too. And in a way I've saved the best for last, because utilizing this third type of learning will tremendously accelerate the other two. It is *knowledge through modeling*.

Throughout human history, and long before there were such things as books, universities, or continuing ed programs, there has been one tried and true path for learning a skill, craft, art, trade, or profession: go study with a master. All the great learning traditions say the same thing: if you want to learn how to do something well, go find someone who has already mastered that skill, and apprentice yourself.

The truth is, this third type of learning isn't simply a valuable add-on to the other two. It's essential. Learning pure information is not enough, and while adding the street smarts you gain from applying that information through personal experience can take you far, even that is not enough to go all the way toward the successful achievement of your goals. You need some way to process all that information and experience and integrate it. And there is only one reliable, solid way to do that: find someone else who has already achieved mastery in the area you're looking at, and model your behavior based on their experience.

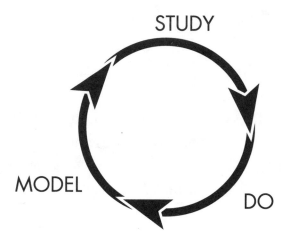

Personal development is not something you can pursue as an arm-chair expert, not something you can master from the sidelines. It has to be a contact sport—one where you are in contact with others who can help you on your journey.

What we're talking about here is the power of a *mentor*.

The Man Who Believed Me into Being

As I said earlier, while growing up I was never anything but average in everything I did. I had average grades, average athletic abilities, average social skills, average everything. When I threw myself back into schoolwork, after my day of disgust on the Daytona golf course, I applied myself like crazy, knowing that the only way I could accomplish anything beyond average would be through sheer effort and persistence. And as I said, it worked: I got straight A's.

But I still saw myself as average.

It wasn't until I got that job as an intern at the Albuquerque airport that my view of myself as "no better than average" started to change, and it changed because of one thing and one thing only: a man named Clyde Share.

My job was not very exciting. As an accounting intern, I would spend my day crunching numbers on an adding machine at a little desk in a hole of an office somewhere in the back of the building. I'm not sure anyone even knew I was there. Then one day, for whatever reason I will never know, Mr. Share stopped over at my desk and asked if I wanted to go get a cup of coffee.

An accomplished and extremely successful guy in his sixties, Clyde Share was the airport director. Airport director was an appointed position, and it meant he ran the entire airport and was in charge of all its 140-odd employees, and he reported directly to the mayor and city council. Clyde was also well respected both in Albuquerque and throughout the national aviation community.

Of course, I knew who he was. In fact, over the months I'd been there I'd passed him in the halls every now and then and said hi. But we'd never had any sort of conversation. And here he was, standing at my little desk, asking if I wanted to join him for a cup of coffee. I knew I had to say something brilliant, so I did.

I said, "Sure."

We went to the staff lounge and talked for a little while over a cup of coffee, and immediately hit it off. We started making that cup of coffee a weekly thing, and then it went from once a week to twice a week, to every other day, to a daily routine.

And that's how it happened that Clyde Share took me under his wing. It was the first time in my life that I felt I was being acknowledged and embraced by a person of importance. And it suddenly changed how others saw me. I could tell that people in the airport were saying, "Why is Mr. Share taking an interest in this college kid? What does he see in him that we don't see? Maybe we should look at him differently, too." And because they started perceiving me differently, I started perceiving myself differently—and started acting differently. I started acting like someone of value, someone who was going places.

Meanwhile, Clyde could see that I was working my way through school and just scraping by, and after a while he created a position called "night supervisor" and offered me the job. Being night supervisor meant I could stay there by myself at night and use the time to do my homework. The rest of the admin staff would get off work at five, so I'd show up at four and stay from then till midnight. There wasn't really anything for me to do, other than be there in case some extra work came up (which was rarely). Essentially, it meant I was being paid to get my homework done.

As my relationship with Clyde kept evolving, through that

connection I started becoming friends with the head of security, the head of maintenance, and the head of field operations. After getting my undergrad degree I went on to grad school—and kept working at the airport. Eventually Clyde encouraged me to apply for the position of airport manager when an opening came up. I did, and so did a ton of other applicants—but I was the one who got the job.

Word started getting around the business community that this twenty-three-year-old kid had taken a position as airport manager at Albuquerque International, and it made a stir. Pretty soon Texas Instruments was knocking on my door. They brought me in to interview, and two days later they were sending me in to see the president. They hired me, put me on a management fast track (after my terrifying experiences in sales), and by the age of twenty-eight I was manager of TI's Intelligent Systems Division.

And it all started with that cup of coffee.

My mom has always said, "Clyde Share was the most important man in your life." And she's right. She saw the transformation that happened when Mr. Share took me under his wing.

It's amazing the impact one person can have on your life, just from the influence of how they see you, and what they see in you that you may not even see in yourself. Clyde Share believed in me. And because he believed in me, I started believing more in myself. It was as if he *believed* me into existence.

Choose Your Heroes

One of the most valuable things I learned from Clyde Share was the power of a mentor: that the quickest and surest path to raising the quality of your life is to start hanging out with people who have been there and done that.

If you want to be a great public speaker, spend time with great speakers. If you want to be a success in business, then find a way to spend time in the company of successful businesspeople. If it's important to you to be a terrific parent, the best thing you can do to further that aim is to spend lots of time with men and women who have mastered parenting.

You can define a society by the heroes it admires. You can also define a person by the heroes he or she aspires to emulate. Who are your heroes? Who are you modeling yourself after?

The 95 percent on the failure curve tend to accept the heroes society plants in front of them: film stars (America's version of royalty), rock stars, sports stars. I can certainly admire these folks, but I always ask myself, "Can I emulate them?" Practically speaking, can I convert my admiration for these people into constructive modeling that pragmatically increases my learning and tangibly moves my own life forward?

If not, maybe I'm better off looking for other heroes.

Too often we make heroes out of people who can't really help us, whose lives are fantasies, not genuine role models. Take a look at who your heroes are—write down a list and examine it. Ask yourself, "Can I become like them? Are these people doing the kinds of things that I aspire to do and living the kinds of lives that I aspire to live? Can they really help me become who I want to become?"

Whatever goals you aspire to, seek out people who have achieved the same or very similar goals or who are well along that path, and go camp on their doorsteps or do whatever you can to associate with them, emulate them, and let their grasp, understanding, and mastery of the subject rub off on you.

What makes Alcoholics Anonymous so successful is not the information they hand out—it's the mentorship they provide, both as a community and as individuals. When you join AA, or any other twelve-step program, you get instant access to a community of people who have gone where you're going, as well as an individual mentor or *sponsor*. If they only handed out DVDs and brochures, put up a website about how to deal with alcoholism, and left it at that, how many people do you think would actually get successfully into recovery? Not many. Of course, they need the information, but what makes the program truly work is the environment and associations that are created around that person.

The same is true for personal development and any change we want to see in our life. It has to consist of information *and* a supportive environment.

In AA, your sponsor isn't just a friend. In a very practical sense, he or she is your hero: the person who goes before, and who lights the path with a torch so you can better see your way. That's what any mentor does. Do they teach you information, show you skills, pass on knowledge? Sometimes. But more than that, they light the way.

Who are you Mentors?

Tweet his or her name and how they lifted you up and include #SlightEdge or post it to our Facebook wall at www.facebook.com/slightedge. Spread their wisdom with the rest of the Slight Edge community!

The Law of Association

Perhaps you've heard it said that your income tends to equal the average of the incomes of your five best friends. It's true, and the same principle applies not only to your finances but to every aspect of your life. Your level of health will tend to be about the average level of health of your five best friends. Your degree of happiness will tend to reflect about how happy your five closest friends are. Your personal development will be at about the average level of personal development of your five best friends. Your relationships, financial health, attitudes, level of success in your career, and everything else about your life will tend to be very close to the average level of each of these conditions in your five closest friends and associates.

We all understand this principle instinctively; our language is shot through with idioms that reflect it:

→ You're known by the company you keep.

→ Show me where you fish and I'll show you what you catch.

→ Birds of a feather flock together.

You are the combined average of the five people you associate with most—including the way you walk, talk, act, think, and dress. Your income, your accomplishments, even your values and philosophy will reflect them.

If the five people around you have negative philosophies, it's virtually impossible for you to have a positive philosophy. If the five people around you are consistently complaining, living in the past, blaming others for their difficulties, and thinking and acting in a generally negative way, then what are the odds of you finding your way onto the success curve? Slim to none. If you consistently associate with negative people, it's highly unlikely you will succeed at having and maintaining a positive approach to your life.

When I was busy being Gorgeous George the beach bum, I was also busily hanging out with a crowd who, frankly, were not really going anywhere in their lives. We had gravitated to the spring break capital of the world for a reason: our lives were a perpetual spring break from everything—from achievement, from accomplishment, from progress, from meaning. A few years later, I was hanging out with a nationally recognized man of accomplishment who spent his days being the director of a major municipal airport. Is it any wonder the path of my life changed?

Become acutely aware of who you are modeling. This has everything to do with your philosophy and your attitudes, which have more to do with your actions and what you're creating in your life than any other factor.

You know why birds of a feather flock together? Because they're all heading in the same direction. Look at the people with whom you flock, the company you keep: what destination are they headed for? And is that where you want to be headed?

Look at the people around you. Are they more successful than you are? Are they people who live the kinds of lives you aspire to live, or the kinds of lives you hope to leave behind? On what side of the slight edge are they living—on the success curve or the failure curve? Is the slight edge working for them or against them? Where will they be in twenty years? And are they pulling you up or dragging you down?

This is a pass or fail test; there is no *maybe* about it. Remember, there is no standing still. Everything curves. We're all going in one of two directions, either up or down. Your association with each person you know is either empowering you, or it's not—taking you up the success curve or down the failure curve.

How can you tell? One way is to go back to the business of future and past, responsibility and blame. When you and this particular friend get together, are your conversations about responsibility, big dreams, and bold initiatives? Or do they often seem to work their way around to blame or its cousins—envy, jealousy, resentment, and irritation?

Do your conversations focus more on the future or on the past? It's only natural, when you share a common history and set of experiences, to enjoy reminiscing over fond memories; that's not what I mean. What I mean is, does your relationship have a forward-looking, positive feeling to it, or do the two of you get together and always seem to circle events of the past, like a cat endlessly turning round and round before it can settle down to sleep? If your relationship with someone has a theme of blame and feeds on the past, it's disempowering. If it has a theme of responsibility, self-reflection, and change and feels like something moving into the future, it's empowering.

We are all either building our own dreams or building somebody else's. To put a sharper point on it, we're either building our own dreams—or building our nightmares.

Sometimes You Need to Run the Other Direction

There are two kinds of people in the world. There are those who brighten the room the moment they enter with their positive energy and excitement for life. I call them *givers*. And then there are the *takers*, those who seem to actually dim the room with their lack of excitement and depressing outlook on life. You know people like this. They dish the latest gossip on who's doing what, complain about how much they hate their job, and make fun of others who are doing their best to be beacons of positivity. *Takers* and *dimmers* are professionals in the art of distraction, experts at drawing people's attention away from the task at hand. They will drive you crazy if you let them.

Longevity experts are now telling us that keeping a positive outlook is just as critical a factor to health and long life as diet and exercise! You can't afford to have people around you who are consistently acting as a drag on your positive outlook.

I can feel a dimmer approaching at a hundred paces. You probably can too. There might be fifty people in the room, but you can feel that one who is sucking the oxygen out of the place and draining the life out of the other forty-nine.

Years ago, when I was in the solar business, I had a mentor named Carol Cooke, who knew everything there was to know about the solar industry. She also knew a valuable thing or two about life, and she shared some sage advice with me about dimmers. "Jeffrey," she said, "here's how I see it. There's one born every minute, and the sad thing is, most of them live. And here's the thing: you're not going to change them. But what you *can* do is run the other direction."

That may not sound like the most compassionate philosophy in the world, but let me tell you, there's nothing compassionate about letting yourself get sucked into a vortex of negativity. The best thing I can do to serve the world around me is to keep myself in a state where I can best contribute—and I can't do that if I'm being dragged down by an environment of cynicism and self-pitying complaint. I want to spend my time with people who have an infectiously positive attitude, who bring energy and vitality to the table, and who brighten the room.

There may be some people with whom you're now spending two days a week where you might decide you need to take that down to two hours. There may also be people with whom you're spending only two minutes, where you'll realize you need to spend far *more* time with them—two hours or two days. And you will find times when what you really need to do is simply disassociate yourself from someone. That's a part of the Law of Association, too.

For many people, I think this can be a tough aspect of the slight edge to understand and accept. Most everything else about the slight edge, as you already know, is easy to do—but disassociating yourself from people who do not empower you can be a painful and difficult thing to do. Especially if you love them. Especially if they are old friends or dear family.

So take heart: by "disassociating" I don't necessarily mean cutting them out of your life completely. But casual relationships deserve casual time—not quality time. There are people with whom you can spend two minutes, but not two hours. There are people with whom you can spend two hours, but not two days.

This part of slight edge thinking requires a compassionate *awareness*. Having compassion and having direction are not mutually exclusive;

they just take careful thought and discernment. You're not judging those people; you're simply asking yourself to be honest about whether or not those relationships are empowering you and helping to support your purpose and realize your dreams.

Form a Mastermind

Of all the books I have ever encountered in my pursuit of excellence and the how-to's of success, Napoleon Hill's masterpiece *Think and Grow Rich* is the most influential. When I ask successful people what factors most contributed to their success, this is the book they most commonly cite.

During the twenty years it took Napoleon Hill to write *Think and Grow Rich*, he interviewed more than 500 of the richest and most successful men and women in the world, and then painstakingly analyzed what he'd learned and spelled it out in the form of thirteen "success secrets." One of the most fascinating success secrets these people shared in common was something he terms the "mastermind."

"No two minds ever come together without thereby creating a third, invisible, intangible force, which may be likened to a third mind," writes Hill. A group of like-minded, achievement-oriented individuals, he explained, could come together to create an association far greater than the sum of its parts, thus dramatically leveraging each other's success.

As two examples from distinctly different sides of the spectrum of human endeavor, he cites Henry Ford and Mahatma Gandhi as masters of the mastermind principle, which he defines as: "The coordination of knowledge and effort of two or more people, who work toward a definite purpose, in the spirit of harmony."

Applying Hill's principle is simple: surround yourself with people of like mind and different talents and temperaments with the purpose of serving the goals of every member of the group. Associate with these people on a regular basis.

Remember that you're always dealing with gravity: one against nineteen, all the time. The 95 percent will always tend to be cynical, skeptical, and negative; even when motivated by the best of intentions, they will attack you and bring you down.

Apply the Law of Association. Create your own mastermind, a group of those who have chosen to live among the 5 percent, and let them support you, let them be the lift beneath the wings of your dreams.

Looking for a Mastermind Partner?

Visit www.facebook.com/yourslightedge. We have a great community of slight-edgers who would love to help you!

Become the Mentor Yourself

I'm often asked, "How do I become a leader?" In our push-button, instant-everything world, people often seem to want to take an express route from the first stages of learning straight to leadership. But of course, it doesn't work that way.

How does it work? Leadership is not something you *do*; it is something that grows organically out of the natural rhythm of learning.

When you start at the beginning of anything, you're at the highest level of anxiety. As you learn—through study and doing, information and experience, book smarts and street smarts—you gradually lower your level of anxiety by raising your level of mastery. As you continue climbing that ladder of knowledge (remember, right foot–left foot, right foot–left foot, study-action, study-action) you keep your eyes on worthy mentors, always using learning through modeling as your learning gyroscope to keep you on track.

Using those three dimensions of learning—study, do, model—with slight edge persistence, in time your level of mastery rises to the point where you turn around and realize others are modeling *you*. You have yourself become worthy of emulating, of serving as a guide and hero to others. The cream has become butter; the hyacinth of knowledge has covered the pond of your effort. You have grown into leadership—and now *you're* the mentor.

Personal Stories from
The Slight Edge Readers

When I first heard of the slight edge philosophy, I had just dropped out of college and had a newborn baby. I was involved with people and activities that I'm now ashamed of. When my wife, Becky, came home, she was blown away to find me with a book in my hand instead of a videogame controller.

Fast-forward … Today I'm proud of who I've become by reading *The Slight Edge* and applying it to my life. I never realized what you can accomplish by adjusting your day-to-day activities, and that I could become a better person by working on myself every day. Reading ten pages a day of a good book has completely changed my thinking. My self-esteem is up, I carry myself so much better, and I'm not afraid to talk to groups of people. Now people ask *me* for advice and to mentor their kids.

My ten-year-old son Camden reads *The Slight Edge*—five pages a day. There is a noticeable difference between him and the other kids in his class. What a blessing to be able to teach your children the proper philosophies so they don't make the same mistakes their parents might have made. We have a nice-sized library of personal development books and I'm looking forward to seeing it grow.

The Slight Edge book started it all. It literally saved my life. Now I'm on my way to becoming successful, and I want to help everyone learn the slight edge philosophy so they, too, can change.

Some people want to make a quantum shift overnight. To those people, I say this: if you follow the slight edge philosophy, you can change *anything* in your life. Your past does not equal your future. Read *The Slight Edge* over and over, apply it to your life and to your business, and watch the transformation!

—*Howard Smith, Macon, Missouri*

Essential Points from Chapter 13

↗ If you want to learn how to do something well, find someone who has mastered that skill and apprentice yourself.

↗ Choose your heroes carefully: are they genuine role models you want to emulate?

↗ Choose your associates: everything about your life will closely reflect the lives of your five closest friends.

↗ Sometimes you need to let go and disassociate.

↗ Form and use a mastermind: two minds are better than one, and five are even better.

14. Use Your Slight Edge Allies

> "Be not afraid of going slowly;
> be afraid only of standing still."
>
> —*Chinese proverb*

The more you become familiar with the slight edge and how it operates, the more you will come to recognize its presence and influence in your life in many forms and under many disguises.

It is the irresistible force delivered by the tidal wash that polishes the sharp edges of a rocky reef to porcelain smoothness. As Lao Tzu said about the *Tao*, "it is like water, giving life to the ten thousand things," and it is as ever-present in all aspects of life as the water molecule is in biology.

The slight edge has many faces—all of them invaluable partners in your pursuit of your fondest aspirations. On your path of mastery onto the success curve, you are not alone. You have powerful allies at your disposal, four slight edge forces that, once you recognize them in your life, you can harness in your pursuit of your dreams, like four wild horses all harnessed to a single chariot. They are momentum, completion, reflection, and celebration.

Use the Power of Momentum

Who won the race—the tortoise or the hare? We all know the answer to that one. Yet we live in a world where most everyone has come to expect instant this and instant that, and if we don't get the results we're after fast and faster, we quit.

Get rich quick. The fast lane. One-click ordering. That fellow standing in front of the microwave muttering, "Hurry uuuup, hurry uuuup...." We've come to expect fast results, to *demand* them—but fast, faster, fastest is a strategy that will eventually take you *down* the slight edge curve to the *unhappy* life.

There's a reason I titled an earlier chapter "Slow Down to Go Fast." The Aesop fable was dead-on accurate: fast is not always optimal, and often does *not* win the race. Here's how MIT professor Peter Senge put it in his business classic, *The Fifth Discipline: The Art & Practice of the Learning Organization*:

> Virtually all natural systems, from ecosystems to animals to organizations, have intrinsically optimal rates of growth. The optimal rate is far less than the fastest possible growth. When growth becomes excessive—as it does in cancer—the system itself will seek to compensate by slowing down; perhaps putting the organization's survival at risk in the process.

You've seen all kinds of examples of things that grow too fast for their own good. The business that expanded too rapidly and then self-destructed. A rock star, movie star, star athlete, or star politician who became a shooting star and came crashing and burning down. The housing bubble of the mid-2000s—and where it ended up in the late 2000s. Going too fast, or growing too fast, often puts the system's (or the person's) survival at risk. Faster can easily turn out to be slower.

Part of learning the slight edge is finding your own "intrinsically optimal rate of growth," and it is always served best by a step-by-step approach of constant, never-ending improvement, which lays solid foundations and builds upon them over and over. The slight edge *is* your optimal rate of growth. Simple disciplines compounded over time. That's how the tortoise won; that's how you get to be a winner, too.

Having said that, now let me ask this: what is the real point of the story of the tortoise and the hare? All together now: *Slow and steady wins the race*, right? But notice something here: the point is not that there's any special virtue to moving slowly. There's nothing inherently good about slowness, and it's just as possible to move too slowly as to move too quickly.

The key word in the Aesop moral is not "slow." The key word here is *steady*.

Steady wins the race. That's the truth of it. Because *steady* is what taps into the power of the slight edge.

The fable of the tortoise and the hare is really about the remarkable power of *momentum*. Newton's second law of thermodynamics: a body at rest tends to stay at rest—and a body in motion tends to remain in motion. That's why your activity is so important. Once you're in motion, it's easy to keep on keeping on. Once you stop, it's hard to change from stop to go.

I coach people on how to build successful businesses by doing very simple, easy-to-do actions every day, just like the Ten Core Commitments our team used after that merger I described in chapter 4. I've found that it's far more effective to take one business-building action every day for a week, than to take seven, or ten, or even two dozen all at once and then take the rest of the week off. People who do the first, week in and week out, build a successful business; people who do the second, don't—*even if they actually take a greater number of those business-building actions than the first group.*

Why not? No momentum. After six days off they have to start all over again, getting themselves geared up and inspired to get back into action. It can take a good amount of energy and initiative to get yourself started in a new activity—but it takes far, far less to keep yourself doing it once you've started.

There's another reason once a day for a week is better than seven times in one day, once a week: the daily rhythm of the thing starts to change you. It becomes part of your routine, and as it does, it becomes part of who you are. That doesn't happen with a once-in-a-while, all-out effort.

Imagine taking a twenty-minute brisk walk in the morning, and then in the late afternoon, working out on a home gym for another twenty minutes. Now imagine that for a week, you did that every day. How would you feel at the end of the week?

Now instead, what if on that first day you took a 140-minute walk (that's more than two hours) and that afternoon, spent another 140 minutes on the home gym—and then did nothing for the next six days? *Steady wins the race.*

When you're in motion, it's also far easier to make positive changes in your direction. It's like steering a car: when the car's sitting still, moving the wheel is hard work, but when it's moving, even at only 10 or 20 mph, turning is a breeze. It's a breeze because you're already *in the flow.*

The slight edge is a flow, and it moves at its own pace, automatically homing in on optimal growth rates. Part of understanding the slight edge is learning to go with the flow. You can be as impatient as you like, but it won't bother the slight edge. It's always moving at its own optimal speed, with or without your consent, whether you are aware of it moving or not. World-class champion athlete Dan Millman, in his magnificent classic *Way of the Peaceful Warrior* (which is my favorite book of all time), said it best:

Let it go and let it flow.

To make the most of the slight edge flow, you'll want to match the speed of your growth and development to the natural progression of the slight edge. And that you accomplish naturally, by having and steadily applying a slight edge strategy. A body in motion, staying in motion. Momentum.

It's easy to stay active. It's also easy not to. And if you stop, it won't kill you today—but that simple error in judgment, compounded over time, will destroy the getting of any goal you're after.

Mary Kay Ash put it simply: "Give yourself something to work toward—*constantly.*"

Use the Power of Completion

Another way you gather momentum and harness it to your advantage is by regularly practicing an activity called *completion.*

Are there any things that are incomplete in your life? Any unpaid bills? Unfinished projects? Did you borrow a book or tool you have yet to return? Is there someone who needs to hear you say, "I love you," or, "I'm sorry," or, "Thank you—I appreciate you"? Do you have any unfinished projects? Any unkept promises—taking a weekend away with your spouse, or taking your kids somewhere special? Are there any agreements or commitments you've left hanging?

Each and every incomplete thing in your life or work exerts a draining force on you, sucking the energy of accomplishment and success out of you as surely as a vampire stealing your blood. Every incomplete promise, commitment, or agreement saps your strength because it blocks your momentum and chokes off your ability to move forward, progress, or improve. Incomplete things keep calling you back to the past to take care of them.

Here's the unfortunate and powerfully destructive truth of being incomplete: it keeps the past alive. Remember, people who live on the success curve are pulled by the future, while those who dwell on the failure curve are pulled by the past. And a surefire way to be forced to live as a prisoner of your past is not to complete things.

Is it easy to do? Yes, and also… —wait. Hang on a second. Let's stop and consider that one for just a moment.

No… you know what, actually it's *not* always easy to complete those incomplete things in life. Not when you've got a truckload of them to take care of. That stack of incompletions can loom larger than the Sears Tower. They can be absolutely overwhelming. Especially when you realize that whatever might have been keeping you from completing them in the first place—fear of confronting the issue, feeling intimidated or overwhelmed by it, worrying it might be difficult or uncomfortable—well, *that* has been compounded by the slight edge, too. That's the slight edge working, again, only working *against* you.

That's how the pile got so big to begin with. And the truth is, even those incompletions that seem difficult to do would have been a lot easier to do when they first came up than they might be now.

Approaching that stack of undones with the slight edge in hand is not only the best way to deal with them, it's the *only* way you'll ever deal with them. Take on those incompletions in your life just as you took on learning to walk. Baby steps, one at a time, letting the force of the slight edge work for you to help you complete whatever needs completing.

Earlier you met Valerie Thomas, whose daughter was able to triumph over unwanted weight gain by applying the slight edge to time on her stationary bike. Here is what Valerie has to say about the power of completion:

"I lived in a house with a huge unfinished basement that had seventeen years' worth of clothes, items, boxes, equipment, toys, you name it all around. There was one small path to walk to the back room to get to the washer and dryer. Eventually, time came when I had to move from that house.

"I thought I would never get to the basement. I cringed every time I thought of it. However, after learning the concept of the slight edge I decided that every time I went down to the basement to do clothes or get food, I would handle just one bag or box. Before I knew it, I saw light, and before long it was all cleared out for a successful move."

Take on any one of your "incomplete" projects, one at a time. And if even that one project seems like too huge a mountain to climb, rummage around its foothills until you find an initial step you can take. The biggest meal is still eaten one bite at a time. Think of the title of Art Williams' bestseller, *All You Can Do Is All You Can Do, But All You Can Do Is Enough*. So find something you *can* do, and do that. Make that phone call. Apologize. Clear out that basement. Write that letter. Give fifteen minutes to completing something every day.

Each time you do complete something, you get to move on with your luggage a little lighter and a bit more spring in your step.

Is it easy not to do? Absolutely. And if you don't do it today, will it destroy you? You know the rest, so sing along…

Use the Power of Reflection

In my business, I often see people make the mistake of thinking they are being productive because they are being busy. Being productive and being busy are not necessarily the same thing. Doing things won't create your success; doing *the right things* will. And if you're doing the wrong things, doing more of them won't increase your odds of success. It will only make you fail faster.

Nobody sets out to fail. We all believe we're headed down the right path, or at least a reasonably right one. People get out of bed, go to work, and work hard. They love their families. They put smiles on their faces. They do everything they're supposed to do and they think they've had a productive day, or at least set out to have one. And all too often, what really happened is that they spent the day treading water like a duck swimming upriver against a strong current, its little webbed feet flailing away underneath but getting him nowhere.

Everybody's busy. Everyone does the actions. But were they the right actions? Were those actions productive? Did you take a step forward? These are questions most people never take the time to think about.

Did you eat well, or did you eat poorly? Who did you associate with today? Did they empower you? How? In what way? Did you listen to good information today, or just zone out to the music? Did you engage in positive conversation, or did you gossip or complain? What did you read that contributed to your success today? Did you do any of the things unsuccessful people aren't willing to do? Whose dream did you build today—yours or somebody else's? In twelve-step programs this is called "taking a searching and fearless personal inventory." I honestly encourage you to get a little searching and get fearless with yourself. Keep your progress, or the lack of it, right in your face.

Here's a powerful exercise: Instead of writing down what you're *going* to do (chances are you've been doing that your whole adult life anyway, and it doesn't make you any better at doing them), write down at the end of the day what you *did* do that day. What actions did you take today that made you successful? Did you read ten pages of a good book? Did you eat healthy food and get some good exercise? Did you engage in positive associations? Did you do the things you need to do to be successful in your business? Did you tell somebody, "I appreciate you"?

At the end of a week, look back over your lists and take inventory. Not only will it tell you a lot about the truth of your everyday life, chances are good that the mere act of recording this daily reflection will have *already started changing* what you do.

Here's what this exercise did for me the first time I did it: after the first few days I found that, by ten in the morning, I was changing my normal course for the day and engaging in more positive slight edge actions, simply because I didn't want to face that man in the mirror empty-handed again that night.

There are lots of different ways to practice consistent self-reflection, and I don't necessarily recommend one over another, simply because everyone's different and what works best for me may not work best for you. Some people accomplish this by keeping a journal. If you choose this approach, here's the key to making it work: don't just write down a record of what happened today, along with your thoughts and feelings about what happened. Ask yourself specific slight edge questions. "In each area of my life, what are the critical, simple little things that are easy to do, and easy not to do? Did I do them? Did I move forward? Did I ride the success curve?"

Some people like keeping a journal but find it difficult to keep up day in and day out, and instead create a specific, written list of slight edge actions that they consult and check off every day. On days they don't make time to write an entry in their journal, they at least go through the list and ask themselves those questions: "In each area of my life, did I do those things that are easy to do, and easy not to do? Did I continue my momentum on the success curve?"

Some people would rather talk than write, and prefer to keep track of the day's actions out loud, in conversation. You can find a slight edge buddy, a friend who also wants to harness the power of reflection, and schedule a little time together to debrief each other. "How did the day go? In each area of my life, did I...?" Doing this every day is ideal, but you can still make it work very well with a twice-a-week call, or even a once-a-week call. The key is consistency; like the tortoise, steady wins the race.

More and more, people are choosing to achieve a higher level of productivity through reflection by working with a coach. A generation ago people thought of "coaching" only in the context of athletics. Then people realized that they had way better chances of pursuing their fitness goals if they used personal trainers. Soon high-level business executives started using individual consulting sessions with productivity consultants to coach them in their high-stakes financial and organizational game. And then the dam burst: people suddenly realized they could hire a coach for anything and everything, and the field of *personal coaching* exploded as one of the hottest new occupations.

So, what does a coach do? More than anything else, a coach holds up a mirror and shows you what you're doing, day in and day out. A coach keeps the slight edge in your face. A coach helps you harness the power of reflection. Whatever method you choose to use, find some way to make reflection an everyday thing, day in and day out, without fail.

When what you didn't improve one day is clear to you and you're aware of it, by ten the next morning you'll be hunting for self-improvements like a heat-seeking missile. You'll be reading and listening to things and associating with people that empower you. You won't be able to *help* it. You'll become so motivated that nothing—*nothing*—will prevent you from improving.

Use the Power of Celebration

There is another critical reason the power of reflection is so important. It's not just to be a nag and remind you when you're slacking off. It's also to point out to you all the positive steps you're taking.

Back in 1980 authors Ken Blanchard and Spencer Johnson wrote, "People who feel good about themselves produce good results." The little book in which these words appeared, *The One Minute Manager*, became one of the most influential business books of all time. Blanchard and Johnson coined what has since become a well-worn phrase in business: they urged managers and business owners not to walk around trying to catch people doing something wrong, but to "catch them doing something right," and then acknowledge it on the spot. They called this a "one minute praising."

It's easy to forget to catch yourself doing something right.

If you have children, chances are that you can still remember the moment they took their first step. Chances are good that step got noticed and celebrated, big time. And chances are even better that within a week, they were walking around for hours a day and nobody even gave it a second thought—including them.

I heard a story once about a woman who had reached a point in her early fifties where she felt she was so badly starving for affection, she didn't know if she could continue in her marriage. She told her husband how she felt, and said that, for years, she had been unable to tell if he still loved her or not. Her husband was sincerely perplexed. "But I told you I loved you thirty years ago," he exclaimed. "Why would you think anything changed?" Poor guy. It had never occurred to him that it's not enough to say, "I love you" just one time. It's something that needs saying every day, and not only in words, but in actions, too, especially those little, thoughtful things that say, "I'm thinking about you and I care about you."

It's the slight edge power of reflection and acknowledgement—celebration.

Keep your slight edge activities, your right choices and incremental successes, right out in the open where you can see them and celebrate them. Remember that all the activity required to apply the slight edge for your success is a series of baby steps. Trust the process. Acknowledge those steps, no matter how small or insignificant they may seem at the time.

Make each successful right choice a celebration. You'll be able to feel, literally, those balance scales shifting in your favor. Nothing breeds success like more success.

It's so simple that it's easy, tragically easy, not to do it. The good news is, *doing* it is just as easy.

Personal Stories from
The Slight Edge Readers

When we were first introduced to the slight edge principles we were financially upside down. We did not have the ability to pay our own bills, let alone bless the lives of others. After learning about the slight edge philosophy, we started applying it to every area of our lives, carefully applying the principles to our family business and using our "slight edge allies."

As a team, we focused on daily activities that we knew would eventually give us the momentum we needed to achieve our goals. We made sure we completed tasks and did what we said we would do so that nothing could hold us back to the past. We spent time reflecting on how our efforts could be more productive as a team and we looked for every opportunity to celebrate our success as well as recognize others who helped us gain those successes.

The results have been greater than we could have possibly imagined. Over the course of the next five years, our income grew tenfold. We have also been able to start a nonprofit foundation to help the less fortunate. Our proudest accomplishment has been raising more than $100,000 for a girls' orphanage in Guatemala. We have also begun to organize trips every ninety days for others to volunteer at the orphanages.

By implementing these simple principles in our lives, we have not only drastically improved the quality of our own lives, but even more importantly, we have been able to reach out and touch those in need.

—*Mike, Steve, and Kim Melia, Wilmington, North Carolina*

Essential Points from Chapter 14

On the path of mastery you have four powerful allies:

→   The power of momentum: *steady* wins the race.

→   The power of completion: clear out your undones and incompletes.

→   The power of reflection: facing the man or woman in the mirror.

→   The power of celebration: catch yourself doing something right.

15. Cultivate Slight Edge Habits

> "Sow an act, reap a habit. Sow a habit, reap a character.
> Sow a character, reap a destiny."
>
> —*Charles Reade (attrib.)*

The chapter on investing in yourself closed with the three words, *it becomes automatic*. In those three simple, magic words lies one of the great, underestimated, underappreciated, misunderstood secrets of the slight edge: the power of habit.

We know all about bad habits. We struggle with them, talk about them, write books about them, and watch endless daytime television shows about them—the bad habits we know we should break but don't, the annoying habits others have and we wish they didn't. We're all aware of the insidious and destructive power bad habits can have in our lives, even if we are not quite as aware of our own as others are. But with all that habit awareness, we tend to overlook the enormous power of positive, *intentional* habits.

It's not that good habits don't exist, or that we don't have them. We do. It's just that we typically take them for granted.

Habit and Choice

There are two kinds of habits: those that serve you, and those that don't. Brushing your teeth is a habit that serves you; biting your nails is one that doesn't. Thinking things through for yourself serves you;

blindly accepting everything you read online or hear through the gossip grapevine doesn't. Looking for the best in people serves you; anticipating their worst doesn't. The first type of habit wields the force of the slight edge on your behalf and moves you along the success curve; the second turns the slight edge subtly but remorselessly against you and pulls you down the failure curve.

A habit is something you do without thinking. You come home from work, walk into the house, pull a beer out of the fridge and flick on the TV while you're talking to someone on the phone. You didn't make a conscious decision that a beer is exactly what you need right now, or that there is something you urgently need to see right now on television. You were focusing on the phone call. The beer and the soap were just habits.

Getting up early can become a habit. So can getting up late and staying up late. Whining, complaining, and criticizing can become a habit; so can praising and appreciating. Spending more than you earn can become a habit; so can putting a piece of every paycheck into a retirement account. Looking for the positive side of every challenge can become a habit, and so can finding the cloud in every silver lining.

And here's the big clincher: every one of those habits, the good and the bad, has its roots in choice—in little decisions you make and over which you have complete control.

Complete control, that is, at first. Until they become automatic and take on a life of their own—a life that will determine the direction of *your* life. So the question is: which behaviors do you want to have take on a life of their own?

The way a behavior turns into a habit is by repeating it over and over and over again until it becomes automatic. The creation of habits is a pure slight edge: simple little actions, repeated over time. The compounded effect of those habits over time will work either for you or against you, depending on whether they're habits that serve you, or habits that don't. Your habits are what will propel you up the success curve or down the failure curve.

Here is how J. Paul Getty, one of the world's first billionaires and during his lifetime considered the richest man in the world, described the power of habit:

"The individual who wants to reach the top in business must appreciate the might of the force of habit—and must understand that practices are what create habits. He must be quick to break those habits that can break him—and hasten to adopt those practices that will become the habits that can help him achieve the success he desires."

It's interesting to note where your habits really come from. They arise out of your actions, true—but where do your actions come from? Remember this?

your
PHILOSOPHY creates your **ATTITUDE**
your **ACTIONS**
your **RESULTS** creates your
LIFE

Your habits come from your daily activities compounded over time. And your activities are the result of the choices you make in the moment. Your choices come from your habits of thought, which are the product of your thinking, which comes from the view you have of the world and your place in it—your philosophy.

Which is why the key to your success, to mastering the slight edge through the long-term effect of your everyday habits of thought and action, is your philosophy.

The point of this book is to give you a structure for designing your success. Once you are aware of and understand how to use the slight edge to work for you, you can go about succeeding on purpose. Your intuitive sense of the slight edge becomes your automatic pilot. It guides you, keeps you on track, and helps you measure your progress. It weighs and measures your every habit, discarding those that don't serve you and designing new ones that do.

The key is making those right choices.

Changing Steel Cables of Behavior

Have you ever seen the huge steel cables that hold up suspension bridges, like the Golden Gate Bridge in San Francisco or the Verrazano-Narrows Bridge in New York? They're flexible, yet so thick and strong you get the sense that no earthly force could break them.

The ropes of behavior made up of your everyday little choices are just like those enormous metal sinews that hold up those bridges. Each choice is like a length of steel wire. By itself, it's not that big a deal—but when braided together, when compounded with all the other choices you make, these slender lengths of wire form tree-trunk-like tension lines of awesome strength. As the Roman poet Ovid wrote, "Nothing is stronger than habit."

The cables made from your right choices uphold and support you. Those made from wrong choices imprison and restrain you. These cables are your habits of thought and attitude.

Want to know where the slight edge is taking you? Look at your predominant habits of thought and the kinds of choices you habitually make.

Your habits operate at the unconscious level, which means you are not normally aware of them. It's only by bringing a habit into your conscious awareness that you can observe what it's doing, how it empowers and serves you ... or doesn't. By developing slight edge thinking—and especially by using the slight edge ally of reflection—you'll shine the bright light of awareness on your habits.

Once you're aware of a habit that doesn't serve you, how do you change it or get rid of it? All it takes is knowing where to focus your energy. That, plus *time*.

Trying to get rid of an unwanted habit is a bit like trying not to think about an elephant (the more you try not to think about it, the more you think about it). That's because what you focus on, grows. Which is why people who put a lot of energy into focusing on what they don't want, by talking about it, thinking about it, complaining about it, or fretting about it, usually get precisely that unwanted thing.

It's tough to get rid of the habit you don't want by facing it head on. The way to accomplish it is to *replace* the unwanted habit with another habit that you *do* want. And creating new and better habits, ones that empower and serve you, is something you know how to do. You do it the same way you built any habit you have: one step at a time. Baby steps. The slight edge.

Here are seven positive, productive habits of attitude and behavior, steel cables that will unflinchingly bear you up under any circumstance and support you on the path to your dreams.

Habit #1: Show Up

Be the frog who not only *decides* to jump off the lily pad but actually *jumps*. The world is rife with hesitation, the cornerstone of mediocrity.

When you talk with people who have achieved extraordinary things and ask them how it was that they accomplished whatever it is they've done, it is stunning how often they will tell you some version of this: *I just decided to do it.* Skill, knowledge, experience, connections, resources, finesse, expertise, all these things are part of the journey—but none of them are possible until the journey itself is initiated.

Do the thing, and you shall have the power.

When my daughter Amber arrived at her first year of college, she was intimidated. She'd been a good student in high school and had graduated with excellent grades, but now she was walking into an environment where *everyone* had graduated with excellent grades.

I got a clear sense of this at her freshman orientation, which took place in a large auditorium on the University of Florida campus. As we sat there with thousands of other students and parents, the dean of students announced from the podium that they had 6,700 incoming freshman that year; that among this group the average GPA was 4.0 (the *average!*); and the SAT scores were in the top 10 percent nationally. I wasn't sure if he was intending to motivate them or frighten them, but from the look on Amber's face, if he was going for fear he'd accomplished his aim.

After the orientation was over she said, "Dad, I'm going up against the best of the best here—how am I ever going to get an edge over my classmates?" She so badly wanted to do well and come out at the top of her class, but she didn't see any way that was possible.

I told her what I'm telling you: *show up.* If you'll just commit to showing up, that's half the battle right there. By simply showing up you can rise above half of the population in any circumstance.

The novelist Anne Lamott, author of *Help, Thanks, Wow: The Three*

Essential Prayers, wrote this about the power of showing up:

> *Hope begins in the dark, the stubborn hope that if you just show up and try to do the right thing, the dawn will come. You wait and watch and work: you don't give up.*

Wait and watch and work—and don't give up.

Habit #2: Be Consistent

According to Woody Allen, 80 percent of success is showing up. That's a philosophy I subscribe to wholeheartedly—but I would add two words: 80 percent of success is showing up *every day*. Now there's a truth that will take you anywhere you want to go. As essential as it is to show up, it is consistency that greatly multiplies its power. Showing up *consistently* is where the magic happens.

The great Baseball Hall-of-Famer Tom Seaver put it perfectly:

> *In baseball, my theory is to strive for consistency, not to worry about the numbers. If you dwell on statistics you get shortsighted; if you aim for consistency, the numbers will be there at the end.*

After that intimidating freshman orientation, I told Amber she not only needed to show up every day for school, but she also had to amplify that with at least two hours of study per day. I knew how easy it was to get off the track, to get caught up in campus life. I knew her new friends would want her to skip out on classes to join them in other activities that are part of the college experience. I knew the seductive but vicious cycle of goofing off and then having to brutally cram for tests. My advice to Amber? Leave that to the others. Show up—and be consistent.

"That's it," I told her. "Show up every day for class. Study for two hours a day." Not that hard to do. Easy, actually. But of course, just as easy not to do.

Three weeks later Amber called and said, "Dad, remember that class I have with 400 students in it? Well, there's only eighty people showing up for class now." Nobody had flunked out; they hadn't even had their first test yet. Yet in just three weeks' time 80 percent of her class was nowhere to be found.

That's the way the world is. That's why mediocrity prevails. That's why 95 percent live on the failure curve, and only 5 percent on the success curve.

Four years later Amber graduated at the top of her business class by doing those two simple things: showing up, and being consistent. She wasn't any better or smarter than any of the other kids. They were *all* the cream of the crop, top-notch students. But Amber had one distinct advantage the others didn't: she had a philosophy that drove her to stay on course even when everyone else was doing the opposite. She showed up consistently and succeeded because she had a simple philosophy that she applied every day, rain or shine.

If you will commit to showing up consistently, every day, no matter what, then you have already won well *more* than half the battle. The rest is up to skill, knowledge, drive, and execution.

Habit #3: Have a Positive Outlook

In the late nineties, a positive psychologist named Marcial Losada conducted some fascinating research with business teams. He placed these groups of businesspeople in different conference rooms that were outfitted with one-way mirrors and a sophisticated system of monitors and software that allowed him to separately track every single statement made by every person in the room over the course of an hour-long conference. He recorded and analyzed them, classifying each as coming from a more positive outlook or negative outlook, more focused on others or on self, and more open (asking questions) or more closed (defending their point of view).

He did this for years.

After analyzing the statements of sixty different business teams, Losada mapped the results against the teams' and individuals' actual performance in real-world business. You'll never guess the results.

Okay, maybe you will.

Turned out, the more positive the individuals' outlook, the more productive and creative the team's interaction—and the greater their actual long-term business success.

This is just one example of hundreds, thousands of research projects in the past two decades that have confirmed what experience and common sense suggest: approaching the events of everyday life with a consistently positive outlook moves you toward your goals.

According to the research, people who consistently practice seeing opportunities instead of problems, who focus on the best in a situation rather than the worst, who notice other people's better qualities and look past their weaker ones, who see the glass as *at least* half-full in every circumstance, are happier, more creative, earn more money, have more friendships, have better immune response, have less heart disease and strokes, have better and longer-lasting marriages, live longer, and are more successful in their careers.

In fact, people who have made a habit of positive outlook don't just see the glass as half-full: they see it as overflowing. And because they see it that way—because that's their attitude—it consistently ends up being that way for them.

Attitude creates actions create results create destiny.

Dan Buettner, author of *Blue Zones: Lessons for Living Longer From the People Who've Lived the Longest*, has traveled the world studying the everyday living habits of people who are healthiest and live the longest of anyone on the planet. Of all the factors possibly influencing health, vitality, and longevity, Buettner and his team compiled a list of nine. These people (1) live an active life, (2) cultivate purpose and a reason to wake up every morning, (3) take time to de-stress (appreciation, prayer, etc.), (4) stop eating when they are 80 percent full, (5) eat a diet emphasizing vegetables, especially beans, (6) have moderate alcohol intake (especially dark red wine), (7) play an active role in a faith-based community, (8) place a strong emphasis on family, and (9) are part of like-minded social circles with similar habits.

As Buettner points out, physiological factors like exercise and diet play a role—but not as big a role as you'd expect. A big part of it is factors that have to do with attitude, habits of behavior, and who they associate with.

And while we're talking about positivity, let me clear up a common misconception about positive outlook, right here and now.

Cultivating positive outlook does *not* mean you are always happy. It does not mean life never gets you down. It does not mean you walk around with an idiotic grin on your face even when you're hurting, and it doesn't mean living in denial, ignoring the realities of pain and struggle, or checking your brain at the door. People who cultivate a genuinely positive outlook go through tough times, too; when we're cut, we bleed red blood just like everyone else.

There are days when I wake up and I'm in a funk. I might not even know why, but life feels heavy and depressing, and I just don't want to get out of bed.

When this happens, the first thing I do is take inventory of my blessings. (According to positive psychologists, a habit of gratitude is one of the most common traits in consistently happier people.) I have people who love me, I have great relationships, I'm healthy, I have a great business, I love what I do, and so on. But sometimes it still doesn't go away. In fact, sometime it takes hours or even days to get out of the funk.

I don't think it matters how successful you are, the funk is still going to get you at times. It comes for everyone. It doesn't discriminate.

And sometimes you have good reason for a funk. Bad things happen, and nobody leads a fully charmed, invulnerable life. The truth is and always will be that sometimes life hurts.

When that happens, first know that you're in good company. The funk finds everyone. But here is what I've learned, and it has saved me and pulled me from the funk more than once: There is no way I can understand love if I haven't felt the hurt of loneliness. I can't know what good is and how good it feels, without knowing bad. I can't feel happy and content without feeling the funk. Life is ebb and flow. Everything curves.

So when bad things are happening to you, embrace the funk. That, too, is cultivating positive outlook. When something is hard or difficult and adversity is at your front door, embrace it, because it will make you stronger and your life richer. You can't know happiness unless you feel sadness. If you embrace it as part of the process, it can be life-altering.

Life is going to get you down and the funk is going to get you. Embrace it and fight through it and know you are not alone. Take baby steps, remember all the slight edge allies you have, and know that there is a path out of the funk.

Habit #4: Be Committed for the Long Haul

Showing up is essential.

Showing up consistently is powerful.

Showing up consistently with a positive outlook is even more powerful.

But doing all that for a week … is just doing it for a week.

You've probably seen those weight-loss and workout programs that promise to change your life and create "a better you" in ninety days. I'm not saying they don't get results, but here's the problem with a ninety-day program: it doesn't give you enough time to build up a new belief level in yourself that you can continue once the ninety days are over.

This wouldn't be a very popular marketing campaign, but it *is* the truth: you don't need a ninety-day program. You need a 250-day program. (That's 365 days with 115 off, just to allow for the human factor.) And hey, if you read ten pages a day of powerful, positive material aimed at improving your life, and you do it consistently for 250 days, that's 2,500 pages, or about ten books.

Absorbing and putting into practice the insights in ten powerful books? Now that *can* create "a better you." Even more so if you do it again the next year, and then again the year after that.

Farmers know they have to wait a full season to reap their harvests. In our post-industrial world, where so much of everyday life is accessible through the click of a mouse, it's easier than ever to forget that. But that doesn't mean it isn't still true.

Plant, cultivate, harvest. And that second comma, the one between *cultivate* and *harvest*, often represents a looooong period of time. As the great literary figure John Leonard once wrote:

It takes a long time to grow an old friend.

In his remarkable book *Outliers*, Malcolm Gladwell traces the actual amount of time that goes into the eventual "overnight success" of superstars from all sorts of fields, from the Beatles to Bill Gates, and documents what he calls the 10,000-hour rule: the key to outrageous success in any endeavor is to put in about 10,000 hours of practice. Seriously. No kidding. Ten thousand. (Gladwell is a pretty good example of that himself, and the book not only debuted at #1 on the *New York Times* bestseller list, but also stayed there for eleven consecutive weeks.)

If you put in eight hours a day, forty hours a week, fifty weeks a year, for five years, that's 10,000 hours. When Amber spent four years studying marketing in college, if you add up the time spent in classes, study, and homework, she probably put in something approaching 10,000 hours. But all the kids who were cutting class by week 4? Not so much.

No matter what you are trying to accomplish, you need to ask yourself, am I willing to put in 10,000 hours or more to get what I want?

Habit #5: Cultivate a Burning Desire Backed by Faith

Early on in this book I said that just wanting something isn't going to get it for you. And that's true—but it doesn't mean desire isn't a necessary ingredient. We think of desire as a powerful force, because we often feel it so strongly. But the truth is, desire in itself is often a pretty fickle, weak thing. You want something, and then the feeling passes. Like an infant, we desire a shiny object, and then once it's in our hands our attention is caught by something else, and the shiny object that was sought so earnestly moments ago now falls from our fingers unnoticed.

Sometimes, though, desire gets deep down on the inside and starts to burn—and when it does it can burn for years. That's the kind of desire that gets you up early and keeps you up late. It's what keeps you motivated to press forward when adversity hits. A desire like that can move mountains and alter the course of rivers.

Here is the truth about burning desire: it is a powerful force, and it works in two directions *depending on what you see.* Most people wish for big things but can't really see themselves getting them. The few who achieve great things are those who not only passionately wanted to achieve them but also clearly *see themselves achieving them.* That's the key to harnessing the power of desire: it is like a team of wild horses that need a driver to steer them in the right direction, and that driver is your *vision.*

I've mentioned Napoleon Hill's classic *Think and Grow Rich* a number of times. Here is how it came about. As a young journalist, Hill was assigned to do a story on Andrew Carnegie, then one of the most successful men in the world. In the course of the interview (which Hill later declared was the signal turning point of his life), the older man outlined his simple philosophy of success, and went on to propose that Hill embark on a project to interview some 500 of the most successful men and women of their day to document the principles and philosophies he found in common. Hill took him up on the challenge, and the years he spent pursuing that project led to one of the best-selling books of all time.

Of the 500-plus subjects Hill interviewed, the number one characteristic he found was what he called *desire backed by faith*.

"I believe in the power of *desire* backed by *faith*," he wrote, "because I have seen this power lift men from lowly beginnings to places of power and wealth; I have seen it rob the grave of its victims; I have seen it serve as the medium by which men staged a comeback after having been defeated in a hundred different ways."

A burning desire backed by faith simply means deeply, passionately wanting to get somewhere and knowing—not hoping, not wishing, but *knowing* that you're going to get there. In other words, there has to be congruence between your desire and your faith. If there is a disconnect there, if you desire something but don't genuinely have the faith that the actions you're taking will get you there, then you're setting yourself up for failure. On the other hand, if what you desire is huge, so big that it seems far, far away at the present moment, yet your faith in the slight edge actions you're taking is congruent with that desire, then you are setting yourself up for exactly the kind of success Hill is writing about.

In the course of your journey all sorts of obstacles will appear in the path. And you can determine the size of the person by the size of the problem that keeps them down. Successful people look at a problem and see opportunity.

A burning desire is what motivates you to confront them, rather than turn tail and run. But it's a burning desire backed by faith that takes you *through* them.

Habit #6: Be Willing to Pay the Price

When I faced that day of disgust on the golf course all those years ago, it hit me that if I didn't choose to do something to become successful, I was going to become unsuccessful *for the rest of my life*. I also realized that making that choice would mean paying a price—and that anything worth having is worth paying that price for.

When I say "be willing to pay the price" I can see people wince. I know what they're thinking: "Aha, I knew it, here it comes—to be successful I'm going to have to make this gigantic, painful sacrifice. What do I have to do, throw away my television? Say goodbye to all fun and forgo all my favorite foods?"

Actually, it's not that dramatic. Your dreams may be big (in fact I hope they're *huge*), but the steps you take to get there are *always* going to be small. Baby steps; easy to do. And the price you pay works the same way. You don't have to pay for your million-dollar dream with a million-dollar personal check. You can pay for it with ... well, a penny a day.

But you do need to understand what that penny is—and you do need to be willing to pay it. Whatever the dream, whatever the goal, there's a price you'll need to pay, and yes, that does mean giving up something.

It may be something as simple as giving up a type of junk food you're attached to, for the sake of your health; or something as subtle as giving up your right to be right, or your habit of exerting control over conversation for the sake of a relationship. It may mean giving up that bit of extra lazy-time sleep-in each morning to take time before work to write down three things you're grateful for, do those sit-ups, and make yourself a decent breakfast instead of grabbing something colorful and tasty and poisonous on the go.

It may mean the delayed gratification of postponing certain purchases or acquisitions, or letting go of some pleasures for the sake of the pursuit of a longer-term aim.

As I've said, I was never more than average in athletic ability, but I was always pretty serious about my athletics. At one point I'd become part of a softball team. We had practiced long and hard and gotten pretty good, to the point where we were traveling and winning tournaments right and left. I don't mind telling you, it was thrilling to be a part of. Until I reached a critical juncture. I hit a decision point where I'd suffered some major setbacks in business and lost everything, and I knew I had to get my career back on track. It was time to pick up the pieces of my life, regroup, and move on.

I also knew I couldn't do this without changing something: I had to pay a price. It was a difficult choice—but I walked away from our softball team.

My friends couldn't believe it. "You're quitting?!" And I said, "Hey you guys, you're still my friends, I love you, but get another outfielder." I had to take that time I was spending on softball and invest it elsewhere. I didn't have to completely change my whole life, I just needed to redirect ten hours a week. I could have taken it from family time or work time, but wherever I took it from, it was going to have to come from *somewhere*. That was the price.

Remember, there aren't many millionaires who bowl over 100. Why not? Because they left the bowling league behind to build their fortunes. "Is that too large a price to pay?" is a question only you can answer. Remember this: whatever price you pay, there's a bigger price to pay for *not* doing it than the price for doing it. The price of neglect is much worse than the price of the discipline. In fact, no matter what price you pay for success, the price for failure is brutal by comparison. It may take five years and 10,000 hours to put your success on track, but it takes a lifetime to fail.

Habit #7: Practice Slight Edge Integrity

Everyone knows that business startups have a high failure rate. The big reason people usually cite is lack of sufficient capital, and it's true, that is an important one. But there is another cause that often lies unseen and unacknowledged, and it is just as big as lack of capital: lack of sufficient slight edge integrity.

There are many definitions of integrity. Honesty. Truthfulness. Congruence between words and deeds. The aspect of integrity that is most applicable to the slight edge is this: *what you do when no one is watching*.

It's bedtime, end of a long, rough day, and you're beat. You head for bed—and there's your book, sitting there looking at you. You've made a commitment to read ten pages a day. But man, you are *tired*. Don't even know if you can keep your eyes open. What to do? "You know," you say to yourself, "if I skip the ten pages, just for tonight, it's no big deal." And you know what? You're absolutely right. It's not going to make a huge difference, one way or the other. It *is* no big deal.

And in that moment, you find out who you really are.

It's in that moment's decision, when nobody else is watching and no one will ever know, when your choice is so slight, so subtle, so insignificant … it's at *that* moment that you find out whether or not you have slight edge integrity.

Finding three new things today that you're grateful for. Putting down the fork before you're stuffed. Putting on your jogging shoes and taking that half-hour walk, even when it's cold. Making the three calls you said you'd make—even when no one will know whether or not you did it.

No one, that is, but you.

Slight edge integrity is one of the great secrets of entrepreneurial success. When you own your own business, there is no one telling you that you need to be at work or shouting in your ear to make sales calls. No one is there to make sure you are on top of your vendors and your books are up to date. This is all up to you now. You have no boss.

Actually, that last statement isn't quite accurate. You *do* have a boss, but that boss is you. Serving as your own boss, and doing so successfully, consistently, day in and day out, takes an uncommon degree of slight edge integrity, and frankly many business owners just don't have it. They become intoxicated by the freedom of being their own boss and fail to maintain the kind of structure it takes to become successful. Without that integrity in the little everyday things, a new business can't keep its head above water for long.

And in case you're thinking this doesn't apply to you because you aren't an entrepreneur and you don't own your own business, have I got a surprise for you: *yes, you are, and yes, you do.*

The truth is, living a life *is* being an entrepreneur. No matter whether you are one of ten thousand employees working at a gigantic corporation, a sole proprietor running your one-man ice cream stand, or a stay-at-home parent managing the household, you are solely in charge of the steadily unfolding course of your life. Your life is an Apollo rocket headed for parts yet unknown, and there is no one at the helm but you.

You are a novelist, and the story you are inventing, with its rich plot and imaginative palette of distinct and believable characters, is your life.

You are the screenwriter, director, and producer of an epic film, one that will run for years.

Like Edison, you are an inventor; like Fritjof Nansen, an explorer; like Emerson, a philosopher; like Steve Martin, an entertainer; like Lincoln, a statesman; like Wilberforce, a patient liberator. You are all these things and more—and the fabric of the tapestry upon which you're assembling this story is made up of tiny threads that few will ever notice as you weave them.

You may think I'm exaggerating. I'm not. You are capable of great things. I know this, because I've observed the human condition, and every soul alive is capable of great things. Most will never achieve them or experience them. But anyone can, if they only understand how the process works.

Show up.

Show up consistently.

Show up consistently with a positive outlook.

Be prepared for and committed to the long haul.

Cultivate a burning desire backed by faith.

Be willing to pay the price.

And do the things you've committed to doing—even when no one else is watching.

Habits that serve you are critical!

Tweet a positive habit and include #SlightEdge or post it on our Facebook wall www.facebook.com/ yourslightedge.com I would love for you to share with the Slight Edge community!

Personal Stories from
The Slight Edge Readers

I have been boxing since I was eleven. I am from a tough neighborhood and my parents were very young and struggling financially, so we didn't have the money for the kind of one-on-one training time I needed, but I applied slight edge principles and just showed up to the gym to practice every single day, no matter what. *Nothing* could stop me from showing up.

For years I would lose at finals or walk away with a bronze. More often than not I lost in the finals of national events. Yet even when I was upset because of losing, I firmly believed in the slight edge principles and the compounding of my efforts. I knew that just by showing up, consistently and with a positive outlook, I was putting myself way ahead of the game.

Now it is ten years later, and I am starting to see the fruits of my labor. As of this writing, I am Featherweight champion with an undefeated win-to-loss record of 15-0, and I recently defended my title in Atlantic City.

Now that I am a little older and wiser I firmly believe in all the philosophies of *The Slight Edge* at a deeper level. I have learned how to use my past as a tool to help make my ride to the future a little easier. I firmly believe that if I keep my simple daily routine consistent, with nothing fancy, just keep refining my craft and keep swimming in the bucket of cream, I know that it will turn into butter.

— *Jorge Diaz, New Brunswick, New Jersey*

By the age of thirty I was worth a million dollars on paper. I owned land, businesses, oil wells, I was even president of our local Chamber of Commerce and an upstanding citizen of the town. Life was good. Over the next decade all that changed, and by the age of forty I found myself divorced and bankrupt, with five children to support. My self-esteem was in the toilet.

A chance encounter with an old acquaintance changed everything. He had an opening at his company, which he offered me. Equally important was that he recommended some great books and resources I should start reading to get my psyche back on the right track. As we discussed my salary, I told him that I would work for free—and he could tell me what I was worth.

I knew I had within me the ability to turn my life around, and that for that to happen, I would need to practice the principles of *The Slight Edge* every single day. It would require that I set goals and do the daily disciplines that would eventually lead me to the vision I was holding for my life. Working as a telemarketer, I made hundreds of cold calls all day, every day, and got every response imaginable, most of them not very favorable. My nights I spent on the office floor, since I couldn't afford my own place. Day in and day out, I slowly mastered the mundane. By six weeks into the job I still had zero total sales—but I persevered, knowing that I was developing my skills as a telemarketer and that it would pay off.

That day came when I was informed that one of the largest insurance companies purchased over 150 tickets for their agents and would be purchasing the same for another event we were promoting. It was the largest single sale anyone had ever made at this company. Eventually I was given the title of vice president and made a 50 percent partner in the company.

All this transpired because I showed up consistently over a long period of time with a good attitude. I had a burning desire and faith and was willing to pay the price. And I was willing to do all this even when no one was watching. I am now living out my dreams and making a positive difference, sharing the profound but simple principles of the slight edge.

—*Steve Fleming, Santa Fe, New Mexico*

Essential Points from Chapter 15

↗ There are two kinds of habits: those that serve you,
and those that don't.

↗ You have choice over your habits through your choice of
everyday actions.

↗ The way to erase a bad habit is to replace it with
a positive habit.

↗ Here are seven powerful, positive slight edge habits:
1. Show up: be the frog who jumps off the lily pad.
2. Show up consistently: keep showing up when others
fade out.
3. Cultivate a positive outlook: see the glass as
overflowing.
4. Be committed for the long haul: remember the
10,000-hour rule.
5. Cultivate a burning desire backed by faith: not hoping
or wishing—knowing.
6. Be willing to pay the price: sometimes you have to quit
the softball team.
7. Practice slight edge integrity: do the things you've
committed to doing, even when no one else is watching.

16. Three Steps
to Your Dreams

> "First comes the thought; then organization of that thought into ideas and plans; then transformation of those plans into reality. The beginning, as you will observe, is in your imagination."
>
> —*Napoleon Hill,* The Law of Success

There are entire books written about how to set, pursue, and achieve your goals, and some of them are actually pretty good. You may or may not need an entire book on that topic; that's up to you. Me, I like to keep things as simple as possible, because simple is usually far more effective. Even more importantly, *simple* is what works best with the slight edge. Remember *easy to do*, and you won't stray far from having your hands on the slight edge.

While everyone has a different approach to goal setting, there are three simple, fundamental steps you need to take for your dreams to turn into reality. Everyone who has ever created success, whether or not they consciously framed it this way or used this specific language to describe them, has gone through some version of these three steps. They are the three universal steps to reaching for a big dream.

For a goal to come true:

You must make it specific, give it a deadline, and write it down.
You must look at it every day.
You must have a plan to start with.

Step One: Write It Down

The most critical skill for achieving success in any area whatsoever, from sports to high finance, radiant health to fulfilling relationships, is the skill of *envisioning*. Envisioning something simply means having the ability to create a vivid picture of something that hasn't factually happened yet, and to make that picture so vivid that it feels real.

Envisioning doesn't happen at its optimum effectiveness simply by creating a picture in your mind. If your dreams and aspirations are happening in your mind only, that easily winds up being no more than wishful thinking. It's like saying, "I'll give it a try," which as Yoda pointed out really doesn't cut it. "Do or do not—there is no *try*" might be only a line in a movie spoken by a puppet posing as a Jedi master, but it's still a potent, sobering truth.

Envisioning means quite literally making something up out of thin air—and *making it real*. By definition, you can't do that within the confines of your brain. It needs to become physical; it needs to involve your senses. In other words, you need to write it down. Making pictures of it, which people sometimes call a dream board, is even better. Speaking it out loud to another person is the most powerful of all. But at the very least, write it down. The moment you do, it has started to become real.

What do you dream about? Pick a dream you have, any dream: your dream house, dream location, dream vacation, dream job, dream marriage, dream career. Pick a dream that you'd truly, deeply love to have come true. Write it down, describing it in just a few words, on the first line below. Then pick another, and another, until you have identified and listed five dreams.

If you're hesitating, know this: these dreams may be as huge or as small as you like; neither is "better" or more or less worthy to be made real.

1. _____

_____

2. _____

_____

3. _____

_____

4. _____

_____

5. _____

_____

Good. Now, let's have you add two descriptors that will make your dream more concrete: *what* and *when*.

First, go back to each dream and add whatever wording you need to make it absolutely specific. (You may need a fresh sheet of paper or text doc on your laptop to do this.) For example, if you had a dream to "be financially free," what does that mean specifically? How much money do you need in the bank or investments, or coming in as annual income, to achieve what you call *financial freedom*? If there are any other conditions that need to be met (such as "being completely debt-free"), add those in, too.

Let's say one of your dreams is "radiant health." How would you make that specific? One way might be to describe exactly how you feel, what kinds of activities you engage in, and what they feel like. Imagine reading your dream to someone you care about, and that person saying, "I'm not sure I quite get what you mean. Can you tell me exactly what you're shooting for?"

Now, the second descriptor: when. It's been said that goals are "dreams with deadlines." Let's reshape your dreams into tangible, practical goals by giving them timelines. Go back through each dream and answer the question, "By when?"

You've probably heard of the Pareto Principle, more popularly known as the 80/20 rule, which says that, for instance, 20 percent of the people in a sales force produce 80 percent of the results. Vilfredo Pareto, the Italian economist who promulgated this theory around the start of the twentieth century, actually arrived at his formula (which is a bit more complex than a simple 80/20) to describe the tendency of wealth, innovation, and initiative to concentrate in a self-selected elite, no matter what the external social or economic system. In plain language, Pareto was really describing the success curve and failure curve—the two sides of the slight edge.

Here is another application of Pareto's Law: 80 percent of everything you do tends to get done in the last 20 percent of the time available. And that can end up being an insidious truth. Because if you don't create a concrete deadline, that last 20 percent never seems to show up—and you're always living in the 80 percent time saying, "Someday..."

Someday ... the day that never comes.

Write your dreams down; make them vivid and specific; give them a concrete timeline for realization; and you've taken a giant step toward making them real.

Step Two: Look at It Every Day

The single most compelling reason for writing down your dreams is so you can look at them and read them every day. The reason you need to look at them every day is the same reason you need to keep yourself in the company of positive people: you need to counteract the force of gravity. Or to put a different name to it, the force of mediocrity.

Remember, the odds are nineteen to one against you, and you need to constantly remind your brain where it is you're headed or you'll drift off the path of mastery and lose your way. If you don't keep yourself constantly, repeatedly focused on your destination, you'll be like a rocket ship without its gyroscope: you'll simply coast off into the outer space of failure, never coming even remotely close to reaching the moon. Or back to earth to again.

After faith and a burning desire, the third factor Napoleon Hill found in his 500-plus of the most successful men and women of his day was what he called *autosuggestion*: the power of regularly, consistently telling and retelling yourself what your goals are. He found that, on average, these people did this twice a day—*every* day. You have to ask yourself, why would titans of industry, world-class statesmen and other figures at the very top of their fields feel they needed to tell themselves every day what it was they were doing? It certainly wasn't because they were stupid, or had bad memories. It was because they understood the power of the subconscious. They knew they had to constantly feed their goals to their subconscious mind, so it would stay attuned to whatever came across their path that supported those goals, and ignore the distractions that detracted from it.

Surround yourself with it, keep your awareness in your face, look at it every single day. Your brain is far more complex and powerful than the biggest computer in the world—and your own subconscious is by far the biggest distraction you have.

Remember how many times you heard the word "no" by the time you hit first grade: more than 40,000 times, and it had *octuple* the impact of those mere 5,000 yeses. Your brain has recorded an eight-to-one preponderance of *No*, which translates into, "You can't do it.... It will never work.... That's impossible.... Why even bother trying?" We all come at this business of success with an imposing baggage of negative conditioning.

And that's okay. You and I can't live our childhoods over again, but we don't need to in order to fulfill our dreams. What we can do—and need to do—is *surround ourselves with our own yeses*. Surround yourself with messages that tell you that your dreams are real, your dreams are real, your dreams are real.

Not only are they possible: they are *inevitable*.

That's the message your subconscious needs to be soaked in constantly.

Having your dreams concretely spelled out, on paper, in the most vivid and specific terms possible, and with a very tangible, concrete timeline, provides you with an "environment of Yes!" for your goals, dreams, and aspirations. And when that nineteen-to-one force of gravity starts leaking in from our subconscious and whispering, "Yeah, but are they *really*?" we need to respond instantly and without hesitation, *Yes! Yes! Yes! Yes! Yes!*

Here is the amazing thing—and I've seen this happen so many times, yet it never ceases to fill me with awe: when you clearly, tangibly set your goals, life has a way of rearranging itself, setting in motion a series of events that you could never have predicted or planned, to get you there. If you just sit there and try to figure it out, it doesn't happen. But when you surround yourself with the vivid expression of your tangible goals, your subconscious brain goes to work on it—and if you have the right philosophy, the philosophy of the slight edge, then you will come up with the right actions and keep repeating those actions ...

and a series of events will kick in, including circumstances you could never have dreamed of, that will take you there.

Step Three: Start with a Plan

This is the point where people are often thrown off track. It's easy to assume that you need to put together the plan that will get you there—in other words, the *right* plan. The plan that will work. No.

The point is not to come up with the brilliant blueprint that is guaranteed to take you all the way to the finish line. The point is simply to come up with a plan that will get you *out of the starting gate*. It's not even that your starting plan doesn't necessarily get you there—it *for sure* won't get you there, at least not the exact plan you conceive at first. Nobody has that degree of perfect precision in long-range planning, and there are too many variables and surprises along the way that will require adjustments to the plan. You have to start with a plan, but the plan you start with will not be the plan that gets you there. In fact, just for emphasis, I'm going to say that once more:

You have to start with a plan, but the plan you start with will not be the plan that gets you there.

Now that may sound like it makes no sense at all. I mean, if this plan isn't going to get you to your goal, why bother designing it? What's the point? The point is that you need a plan to start with, the same way you need a penny to start with before anything can double. The way you took your first baby step. The way you furrowed your brows, pursed your lips, and struggled to sound out the first sentence you read.

Would that penny have financed an empire? Of course not. Would that first step have won the Boston Marathon? Would that first sentence have earned you a master's degree in literature? No, and no, and no. But without that penny, without that first wobbling step, without that first stumbling sentence, your dream—no matter how deeply you wanted it—would never have materialized.

The power of a plan is not that it will get you there. The power of a plan is that it will get you started.

People make the mistake of thinking they need the perfect plan. There is no perfect plan. By definition, there can't be, because *a plan is not getting there—it's only your jumping-off point*. And that's exactly the reason you need a plan: if you have no jumping-off point, there won't be any jumping off happening. Tomorrow, you'll still be on your lily pad with the other frogs. In fact, if you put too much energy into the plan and fuss around trying to make it perfect, you're likely to squelch all the life, spontaneity, intuition, and joy out of the *doing* of it.

Do the thing, and you shall have the power.

Don't try to figure it all out.

If you want twice the success, double your rate of failure.

You start with a plan, then go through the process of continuous learning through both study and doing, adjusting all the time like a rocket ship on the way to the moon, off track 97 percent of the time, your gyroscope feeding information to your dream computer to bring you back on track, and continuing on the path of mastery toward your passionately dreamed-for objective.

Success is the progressive realization of a worthy ideal.

Keep holding that as your philosophy, and you will generate the attitudes and actions you need to keep progressively realizing a better and better plan. You need a first plan so you can get to your second plan, so you can get to your third plan, so you can get to your fourth plan. Your starting plan is not the plan that will ultimately get you there—but you need it so you have a place to start.

In my profession, training is a huge part of what drives a business's success. Training is the great equalizer. Because we work with such large numbers and such a sweeping diversity of people from all types of backgrounds and walks of life, we train, train, and train some more. It's not that there's all that much to learn. It's like learning to play music: there are only twelve notes, after all. But to learn it, you need to hear it, and play it, over and over. It's as vivid an illustration of slight edge success as I've ever seen.

At the same time, I have little regard for trainings that tell you, "This is exactly how you have to do it," because the actual sequence of actions and events that works will be different for everyone, every time. You can train people in the concepts, in how to think and what kinds of actions have worked, but you can't blueprint the specific sequence in every detail because circumstances are always different and always changing. Life curves.

This is why you need to have a plan to start with—but you cannot start with the plan that will get you there. You have to start with the *philosophy* that will take you there; with the right philosophy, you'll find the plan.

To give you a real-life example of the perfect power of an imperfect plan, here is the true story of how I built the largest sales and distribution forces in all of Germany for one of my past companies, which has since become one of the largest such organizations in all of Europe and one of the most successful in the history of that industry.

Anatomy of a Breakthrough: How I Built a German Sales Force

One Friday morning, I woke up and turned on the television while I was getting dressed. On television, someone was talking about a business trade show in Albuquerque. I thought, "Hey, maybe I should be in that." I called the people running the show, asked if they had an opening, they said, "Yeah," so I changed my plans for the day and spent the next eight or ten hours shopping around, buying things for my booth, and making little signs and packages to hand out.

The next morning I showed up at the franchise show and found my way to my little booth. I'd never done this before. I was surrounded by really nice, professional booths—and I stood in my stupid little homemade booth, trying to hand out my little brochures. Across from me, another person with a booth was blowing up balloons shaped like bears. There we were. Bear Man and me.

All day long, people would come over to see the Bear Man's balloons and I would try to hand out my information, but nobody paid any attention to me. I had three hundred packages to give out and hoped to get names and phone numbers from maybe ten or twenty people—but I could not even *give* my stuff away.

Finally I found a line that worked. As one person walked past me to go see the Bear Man's balloons, I caught his eye and said, "Would you be interested in some great propaganda?" He stopped and laughed, and said, "Sure." I used that line for the entire weekend, gave out all three hundred packages, and got about twenty names.

One of them happened to be a doctor named Shapiro. The next week, I called Dr. Shapiro; we had a pleasant conversation, but nothing happened. I called him again, and then kept calling him. After about a month and a half of following up with him, he joined me in my business.

About this same time I learned that our company was planning to open in Germany in about six months. I got my mastermind group together and said, "Guys, this is it, we're going to open up Germany." They said, "How?" Well, I had no idea how. The only thing I knew how to do was to double my rate of failure.

Do the thing and have the power.

We talked it over, and I decided what we needed to do was find Germans. So at our meetings we began teaching this amazing, sophisticated strategy we had developed: *Find Germans.* Eventually somebody came up with the idea of dropping in on the local Mercedes dealership; someone else visited the local German club. One by one, ideas started to percolate.

About two weeks later Dr. Shapiro showed up at a meeting and said, "Hey, I found a German." I asked him, "What do you mean?" He said, "I'm talking to my neighbor while he's mowing his lawn and I say, 'Hey by the way, Bob, you know any Germans?' and he says, 'Well, yeah, I know a guy who lives in Germany,' and I say, '*Really?*'"

I told Dr. Shapiro to send this German person all my information, because I was planning to go over there in a few months. He said, "Hey Jeff, aren't you speaking over in Miami in a few months?" Yes, I was. "Well, this guy's coming over to the U.S., and I think he's going to be in Miami then, too!"

A few months later, I go to Miami and sure enough, this fellow comes up to me afterward and talks to me: his name is Vin, he's from Germany, and he gets quite excited about going back to Germany and helping us open up there in a few months.

Except after Vin flies back to Germany, three months go by—and the company doesn't open in Germany after all. Things aren't ready. The plan has to change. We have to delay the opening by at least another three or four months.

So I call Vin and tell him, "Hey, we're not opening in Germany yet after all, but listen, we're open in England now, why don't you go over to England and start working over there? You can get some practice, and then when Germany does open up, you'll already know the ropes and be really ready."

So Vin and his wife Birgitte go to England, rent a little flat and start working there.

One day Vin and Birgitte are walking around England when they happen to stop to talk to a man who's painting a house. As they get talking, they ask him—are you ready for this? Have you already guessed what brilliant question it is they ask? You got it: they say, "Hey, do you know any Germans?" and the man says, "Oh, yeah, I know this guy in

Germany, he's really successful there."

Months later, when I finally get to Germany, I go from city to city, meeting with people in hotel lobby after hotel lobby—Hamburg, Düsseldorf, Cologne, Heidelberg, Munich, Frankfurt.... I don't know a thing about Germany, and I don't speak a word of German. But Vin was with me the whole time, side by side, translating and helping me out and showing me around.

At first, I'll be speaking to a group, then Vin will translate, then I'll say something else, then he'll translate. But soon something weird starts happening: I'll say something—and before I've even finished my thought, Vin takes off in rapid-fire German and talks for five minutes straight before coming up for air. He doesn't need me to finish my sentences. He's doing fine without me!

By the time I left Frankfurt we had launched Germany—and today Vin and the housepainter's German friend are both multimillionaires with sales forces in all of Europe.

So here's the question I want to ask you: did I *plan* all that?

Maybe it went like this:

One day I was sitting on my bed, putting on my socks, and mumbling to myself, "Now how can I build a huge European sales force?" I thought about that for a while, then slapped my forehead and said, "I got it! All I need to do is turn on the TV, they'll probably be talking about a business trade show....

"And if I go to the trade show, chances are really good that I'll be stuck in a corner with some guy called the Bear Man who'll take everyone's attention off me so I won't have any success handing out my little brochures, which will make me figure out that what I should say to people is something like, 'Hey, would you be interested in some propaganda?' and if I do that not only will I hand out all three hundred of my little packages but I'll also get about twenty names....

"And one of those names just might be a doctor from Albuquerque who won't really be that interested at first, but even though it could take me, oh, three weeks of calling him, maybe the doctor will finally show up when I'm teaching people about how to ask everyone if they know any Germans, and this doctor will talk to his next-door neighbor one day while he's cutting his grass (and it's a good thing it won't be raining that day, because it if did then this carefully laid plan wouldn't work) if he happens to know any Germans....

"And he will! He'll know this one person who not only lives in Germany, but also happens to be coming over to Miami at the same time I'm going over there, which will work out really well….

"Because even though this guy'll go back to Germany all excited about opening up there, if this plan I'm developing here works just right then that won't happen because it'll turn out that the company isn't ready to open up in Germany yet after all and that'll be just perfect because then I'll tell this guy, 'Hey, why don't you go over to England instead for a few months?' which my guess is he'll probably go ahead and do, maybe even renting a flat with his wife….

"Which will be just perfect, just like I planned it, because one day when they're out walking they'll walk right past this house, which will be timed just right (because of course it won't be raining on *that* day either) so they'll stop and strike up a conversation with this house-painter, which is *perfect* because I will have trained them to ask, 'Hey, do you know any Germans?' so they'll ask that question and if this all goes just according to my plan then the housepainter won't even have to stop and think about it 'cause he'll just say, 'Yes, actually, I do know a fellow in Germany, and in fact he's quite a successful bloke over there,' and that'll be perfect too because when I do finally get over there to Hamburg, even though it will look like I don't have the slightest clue about what I am trying to accomplish in Germany, the truth is that this guy who met me in Miami (the trade show doctor's next-door-neighbor's friend) and the successful guy in Germany (the guy that the Miami guy's neighborhood housepainter knows) will meet me in the hotel and travel with me as my translators and because they'll be translating for me they'll understand the business better than anyone else I talk to by the end of visit….

"And then maybe those two guys will go on to build the largest sales organizations in Germany, and one of the largest in all of Europe.

"Yeah," and I nodded sagely. "That should work without a hitch. Good plan, Olson!"

And I finished putting on my socks and shoes.

Do you think that's how it happened? Of course not. Then how *did* it all happen?

The simple truth is, *I started with a plan.* My plan was this: I told people to ask other people, "Do you know any Germans?" That was it. That was the brilliant master plan.

And you know, it worked. A simple plan—you could even say it was so simple it looked stupid. But if you start with a plan, and you practice those simple daily disciplines, then one plan leads to the next plan, which leads to the next plan, which leads to the next.

Can you imagine how many times this ridiculously unlikely chain of events could have fallen apart? Something as innocuous as an afternoon rain shower would have completely scuttled it—not once, but *twice*. Why didn't it? Because we started with a plan, and then allowed the slight edge to work.

The unerring way a simple plan works, when coupled with the earnest pursuit of slight edge habits and disciplines, was beautifully expressed in this famous passage from *The Second Himalayan Expedition*, by the Scottish mountaineer W. H. Murray:

> *Until one is committed there is hesitancy, the chance to draw back, always ineffectiveness. Concerning all acts of initiative (and creation), there is one elementary truth, the ignorance of which kills countless ideas and splendid plans: that the moment one definitely commits oneself, then Providence moves too. All sorts of things occur to help one that would never otherwise have occurred. A whole stream of events issues from the decision, raising in one's favour all manner of unforeseen incidents and meetings and material assistance, which no man could have dreamt would have come his way. I have learned a great respect for one of Goethe's couplets:*
> *"Whatever you can do or dream you can, begin it.*
> *Boldness has genius, power and magic in it!"*

A whole stream of events … which no man could have dreamt would have come his way. That strikes me as an excellent description of how our German sales force came into being.

Don't try to figure out the whole race. Just figure out where to put your foot for the starting line. Just start. Take a bold step onto the path of mastery. The result looks incredibly complex, but it's not. It never is. It's always the simple little things that take you there.

Everything you do, every decision you make, is either building your dream or building someone else's dream. Every single thing you do is either leading you away from the masses—or leading you away *with* the masses. Every single thing you do is a slight edge decision.

Our strategy for opening Germany seemed absurdly simple. What made the difference was that we did it every day. Did we have success in Germany after one day, one week, even one month? Of course not. We had nothing—just a few names. That was our penny. And one day, not more than a handful of months later, those few names had blanketed Europe with a financial empire.

Just like the water hyacinth.

Personal Stories from
The Slight Edge Readers

After many years of working in the real estate industry, I woke up one morning and realized I couldn't do it anymore. I was almost forty years old and already in full burn-out mode. I took a vacation to Montana to try to rejuvenate and fell in love with "big sky country." Everything about the mountains and rivers spoke to me, and I knew that this was where I was going to live someday.

I went back to Texas, left the real estate industry and began my own business, rejuvenated by my dream of living in big sky country.

I started dreaming big—*really* big. I thought about my ranch in the Montana mountains, backing up to thousands of Forest Service acres with trees, rivers, and streams running through the property. I would have horses, of course, and lots of room for all my friends and family to visit and enjoy. I would build a convention center on the property so I could have retreats for women and hold family reunions, all right there at my ranch.

Of course, the reality of my living conditions at the time were pretty stark in comparison. But I didn't pay attention to that. Instead I focused 100 percent on where I was going to be in five to ten years, looked at my goals every day and envisioned myself attaining them—and dedicated myself to consistent daily actions that would take me there.

For years I pored over floor plans for my dream home, all the while working on my business steadily and with intensity. Then, one fall day, as I was taking a Sunday afternoon drive to look at the aspen trees turning gold, I literally drove up to my dream place.

There it was, sitting in the middle of the national forest, with lots of trees and a stream running beside it—and up on the fence post by the gate was a sign that read, FOR SALE BY OWNER. I drove up the hill and knocked on the door, and as they say, the rest is history. Within thirty days I had purchased a beautiful eighty-acre property that looked exactly like what I have been envisioning for over ten years! I spent a year renovating the house to get it exactly like all the pictures I had collected over the years.

My friends and family wondered, how did she do it? I can tell you exactly how: by applying the slight edge in every part of my life. From my beliefs, philosophies, actions, disciplines, every single day. I changed language from "can't, maybe, don't know" to "can, sure, I will figure it out." I changed my thought pattern and when faced with disappointment or so-called failure I asked myself, "What did you learn?" The slight edge philosophy is life altering and now I am passing it on. I am teaching my children and grandchildren the same principles so they can be as blessed as I have been.

I hope you dream big and go for your dreams with your whole heart. If you will consistently apply the slight edge in every decision you make you will realize them very soon.

—*Kathy Aaron, Helena, Montana*

Essential Points from Chapter 16

There are three simple, essential steps to achieving a goal:

➤ Write it down: give it a *what* (clear description) and a *when* (timeline).

➤ Look at it every day: keep it in your face; soak your subconscious in it.

➤ Start with a plan: make the plan simple. The point of the plan is not that it will get you there, but that it will get you started.

17. Living the Slight Edge

> "Gentlemen, this is a football."
>
> —*Vince Lombardi*

With these words the legendary football coach would begin each new season of training, never taking anything for granted and always viewing each of his players as a blank slate, despite the fact that they were all seasoned pros. The first time Lombardi came out with this now-famous line, Green Bay Packer great Max McGee delivered his own immortal retort: "Uh, Coach, could you slow down a little? You're going too fast for us," and got a chuckle even from the unflappable Lombardi.

The modern business world has an expression for this mindset: "Assume nothing." The Zen Buddhists call it "beginner's mind." It's a mindset of humility and fresh inquiry, always looking for the most meaning and importance in the smallest things. I can't think of a better or more eloquent way of expressing it than, "Gentlemen, this is a football."

No matter how great your aspirations, how tall the dream and great the leap it means, the eternally repeating truth of the slight edge is that it is always built of small, simple steps. Easy to do—and just as easy not to do. Don't go too fast, and don't be too proud to stop, look at your life, and tell yourself, "This is a football."

To the coach, the football was the single step that began the players' thousand-mile journey. The football was Lombardi's penny.

Now it's time to find yours.

What one simple, single, easy-to-do activity can you do, day in and day out, that will have the greatest impact on your health, your happiness, your relationships, your personal development, your finances, your career, and your impact on the world?

Earlier in this book you walked through a brief exercise where you assessed your life as being on the success curve or failure curve in these seven specific areas. Now let's revisit them, only this time I'm going to ask you to make a simple roadmap for each one, consisting of three elements: 1) your dreams for that area, expressed as goals—specific, vivid, and with a timeline; 2) a simple plan to start (and when I say *simple* think: "find Germans"); and 3) one simple daily discipline that you will commit to doing each and every day from now on.

Go ahead, now, and take this stroll through your life; take a pencil as a walking stick.

The Slight Edge and Your Health

They say the way to a man's heart is through his stomach. I don't know about that, but I do know this: it is the way to his destiny. That is perhaps your most important choice, day by day and hour by hour: whether to let your eating and physical activity build your fondest dreams—or dig your grave. Hamlet wondered, "To be, or not to be?" You get to ask yourself that great question, and answer it, with every meal.

I always start with the area of health because when I'm in good physical shape I think more clearly, get more accomplished, and feel better about everything. There is nothing more basic to your life than your health, and there is no area of life where the slight edge is more vividly in operation, working either for you or against you.

My simple daily discipline for my health used to be running for at least half an hour a day. When I started doing this, I have to admit, it didn't thrill me. That first day I went running was a real drag. I'd let myself go physically; it was harder than I'd expected it would be. That first day I ran for only about ten minutes; over the next several weeks, I slowly worked my way up to my daily half hour. But even before that first week was over, I actually felt better than I had in months. I usually say that the slight edge does not work quickly, but the truth is, when it comes to your health you often *will* get positive results fairly quickly. That's the way it was with my running.

These days, instead of running, my daily health discipline is to work out for thirty-five minutes a day. When I say this people often ask, why thirty-five minutes? The answer is simple: I've found that's my workout equivalent of ten pages of reading a day. If I said I would do forty-five minutes or an hour, I know there are days I would have a hard time getting it in. But I know that no matter how busy I am, I can do thirty-five minutes—so thirty-five minutes it is.

Among the thousands of readers who've written to us since the first edition of this book came out, quite a few have been doctors who report that they have incorporated slight edge principles into the health regimen they recommend to their patients. Taking control of your health is just a few daily actions away.

Take a few moments to work out your own slight edge plan for your health. You don't need to feel limited or constricted by this exercise; you can always change and modify what you write here. Use a pencil. Do yourself a favor: don't skip over this and read on to the next. Actually take the time to fill out each section, at least jotting down some ideas to start with. You can always add to it and refine it later.

That's how the slight edge works: you're not supposed to get it perfect the first time.

My dreams for my health (specific, vivid and with a timeline):

_____

_____

_____

_____

Plan to start:

_____

_____

_____

_____

One simple daily discipline:

_____

_____

_____

_____

The Slight Edge and Your Happiness

If health comes first, happiness is right on its heels, because once you start practicing simple daily disciplines that increase your levels of happiness you'll find it feeds every other aspect of self-improvement you're trying to implement.

Remember: success does not lead to happiness—it's the other way around. Greater happiness is what leads to greater success. And creating greater happiness is a lot simpler, a lot easier, and a lot more accessible than most people think.

The first step to increasing your happiness is to understand what positive psychology research has been telling us for the past fifteen years: the most significant factors in your day-to-day, moment-to-moment level of happiness are not circumstantial. They're not heredity. They're not dictated by your genes or caused by outside events. The most significant factors in your happiness are *your actions*. What you do every day.

You can break down the bulk of happiness research into three areas. Your happiness is affected by 1) your outlook, that is, how you choose to view the events and circumstances of your everyday life; 2) specific actions with positive impact—things like writing down three things your grateful for, or sending appreciative emails, doing random acts of kindness, practicing forgiveness, meditating, and exercising; and 3) where you put your time and energy, and especially investing more time into important relationships and personally meaningful pursuits.

It's easy to create your own happiness workout plan, just like a personal exercise program, and you don't even need a coach or trainer. (There are no muscles you're going to pull if you do it wrong; in fact, there is no "wrong" here.) We're including a handful of the best happiness books at the back of this book.

The most important thing to know about increasing your happiness is that it is something you can consciously, intentionally do—but it doesn't happen automatically or just by saying, "I resolve to be happier." Happiness is like health. There are concrete steps you need to take to make it happen.

No doubt you'll change and develop your plan and *happy habits* routine further as you learn more in this area, but go ahead and put down a starting plan now, based on what you know so far.

My dreams for my happiness (specific, vivid and with a timeline):

_____

_____

_____

_____

Plan to start:

_____

_____

_____

_____

One simple daily discipline:

_____

_____

_____

_____

The Slight Edge and Your Relationships

Here is the ironic truth of human existence: no matter how great our accomplishments, it is ultimately other people who give them meaning. One reason *Citizen Kane* continues to rank among the greatest films ever made, more than seventy years after it first appeared, is that it makes such a powerful statement of this truth. Despite all his millions, his power, and his larger-than-life accomplishments, in the final hour of his life Charles Foster Kane was consumed by a single thought: anguish over being ripped from his childhood and thrust into the world alone at the age of eight. The "great man" had no one to share his conquests and accomplishments with.

All the success in the world means little if there is no one to share it with.

Your relationships, like your health, are built up or torn down in the subtlest ways. Because most people are not aware of the slight edge, the progress of their relationships tends to be a mystery. What makes a marriage grow richer over the years for one couple, and grow stale, empty, and bitter for another? Nineteen times out of twenty there is no single big, significant answer. It is the little things, day by day, that add up over time to unshakable contentment or unsalvageable misery.

It is, as the expression goes, the little things that count. The remembered birthdays, the little gifts, the gestures, the kind words, the remembered favorite color. The five minutes, snatched from an impossibly hectic day, to drop everything and hear the other's news. The word of encouragement; the reminder of your own belief in the other person. The listening. It's been said that the most important statements of friendship are usually spoken in five words or less. That is the wisdom of the slight edge: those tiny thoughts and gestures that are surprisingly easy to do—and tragically easy not to do.

The future of every relationship you have, like that of your health, is a choice that is always in your hands, and it's no bigger than a penny. The key is to make the choice—and keep making it.

Take a little time to think about the relationships in your life, and jot down a few thoughts about how you might work out your own slight edge plan for deepening, strengthening, and enriching those relationships. This is perhaps the most personal area of the five, and if you feel safer (since someone else might later be reading this copy of *The Slight Edge*), copy the worksheet below into a diary or journal, and fill in your answers there. Either way, do take the time to give it some thought and come up with your own answers. This is your life; this is the reason you're reading this book.

My dreams for my relationships (specific, vivid and with a timeline):

_____

_____

_____

_____

Plan to start:

_____

_____

_____

_____

One simple daily discipline:

_____

_____

_____

_____

The Slight Edge and Your Personal Development

If you could wave a magic wand and have either a million dollars in the bank or a million-dollar mindset, which would you choose? I wouldn't hesitate for an instant: I'd rather be *worth* a million than *have* a million. If I'm penniless but I have a million-dollar mindset, then it won't be long before I have the million dollars, too. But if I don't have a million-dollar mindset, then even with a cool million in the bank it won't be long before I'm back to being penniless again.

Your income will never long exceed your own level of personal development. It may take a jump through fortuitous circumstances or a lucky break. But if your own development does not quickly rise to meet that new level, it will quickly bounce back down to the plateau where your personal development limits it, sure as if it were on a rubber band. Just like lottery winners.

In that great classic of personal development, *As a Man Thinketh*, James Allen put it this way:

> *You will become as small as your controlling desire, or as great as your dominant aspiration.*

You already know my number one slight edge recommendation here: read at least ten pages of a powerful, life-transforming book each and every day. At the back of this book I provide a list of some of my favorites. Add to that list; make it yours. Building your own personal self-improvement library may be the single most valuable and important investment (after your personal health) that you can make.

Audiobooks are a great way to do this. The average person spends 250 to 350 hours every year driving from this place to that. That's forty minutes to an hour every day. If you spend that time listening to educational and self-improvement material, you'll have the equivalent of a Ph.D. on any subject you choose in just a few years. And you'll start noticing a difference in how you look at life in months, maybe even sooner.

Listening to audios is an especially powerful slight edge tool because it can turn your "down time" into *up* time and double your productivity. Listen while you drive to the store, to work, to school. Listen while you jog, walk, or exercise, while you sit on planes or stand in line. Feed your mind with life-transforming information and insight.

Easy to do. Easy not to do. Which is why 95 percent don't do it. Will you?

Take a few moments to work out your own slight edge plan for your personal development. Don't skip on to the next step: do yourself a favor and put down some initial thoughts.

My dreams for my personal development (specific, vivid and with a timeline):

_____

_____

_____

_____

Plan to start:

_____

_____

_____

_____

One simple daily discipline:

_____

_____

_____

_____

The Slight Edge and Your Finances

It's no accident that our exploration of the slight edge began with the story of a penny doubled. The world of finance is one of the easiest places to see, objectively and logically, the power of the slight edge in action.

As I said earlier, everyone *thinks* they know about the power of compound interest—but most don't, not really. In fact, only about 5 percent really understand this power: the ones on the success curve side of the slight edge. Here's another pithy bit of Vince Lombardi wisdom, and this one applies perfectly to personal finance:

Winning is a habit. Unfortunately, so is losing.

If you have developed losing habits in your finances, it's time to replace them with winning habits. Resolve to stop following that Parkinson's Law lament: *Whatever I have, I spend.* Choose not to be part of the 95 percent. Treat your personal finances like the precious resource it is. Emulate the masters of slight edge economics described in *The Millionaire Next Door.* Be like my mom: live below your means. Set up a modest savings plan and stick to it.

You probably have some concrete thoughts about this area already. Maybe you've been working this part out in the back of your mind ever since you read the story of the wealthy man and his two sons. Now's the time to start putting some of your thoughts to paper, and sketch out an initial plan for realizing your financial dreams and goals.

My dreams for my finances (specific, vivid and with a timeline):

_____

_____

_____

_____

Plan to start:

_____

_____

_____

_____

One simple daily discipline:

_____

_____

_____

_____

The Slight Edge and Your Career

Sigmund Freud was once asked what people need in order to be able to live a full and happy life. His reply was three words: "Lieben und arbeiten." *Love and work*.

Work is one of the most defining, overarching aspects of our lives. It molds and establishes nearly everything about our everyday existence; it is something we do practically every day and *will* do practically every day for most of our lives. When someone asks you, "What do you do?" what they are really asking is, "What is your work? What is your career?" Yet here is the sad irony of work in the world of the 95 percent: most people don't love their work. A pretty good number, in fact, hate it.

Not the 5 percent. The 5 percent have learned one of the great secrets of long and happy life: loving your work.

Before you go to work tomorrow, ask yourself this question: "Why am I doing this?" There could be all sorts of reasons, but they generally come down to one of these two:

a) Because I have to.

b) Because I want to.

Now, if you're going to be honest, your answer probably needs to involve some of the first. Just make sure it also includes a healthy dose of the second.

And here is the good news: your newfound understanding of how the slight works, your new philosophy, can transform your career just as surely as it will transform your health, your happiness, and your relationships. Take a few moments now to map out where you want to go in your career, and make a simple starting plan (no more complex than "Find Germans") for getting onto that path, along with a simple daily action that will put you there.

My dreams for my career (specific, vivid and with a timeline):

_____

_____

_____

_____

Plan to start:

_____

_____

_____

_____

One simple daily discipline:

_____

_____

_____

_____

The Slight Edge and Your Positive Impact on the World

In a typical goal-setting workshop, participants are often asked to set goals for a year ahead, five years, even ten years ahead. I went to a seminar once that had a unique approach: we were asked to set *one-hundred-year* goals.

What kind of goal would you set for one hundred years from now? What kind of impact can you imagine yourself having on the world that will last long after your own life has run its course? What will people remember you for after you have come and gone?

I used to ask people to think about their careers, their social and community activities, and their spiritual lives as distinct, different areas, much like their health and finances. I've come to see this a little differently, and now ask a larger question that embraces all these—career, social impact, and spiritual life—as well as many others: *What do I want my life to mean?*

This is the biggest area of all, because it includes all the others. But don't let its size and scope intimidate you. After all, what we're looking for here is simple, little things you can do every day—things that are easy to do. (Though also easy not to do.) The key is not to spend too much time on this. Do the thing, and you shall have the power. Go ahead: take a pencil in hand and sketch it out. Remember, it's your life; what would you like it to mean?

My dreams for my life (specific, vivid and with a timeline):

_____

_____

_____

_____

Plan to start:

_____

_____

_____

_____

One simple daily discipline:

_____

_____

_____

_____

Everything You Do is Important

Toss a rock into a pond, and you'll see ripples from its impact spreading out until they reach the opposite shore. The same thing happens in life. In most cases you never see those ripples. Clyde Share left this earth long before he had a chance to see the multiple successes that I've had the privilege of being involved with, but it's Clyde's ripples that built them.

Everything you do is important. When you smile at a child and encourage him, or scold him and tell him he's no good—in either case, you may see the splash it makes, and you may see the first or second ripple, but the impact goes far, far beyond what you see. You don't see all the ripples.

You teach someone to read ten pages of a good book a day, and you may see how it changes her, but chances are you won't see how it changes her kids, and her kids' friends, and their friends. And as these ripples spread out, they grow bigger and run deeper. For better or for worse, with positive impact or negative impact, even your smallest actions create a ripple effect that has an incalculably great impact on the world around you.

And remember this, too, no matter how high-minded or long-term your life dreams may seem: "Gentlemen, this is a football." It starts with a penny. Start finding your pennies.

Are you ready to live the slight edge?

Make your commitment public and send a tweet, including #SlightEdge or post them to our Facebook wall at www.facebook.com/yourslightedge.com. I would love to hear what daily slight edge activity you are doing today!

Personal Stories from
The Slight Edge Readers

Soon after reading *The Slight Edge*, we decided to launch our home health seminars as a business that now touches individuals and families all over the world. The name we chose for our company, The Healthy Edge, was inspired by *The Slight Edge*. The foundation of The Healthy Edge is five daily goals that when done consistently, transform people's health, attitude, esteem, and weight.

The principles in *The Slight Edge* exemplify the *exact* approach we use to teach people how to get to their ideal health and weight. We focus on empowering people to make small decisions every day, taking the focus away from the scale and focusing on the journey instead. It's not the one unhealthy meal or one skipped workout that causes you to gain twenty-five pounds; it's the daily unhealthy decisions that add up over the course of a year or two that causes the twenty-five pounds.

The same principle applies to releasing twenty-five pounds. It's not one or two healthy decisions, but the compounding effect of daily healthy decisions over a long period of time.

—Amber Thiel, Seattle, Washington

I was having a hard time staying focused in my studies and was struggling to keep up. At my dad's house I began reading at least ten pages of a good book a day, starting with *SUCCESS for Teens: Real Teens Talk About Using the Slight Edge*. I started implementing daily study habits in my schedule and took small steps to improving my academic success.

In time my grades improved to the rank of AB honor roll. At the end of the school year I received an award for "most improved student." The next year I continued the regimen of ten pages a night. That year I received a letter of commendation from President Obama for scholastic achievement and have been on AB honor roll ever since. I even recently received a commendation from Duke University for testing in the top 5 percent in the nation in a standardized test.

—*Alex Cross, Dallas, Texas*

Essential Points from Chapter 17

Write out your goals and dreams, a simple starting plan, and a single daily discipline:

- For your health
- For your happiness
- For your relationships
- For your personal development
- For your finances
- For your career
- For your impact on the world

18. Where to Go From Here

> "Keep your eyes on the prize."
> —*Alice Wine, civil rights activist*

braham Lincoln spoke about taking twice as long to sharpen the axe as to hack at the tree. In your life, you are the axe; the slight edge is how you sharpen it. Sharpen yourself and pursue your path through those simple, small, easy disciplines, and compounded over time, they will take you to the top.

If you will:

→ Do one simple, daily discipline in each of these seven key areas of your life—your health, your happiness, your relationships, your personal development, your finances, your career, and your impact—that forwards your success in each of those areas; and

→ Make a habit of doing some sort of daily review of these slight edge activities, either through keeping a journal, a list, working with a slight edge buddy, a coach, or some other regular, consistent means; and

⟶ Spend high-quality time with men and women who have achieved goals and dreams similar to yours; in other words, model successful mentors, teachers, and allies, and do it daily, weekly and monthly…

Then you will find yourself on the success curve, and you *will* turn your dreams into realities.

You Know the Rest

You'll notice that, compared with every other chapter in this book, this chapter is short. Very short. There's a reason for that: there's nothing else you need to know. You don't need another big chapter. Your life is waiting.

You know what it takes to follow your dreams and realize them. You know what it takes to set your foot on the path of mastery, to start living your life up on the success side of the slight edge curve.

You know what you need to do to be successful, because you know what successful people do.

Successful people do what unsuccessful people are not willing to do; they put the slight edge to work for them, rather than against them, every day. They refuse to let themselves be swayed by their feelings, moods, or attitudes; they rule their lives by their philosophies and do what it takes to get the job done, whether they feel like it or not.

Successful people don't look for shortcuts, nor do they hope for the "big break." They are always open to quantum leaps, knowing that such opportune moments do present themselves from time to time, but they focus on sticking to their knitting and doing what they've put in front of themselves to do. They step onto the path of mastery and, once having set foot there, they stay on that path for the rest of their lives.

Successful people never blame circumstances or other people; instead, they take full responsibility for their lives. They use the past as a lesson but do not dwell in it, and instead let themselves be pulled up and forward by the compelling force of the future. They know that the path that leads to the success curve and the one that leads to the failure curve are only a hair's breadth apart, separated only by the distinction of simple, "insignificant" actions that are just as easy not to do as they are to do—and that this difference will ultimately make all the difference.

Successful people know how to use the natural tension to close the gap from point A, where they are, to point B, where they want to be. They understand why the tortoise beat the hare and why the one frog lived while the other died; they know that "steady wins the race," and that the slight edge is the optimal rate of growth for them.

Successful people practice the daily disciplines that are assured to take them to their final destination. They show up consistently with a good attitude over a long period of time, with a burning desire backed by faith. They are willing to pay the price and practice slight edge integrity.

Successful people focus on having a positive outlook. They understand that the funk gets everyone, and when it comes for them they embrace it, knowing it is refining them and deepening their appreciation of the rhythm of life. They take baby steps out of the funk and step back into positivity.

Successful people use inertia to build momentum, making their upward journey of success easier and easier. They know how to identify habits that don't serve them and replace them with those that do. They understand the powers of reflection, completion, and celebration and they harness them constantly, using their radar for unfinished business to propel them forward rather than being sucked backward and downward.

Successful people acquire the three kinds of knowledge they need to succeed. They create an ongoing support system of both book smarts and street smarts, learning through study and through doing, and they catalyze and accelerate that knowledge by finding mentors and modeling their successful behavior.

Successful people are always asking: "Who am I spending time with? Are they the people who best represent where I want to be headed?" They form powerful relationships with positive people; they carefully build mastermind groups, work with those groups regularly, and take them seriously; and they do not hesitate to disassociate themselves, when necessary, from people who are consistently negative and threaten to drag them down.

Successful people read at least ten pages of a powerful, life-transforming book or listen to at least fifteen minutes of educational and inspirational audio information every day.

Successful people go to work on their philosophy first, because they know it is the source of their attitudes, actions, results, and the quality of their lives.

They understand that they can increase their success by *doubling their rate of failure.*

They understand activity and because they *do the thing*, they *have the power.*

They understand the power of simple things.

They understand the power of daily disciplines.

They understand the power of the water hyacinth, and know how to use it.

They know how to keep paddling when others give up and sink.

They know when they are being offered the choice of wisdom.

Successful people understand the slight edge, and they put it to work for them.

So, where do you go from here?

Find your penny.

And then start doubling it.

A Personal Invitation

Well, you've reached the end. Congratulations: you've read the book! Unless you're doing what a lot of people do and thumbing through the last few pages before you even make the decision to buy the thing, just to see how it ends.

Either way, it brings up a good question: How *does* it end? Because this isn't a novel, where the author supplies you with a satisfying ending in the last ten pages. This is nonfiction, which means it's about real life—which means the ending hasn't *been* written yet. And the only one who can write it is you.

So, let me ask *you*: How does it end?

It could end like this:

> … and then [your name here] closed the book, nodded a few times, thought, *That was good, I'll have to remember that stuff*, slipped the book up onto a bookshelf where it would be slowly forgotten, and then went on with [your name here]'s life, much as it was the day before and the day before that.

The Slight Edge could end here for you right here and now. Or you could, in the late great Stephen Covey's immortal phrase, *start with the end in mind*, and decide today to put your foot on a path that will change your life forever.

You can put this book down and forget about it. Or you can become a part of a movement—a movement of things that are easy to do, easy not to do, yet make all the difference in the world.

Throughout this book we talked about the ripple effect, that is, the long-term impact that your everyday decisions and actions have on others. In the seven areas of life we looked at where the slight edge can make a transformational difference—health, happiness, relationships, personal development, finances, career, impact—the final and largest of all is *impact*, the difference you make in the world around you. Your personal butterfly effect, if you will. In many ways, that ripple effect is where the slight edge matters most.

Not only for the world around you, but for you, too.

Because here's something we didn't mention before: once you become aware of your own ripple effect, once you start seeing and hearing and feeling the positive, life-changing impact that sharing your own slight edge experiences can have on others, the act of that sharing will also have a life-changing impact on you. In fact, your life will never be the same.

We encourage you to join us online to help you stay on track with your daily habits, and also provides a forum where you can experience the power of association by being a part of a positive group of like-minded people. A place where you can interact with and touch the lives of others, and keep the slight edge experience alive in your life. Slight Edge Community:

twitter.com/yourslightedge   **facebook.com/yourslightedge**   **slightedge.org**

I look forward to seeing you there!

Life-Transforming Books

The Happiness Advantage, Shawn Achor

Before Happiness, Shawn Achor

As a Man Thinketh, James Allen

Multiple Streams of Income, Robert G. Allen

The Automatic Millionaire, David Bach

Start Over, Finish Rich, David Bach

The Go-Giver, Bob Burg and John David Mann

Go-Givers Sell More, Bob Burg and John David Mann

It's Not About You, Bob Burg and John David Mann

The Aladdin Factor, Jack Canfield and Mark Victor Hansen

How to Win Friends and Influence People, Dale Carnegie

Acres of Diamonds, Russell H. Conwell

The Richest Man in Babylon, George S. Clason

The 7 Habits of Highly Effective People, Stephen R. Covey

The Power of Habit: Why We Do What We Do in Life and Business, Charles Duhigg

Positivity, Barbara Fredrickson

Outliers, Malcolm Gladwell

The Dip, Seth Godin

Think and Grow Rich, Napoleon Hill

Delivering Happiness, Tony Hsieh

Conversations with Millionaires, Mike Litman, Jason Oman, et al.

The How of Happiness, Sonja Lyubomirsky

The Myths of Happiness, Sonja Lyubomirsky

The Greatest Salesman in the World, Og Mandino

Failing Forward, John C. Maxwell

The Power of Positive Thinking, Norman Vincent Peale

Drive: The Surprising Truth about What Motivates Us, Daniel Pink

Cultivating an Unshakable Character, Jim Rohn

Seven Strategies for Wealth and Happiness, Jim Rohn

The Art of Exceptional Living, Jim Rohn

The Challenge to Succeed, Jim Rohn

The Five Major Pieces to the Life Puzzle, Jim Rohn

The Seasons of Life, Jim Rohn

The Happiness Project, Gretchen Rubin

The Magic of Thinking Big, David Schwartz

Authentic Happiness, Martin Seligman

Flourish, Martin Seligman

Little Things Matter, Todd Smith

The Millionaire Next Door, Thomas J. Stanley
and William D. Danko

SUCCESS for Teens: Real Teens Talk about Using the Slight Edge,
The Success Foundation

21 Success Secrets of Self-Made Millionaires, Brian Tracy

The Thank You Economy, Gary Vaynerchuk

The Science of Getting Rich, Wallace D. Wattles

Many of these books are also available on audio.

Acknowledgments

To John David Mann, my coauthor, who brought his craft, passion, literary magic, and good cheer to the project and made our book shine. To John Milton Fogg for his insights and support, and for helping to get the ball rolling. To Todd Eliason, who brought his brilliance to the 2011 edition, and to Al Desetta, Keith Hafner, and the staff at Youth Communication for their help in adapting the slight edge material in to a book for teens, *SUCCESS for Teens: Real Teens Talk about Using the Slight Edge.* To Reed Bilbray, who has been a pivotal force in bringing *The Slight Edge* in all its various versions and editions from idea to realization. To my close friend Stuart Johnson for helping this book, a dream of mine for many years, to finally come to pass.

My thanks go to my mother, Rosemary, who has always believed in me. To my precious daughter, Amber Olson Rourke, who contributed chapter 8 ("The Ripple Effect") and is the driving force behind the "Ripple Effect" in our company, and who continues to make me proud by living the slight edge in every area of her life. And to Renée Olson, a great friend and my former wife who has always stood by me.

And to all who know they have greatness deep inside them—and that it's just a slight edge away.

About the Author

JEFF OLSON has spoken to more than a thousand audiences throughout the United States and around the world. Over the past thirty years he has helped hundreds of thousands of individuals achieve better levels of financial freedom and personal excellence.

Born and raised in Albuquerque, New Mexico, Jeff took his undergraduate degree in marketing from the University of New Mexico, graduating at the top of his class. While in graduate school, he was hired by the Albuquerque Airport as one of the youngest airport managers in the industry. He then went to work for Texas Instruments, where he worked his way through its sales ranks to become an intelligence systems manager in less than five years. He left TI to form Sun Aire of America, a company devoted to all aspects of solar energy, from design and manufacturing to marketing and distribution. Through all of this Jeff acquired exhaustive "street smarts" and formal business training in every aspect of sales, marketing, and distribution, and within four years Sun Aire was one of the largest solar companies in the United States. In 2012 Jeff founded a direct selling company that grew from zero to $100 million in one year, becoming the first company in its industry to do so, and which is on track to grow to several hundred million in less than two years.

Since his experiences with TI and Sun Aire, Jeff has worked with a series of sales, marketing, and distribution companies, building three different sales and distribution forces from scratch to multimillion-dollar organizations and being appointed CEO to one. In the early nineties he created a national training program for an independent sales force by placing 30,000 satellite dishes in homes across the country. Based on that experience, he went on to found The People's Network, one of the largest personal development training companies in the nation, where he worked with such legendary figures of personal development as Tony Alessandra, Les Brown, Nido Qubein, Jim Rohn, Brian Tracy, and many others, producing nearly 1,000 television programs and presenting seminars in every major city in the United States. He has been featured on the cover of *The Wall Street Journal*, *Entrepreneur*, and *SUCCESS*.

Jeff's original edition of *The Slight Edge* appeared in 2005 and immediately became a national bestseller. Three years later Jeff partnered with the SUCCESS Foundation to produce a version of the book for teens, titled *SUCCESS for Teens: Real Teens Talk About Using the Slight Edge*, which has been distributed to nearly two million teenagers.

Jeff describes himself as "a perpetual student of personal development," and he is as devoted to health and happiness as he is to personal and financial success. Jeff currently divides his time between his business in Dallas, Texas, and his home in Fort Lauderdale, Florida.

twitter.com/yourslightedge   facebook.com/yourslightedge   slightedge.org